The Labour Party under Ed Miliband

MANCHESTER
1824

Manchester University Press

The Labour Party under Ed Miliband

Trying but failing to renew social democracy

Eunice Goes

Manchester University Press

Published by Manchester University Press
Altrincham Street, Manchester M1 7JA
www.manchesteruniversitypress.co.uk

British Library Cataloguing-in-Publication Data
A catalogue record for this book is available from the British Library

Library of Congress Cataloguing-in-Publication Data applied for

ISBN 978 0 7190 9070 7 hardback
ISBN 978 1 7849 9423 5 paperback

First published 2016

Typeset by Out of House Publishing
Printed in Great Britain by CPI Group (UK) Ltd, Croydon, CR0 4YY

To Inês
and
Philippe

Contents

Acknowledgements

I have accumulated a great number of debts while writing this book. First, I would like to thank my editor, Tony Mason, for believing in this project and for his encouraging support throughout the process of researching and writing this book.

I am also indebted to people who took time off from their very busy schedules to talk to me about the Labour Party under Ed Miliband. I am particularly grateful to Jon Cruddas, Stewart Wood, Marc Stears, John Denham, Peter Hain, Patrick Diamond, Rafael Behr, Mark Ferguson, and Barry Sheerman, who were extremely generous with their time. Thanks to their insights I gained a better understanding of what Ed Miliband tried to achieve as Labour leader, but also of the obstacles he encountered. Obviously I am fully responsible for any lacunae or mistakes.

I owe a big thanks to Michele Cohen, Judi Atkins, Steven Fielding, Philippe Marlière, and an anonymous reviewer for reading and commenting on earlier drafts of some of the chapters of this book. I would like to thank the librarians at Richmond University who helped me to find relevant material for this book, and the editorial and production teams at Manchester University Press for their work in bringing the book through to publication. I am also grateful for the encouragement and support I received from Luke Martell, James Connelly, Charles Grant, and Anthony Barnett.

Last but not least, I would like to thank my partner Philippe for his loving and practical support and infinite patience, and my daughter Inês, whose sunny disposition helped me to keep things in perspective.

Abbreviations

BSA	*British Social Attitudes*
EC	European Commission
ECB	European Central Bank
EMU	Economic monetary union
EP	European Parliament
EU	European Union
GDP	Gross domestic product
ILP	Independent Labour Party
IMF	International Monetary Fund
IPPR	Institute for Public Policy Research
NF	National Front
NHS	National Health Service
NPM	New Public Management
OECD	Organisation for Economic Co-operation and Development
PASOK	Panhellenic Socialist Movement (Greece)
PS	Parti socialiste (France)
PSOE	Partido Socialista Obrero Español (Spain)
SNP	Scottish National Party
SPD	Sozialdemokratische Partei Deutschlands (Germany)
TTIP	Transatlantic Trade and Investment Partnership Treaty
UKIP	UK Independence Party

Introduction

Context and some theoretical considerations

I stand before you, clear in my task: to once again make Labour a force that takes on established thinking, doesn't succumb to it, speaks for the majority and shapes the centre ground of politics.

Ed Miliband[1]

When Ed Miliband became leader of the Labour Party in the autumn of 2010 he promised to turn a page on New Labour. For him, the global financial and economic crisis had shown the limits of New Labour, in particular the party's 'naïve' embrace of lightly regulated capitalism, globalisation, flexible labour markets, and its acceptance of rising social inequalities.[2] Miliband's epiphany seems to have been inspired by what political scientists call 'critical junctures' or 'external shocks'; that is, periods in history when crises open 'windows of opportunity' for change to occur. When those moments arrive, political actors look for new ideas and solutions to address new policy problems that can no longer be addressed by old recipes.[3]

The global financial crisis that started in the United States in 2007 as a credit crunch raised fundamental questions about the ideational paradigm – neoliberalism – that had become the governing economic and political philosophy of centre-right but also of centre-left political parties since the 1980s in Europe and North America. Many of its axioms and assumptions were challenged by the events that unfolded in Wall Street and that soon spread to Europe.

The significance of this crisis – which was not just economic, but was also political, social, and ideational – cannot be overstated. The neoliberal assumptions about the rationality of economic agents, about the self-regulating attributes of free markets, about the ability of the market to produce economic growth that would trickledown across society, could not explain the bankruptcy of major financial institutions and the near collapse of the global economy. Even the defenders of the system were utterly confused with the sequence of events that led to the collapse of Lehman Brothers and to the bailout of financial institutions that were seen as the foundations of financialised capitalism. The former president of the Federal Reserve, Alan Greenspan, reflected this mindset when he told the American Congress that the 'whole intellectual edifice ... collapsed'.[4]

Greenspan was not the only one to be confused with the events of 2007–08. Uncertainty was the prevailing sentiment during those turbulent two years. Newspapers like the *Financial Times* tried to make sense of what happened with a series of articles on the 'crisis of capitalism'. Popular culture also contributed to this debate with theatre productions, films, and novels. David Hare's *The Power of Yes*, Lucy Prebble's *Enron*, John Lanchester's *Capital*, Oliver Stone's *Wall Street: Money Never Sleeps*, and Laura Wade's *Posh* sought to explain the culture that led economic actors to engage in such risky behaviour.

Across the United States and Europe, millions of protesters, inspired by the Occupy movement, debated alternatives to capitalism. On the left, socialists and social democrats felt (to paraphrase President Obama's former chief-of-staff Rahm Emanuel) that this crisis of capitalism should 'not go to waste'.[5] In other words, the massive bailouts to the banks, coordinated at the international level and with the blessing of institutions like the International Monetary Fund (IMF) and the European Union (EU), led some social democrats to believe that they had been right all the time about the instability of capitalism and that a 'social democratic moment' was within their grasp. But in the corridors of power, policy-makers acted with the hesitancy of individuals who were not sure about how to respond to events of such magnitude. The easy reflex was to rely on the solutions and policy instruments they knew. And that is roughly what they did.

Miliband and the global financial crisis

If caution prevailed in the corridors of power, the mood was somewhat different within the Labour Party, and in particular in Ed Miliband's close-knit circle of advisers, experts, and supporters. In the early days of his leadership, the pervasive feeling within Miliband's circle was that Labour should use the opportunity to develop a social democratic response to the big policy puzzles created by the global financial crisis. Indeed, Miliband and his team of advisers spoke openly about 're-imagining social democracy'.

The idea of transformative change, but also the sense of possibility, was at the heart of Miliband's bid for Labour's leadership. His promise of change was informed by a critique of neoliberalism (and obviously of New Labour's legacy) but also by a reappraisal of social democratic values and solutions. Miliband's reasoning was simple enough to understand. For him it was clear that the global financial crisis had exposed the limits and flaws of neoliberalism and of New Labour's economic paradigm. The belief in unregulated markets had sown the seeds of the financial crisis and created great disparities of wealth in Britain. It had also created a dysfunctional economy that was over-reliant on the financial services industry and suffered from serious productivity problems as a result. From Miliband's perspective, that economy was also inefficient at distributing the rewards of economic growth.

This book seeks to examine whether the Labour leader was able to use the global financial crisis as a trigger to change the prevailing neoliberal paradigm in Britain. Does Miliband's blueprint represent a successful attempt to renew social democracy, or does it represent a capitulation to the austerity paradigm? What were the factors that contributed to either of these outcomes? By offering answers to these questions, this study will shed some light on some of the causes of Labour's catastrophic defeat at the 2015 general election.

This study argues that under Ed Miliband the Labour Party has sought to re-imagine social democracy by rejecting the main tenets of New Labour, but was only marginally successful in this enterprise. In contrast with New Labour, the Labour Party under Ed Miliband has adopted a critical approach to capitalism, it has placed egalitarian concerns at the centre-stage of its programme, and has developed a new approach to the State that sought to empower individuals. However, the departure from New Labour was not as dramatic as Miliband promised. He faced substantial ideational, institutional, and political constraints that led to the watering down of his initial thinking and plans. His critique of unregulated capitalism was not matched by policy proposals that would reform capitalism along social democratic lines.[6] Surely, he proposed policies that were presented as solutions (or as beginnings of solutions) to those specific policy puzzles, but their scope was far less ambitious than the rhetoric suggested. Likewise, his concern with rising inequalities and low pay was not matched with robust policy commitments. His pledge to address the crisis of capitalism and the problems of the unresponsive State with a commitment to democratic renewal was timid at best. Last, his attempt to address popular concerns with immigration and the politics of belonging were too nuanced and timid to gain any traction with voters. In short, the blueprint Miliband presented to voters on 7 May lacked clarity, definition, and a unifying message. This lack of definition and clarity was one of the reasons why Milibandism was so overwhelmingly rejected by voters.

Politics and ideas

This book focuses on the ideas that have informed and shaped Ed Miliband's agenda of renewal of the Labour Party[7] since 2010 and until the run-up to the 2015 general election, and it seeks to contribute to scholarship on the political thought of the Labour Party. As such, it will look at ideas as agents of political change, and assumes, following Sheri Berman, that 'the development of parties cannot be understood without a focus on ideology' because the organisations, political strategies, and electoral coalitions of political parties are shaped 'by the ideological projects they champion.'[8]

Asserting the crucial importance of ideas does not mean that ideas alone can explain the behaviour of a political party, or that ideas are the sole 'triggers' for political change, but rather that ideas offer political actors 'interpretative frameworks' that help them understand how the world works and develop blueprints that address particular problems.[9] This is particularly true in moments of crisis and institutional change. As Mark Blyth put it, in these circumstances, ideas enable actors 'to reduce uncertainty, redefine their interests, and contest and replace institutions'.[10] Ideas can also be 'facilitators of radical change and a pre-requisite of it'.[11]

But if ideas can be agents of change they do not operate on their own. When developing a political agenda, political actors can be constrained by a variety of factors. One powerful constraint can be the dominant ideas of the time. As Richard Heffernan argued, it is within the prevailing orthodoxy that 'political attitudes are forged'.[12] In other words, 'prevailing orthodoxies' set the parameters of political debate and often limit the number of options that can be considered plausible and viable. Political actors, no matter how authoritative and prescient, can only do so much.

Other constraints can be institutional arrangements, financial and fiscal constraints, public opinion, electoral considerations, and not forgetting Harold Macmillan's famous 'events'. It follows from here that political actors rarely if ever adopt ideas without transforming them and adapting them to the particular contextual circumstances in which they operate, and to the aims they seek to achieve. In the case of political parties, the process of developing a programme of government is heavily constrained by electoral considerations – that is, by power-seeking calculations. These electoral considerations impose on political parties the need to develop an electorally enticing or at the very least a credible programme of government that has the potential to result in an electoral victory.

Having in mind these considerations about ideas, interests, and institutions this book will map out the ideas – old and new – that were debated, adopted, and adapted by the Labour Party under Ed Miliband. In the process, it will explain how the interaction among ideas, institutional, political, and contextual factors informed the development of the Labour Party's electoral blueprint.

The power of ideas

As a book that focuses on the role of ideas in the life of a political party, it will borrow liberally – as encouraged by Kathleen Thelen[13] – from the literature on discursive and historical institutionalisms. Both 'new instutionalisms' emphasise the role of ideas in politics but they place different emphasis on their importance. Whereas discursive institutionalists see ideas as agents and stress their transformative role, historical institutionalists emphasise the role of structures as facilitators or as constraints to their success. Discursive institutionalists also see institutions as simultaneously 'constraining structures and enabling constructs of meaning'[14] but they pay far less attention to those institutions than historical institutionalists. I will now explain how I will use both approaches.

Like historical institutionalism, discursive institutionalism looks at ideas as agents of change but it is perhaps better placed to explain that process. Indeed, discursive institutionalism allows us to identify and to map what Alan Finlayson aptly defined as 'political thinking in the wild'; that is, the way whereby political actors participate in the interpretation but also in the development of political ideologies.[15] As a methodological tool, discursive institutionalism enables us to look at an often neglected facet of politics. By mapping out the ideas that inform and shape a political project we are able to look at politicians as 'thinking' beings and not just as strategic actors. That is, by mapping out ideas we are in a better position to understand how political actors think about and approach policy problems, how they develop proposals, and how they justify them to voters.

According to Vivien A. Schmidt, this is so because discursive institutionalism sees political action as 'the process in which agents create and maintain institutions by using … their background ideational abilities' and 'foreground discursive abilities, through which agents may change (or maintain) their institutions'.[16] As a result, discursive institutionalism sees institutional change as 'dynamic and explainable across time through agents' ideas and discourse, rather than largely static because of path-dependent and unexplainable moments'.[17]

The mapping of ideas – in particular of conflicting ideas – also sheds light on the distribution of power within political institutions. Stronger or more persuasive actors often present the winning arguments. In short, political change has the potential to occur as a result of a congenial ideational process. More importantly, the mapping out of ideational processes enable us to answer a few 'why' questions about the choices made by political actors.

Because discursive institutionalism emphasises the communicative and/or discursive processes whereby ideas are discussed, adopted, and adapted, discursive institutionalists prefer to talk about 'discourse' instead of ideas.[18] Schmidt argues that 'by using the term discourse, we can simultaneously indicate the ideas represented in the discourse … and the interactive processes by which ideas are conveyed'.[19] In particular, it enables us to understand the process whereby ideas evolve 'from thought to word to deed'.[20]

Schmidt's approach involves the tracing of different steps. First, it involves the use of a concept of discourse that includes not only what is said (ideas) but also the context of where, when, how, and why it was said. Second, Schmidt's approach categorises ideas by degree of generality – policies, programmes, and philosophies – and type of content (cognitive or normative). While cognitive ideas provide recipes and guidelines for political action as well as justifications, normative ideas attach values to political action and legitimise the policies of a political programme. Third, she makes a distinction between two main types of discourse: coordinative, which is among political actors – and the communicative discourse, which is between political actors and the public.[21]

Alan Finlayson rightly pointed out a missing element in Schmidt's analytical framework. Whilst she stressed the role of experts and political actors in ideational processes she overlooked what Finlayson identified as the intermediate public sphere, which is located between the 'coordinative' and 'communicative' discourses. This public sphere joins formal expertise with political activists, party supporters, and interested citizens.[22] Finlayson's intermediate public sphere is an important addition to Schmidt's analytical framework; however, it creates too stark a distinction between the coordinative discourse and the public sphere. The links between the two, in particular in ideational processes that occur in political parties, is more fluid than Finlayson implies. The process of developing a political programme in the coordinative sphere often puts the policy expert, the political activist, and the elected representative together in the same seminar room. Thus, the output of these interactions is a joint effort.

The production of different types of discourses and ideas is carried out by a variety of actors: first, the epistemic community of experts, public intellectuals, and party intellectuals who prioritise issues and policy puzzles, provide cause–effect analysis and theories to policy puzzles, and in some instances can offer solutions;[23] second, political actors who include party leaders and other elected politicians, political advisers, activists, and influential media commentators; and third, the audience, who are the target of the communicative action of political actors. The process of mapping out this ideational activity involves, as Finlayson suggested, the examination 'of how they do or do not connect with each other, and how they cohere as part of an evolving yet traditional ideology'.[24]

By applying this analytical framework, discursive institutionalism enables us to identify and create a map of the political ideas that shaped a political programme, to ascertain whether the programme as a whole has some intellectual and ideological coherence, and to identify which goals it seeks to achieve. However, it does not offer sufficiently solid hermeneutical tools to evaluate whether and why the ideas in question succeeded or failed at provoking change. Schmidt seemed to be aware of this weakness. She argued that ideas need to be plausible, pertinent, and accepted by relevant actors; however, these elements seldom enter into her analysis.[25] And yet, considerations about power and administrative arrangements, as well as considerations about the ability of political actors to build coalitions of support for their ideas, are crucial to explain how they can be agents of political change.

Historical institutionalism helps to bridge this gap because it offers an explanation of the process of ideas-induced political change or stasis. For instance, Margaret Weir argued that in order for ideas to be agents of change, (a) they need to be available, (b) administrative and institutional arrangements should facilitate the diffusion of those ideas, and (c) relevant actors or coalitions of support must have a role in either endorsing or rejecting those ideas.[26] A neater formula is proposed by Peter A. Hall. Indeed, Hall argued that ideas can explain processes of political change. As he put it, ideas 'can alter the composition of other elements in the political sphere, like a catalyst or binding agent that allows existing ingredients to combine in new ways'.[27] Hall also argued that some of the effects of ideas are unintended, as 'new ideas have the capacity to change the very perceptions of those who wield them as well as the world itself in ways that their advocates often do not fully anticipate or desire'.[28]

However, the power of ideas is not merely conditional on their innate qualities. As he argued, there are at least three external circumstances that can affect the power of an idea. The first is related to their ability to persuade. The ideas in question need to offer a plausible response to a current policy puzzle. For political parties this is a particularly important, if not difficult, condition, as they have to persuade voters of the appropriateness of their ideas in order to win power.

But persuasiveness is not merely dependent on the intellectual coherence of an idea or on its technical viability. Indeed, there are coherent and viable ideas that are difficult to explain. Hence, in Hall's model, ideas also need to be comprehensible, and that comprehension is reliant on individuals' 'stock of knowledge that is generally conditioned by prior historical experience'.[29] Putting it differently, in order to be persuasive ideas need to resonate with people's cause–effect understanding of policy problems and to a certain extent with their worldviews.

Finally, in order to influence policy, 'an idea must come to the attention of those who make policy, generally with a favourable endorsement from the relevant authorities'.[30] The endorsement of new ideas that can potentially result in the movement from one paradigm to another will depend, according to Hall, 'not only on the arguments of competing factions, but on their positional advantages within a broader institutional framework, on the ancillary resources they can command in the relevant conflicts, and on exogenous factors affecting the power of one set of actors to impose its paradigm over others'.[31]

There are other external circumstances or conditions that limit the ability of political actors to adopt new ideas. Political actors, and in this case party leaders, are also constrained by the traditions, the rhetorical styles, and the rituals and values of the institutions they represent. From here it follows, as suggested by Finlayson, that political actors need to formulate ideas and policy proposals that are congruent with the ideological tradition of their parties.[32] The reason is simple. If parties leapfrog ideologically, they can lose the trust of voters.[33]

This being said, political parties as carriers (though they are also interpreters and makers) of ideologies can be – and indeed are – selective in the use of their party's ideology and traditions. This is so because ideologies are flexible and sufficiently ambiguous to allow for these movements. To use Michael Freeden's fitting expression, ideologies can be 'trimmed to fit within an institutional framework'.[34] As historical organisations, political parties use their ideological repertoire to respond to particular contexts. In so doing, they reveal interesting aspects of their thought processes but also of their programmatic aims. For example, New Labour used the traditions of ethical socialism to articulate a new role for the State that dovetailed with the requirements of the neoliberal economy, whilst the Labour Party under Ed Miliband used the traditions of guild socialism, mutualism, and the New Left to articulate a critique of unregulated capitalism and of the unresponsive State.

Mapping the development of Miliband's agenda

Interweaving Schmidt's discursive institutionalism with Weir's and Hall's analytical frameworks to determine whether ideas have succeeded at provoking change, this book will look at the discursive activities centred around the leader of the Labour Party and around the party's frontbench team. The purpose of the exercise is to map out the ideational processes that led to the development of the political agenda of the Labour Party under Ed Miliband from (and following Schmidt) 'thought, to word, to deed'. This will involve, in a first stage, the mapping of coordinative discourse that takes place in the policy and public sphere, and, in a second stage, it will examine the party's communicative discourse targeted at the public.

The focus on the leader of the Labour Party reflects the fact that Labour is a highly centralised party. The leader and his group of advisers are in almost full control of the policy-making process. Party members, backbenchers, and activists have little influence over policy-making and have often complained about it. According to Richard Heffernan, 'the last four Labour manifestos were written by – or for – the leader's office with the Labour Party at large – its conference, national executive or National Policy Forum – merely consulted by being provided with a *fait-accompli*'.[35] Despite Miliband's difficulties in imposing his authority and vision on the party, there is little evidence that he changed this modus operandi. Indeed, the drafting of Labour's 2015 manifesto followed a similar pattern. The process of policy renewal was long, and involved a wide party consultation process, but the manifesto was drafted by Miliband's team.

However, the predominance of the leader does not imply that he can impose his vision on the party. Not even the most authoritative and strong leader is able to do that. In the case of Ed Miliband, this book will show that he compromised his policy goals with the members of the party's frontbench team and with powerful party factions in a number of areas in order to obtain their support. In some instances, the process of securing support for his ideas delayed the development of his programme. In others, it blurred the shape and contours of his agenda.

In order to explain how certain ideas shaped Miliband's agenda from 'thought to word to deed', I will examine both the coordinative and communicative discourses deployed by the Labour Party leadership.[36] In other words, I will analyse how certain ideas arrived within Labour circles; how they were discussed and interpreted by Miliband and his advisers, public intellectuals associated with or close to the Labour Party, think-tank reports and researchers (mainly from the Institute for Public Policy

Research (IPPR), the Resolution Foundation, the Policy Network, and the Fabian Society), party groupings, and some salient activists (such as Compass, LabourList, and Progress); how they were adopted and adapted by Ed Miliband and the shadow cabinet in their communications to the public; and finally how they were transformed into policy proposals. For that purpose I will analyse speeches and articles from politicians, think-tank reports, activists' blogs, and publications, as well as some interviews that I conducted with members of Ed Miliband's inner circle, Labour politicians and activists, and researchers from think-tanks close to the Labour Party.

It is important to bear in mind that this ideational activity did not happen in a vacuum. It reflected but was also conditioned by a particular political, ideological, and economic context. In addition, Labour's ideational activity was also limited by electoral considerations and institutional constraints. Indeed, one important ideational constraint was the dominance of the austerity paradigm in British and European politics.[37] Though there is little evidence that austerity policies are successful at eliminating public deficits,[38] the neoliberal paradigm, which fathered the austerian response to the debt crisis, was dominant at the time when the Labour Party was developing its post-2010 programme of government. As will become clear in this book, this proved to be a major obstacle that severely hindered Miliband's attempts to develop a credible programme of social democratic renewal. It turns out that other social democratic parties faced a very similar constraint.

The parties of the Coalition Government, influential commentators, international institutions like the EU and the IMF, and even important sections of the Labour Party fully subscribed to the idea that the public deficit was the most important economic problem facing Britain and that austerity was the most plausible response to it. The prevailing belief in austerity at this time had almost a coercive effect, in the sense that it became almost unchallengeable.[39] It also had, as Blyth argued, a persuasive simplicity that resonated with individuals' experiences of domestic economy and public perceptions of how debt could be eliminated.[40]

By contrast, Keynes's 'paradox of thrift', which explained why austerity did not work,[41] was difficult to grasp. It did not help that Conservative politicians and commentators used the language of domestic economy to discuss public finances. References to how the previous Labour Government had 'maxed-up the nation's credit card' were never followed by the explanation that public finances cannot be compared to citizens' personal balance sheets because the State has other resources. It also did not help that Labour did little to challenge this facile but misleading idea. Nor did it help that Labour's response to the deficit was confused and intellectually incoherent as it simultaneously embraced 'austerity lite' whilst claiming that austerity did not work.

Some of Miliband's proposals also lacked Hall's 'comprehensibleness' – that is, they were not easy to grasp. Ideas such as pre-distribution, the relational State, liberal nationalism, or the entrepreneurial State galvanised Miliband's highly intellectual inner circle of advisers and promoted a creative buzz in think-tanks and academic circles, but they were not easily translated into attractive and easily understood policy proposals on the doorstep. And when they were transformed into concrete ideas, such as the freeze on energy bills, or the attack on zero-hours contracts, they were presented as individual retail offers that were tenuously connected to a coherent political agenda and enticing narrative.

But perhaps the main constraint Miliband faced was the legacy of New Labour. After all, it was under the watch of New Labour that the global financial crisis and the deficit crisis emerged. Though New Labour was not responsible for the credit crunch that happened in the United States, or for the irresponsible behaviour of British banks like Northern Rock and RBS, it had facilitated it by supporting light-touch regulation of the financial services industry. In fact, Ed Miliband admitted as much. But more importantly, voters blamed New Labour for the deficit and economic recession that followed the massive bailouts to the banks. Thus, in some party circles it was understood that the only way to overcome the legacy of New Labour was to recognise past mistakes and to articulate a credible economic approach. Miliband resisted the 'concede, and move on' strategy perhaps because he felt there were no guarantees that Labour could really 'move on'. Indeed, it is highly likely that admitting to having overspent whilst in power would open a whole new set of questions that would impose new constraints on the Labour leader.

Another constraint Miliband faced was his party. Much has been made of his ability to keep the party united while in opposition; however, he failed to generate enthusiasm on the Labour benches. To use Hall's criteria, Miliband was unable to build a 'coalition of support' within the Labour Party for his own programme. The level of party support that he encountered was reflective of his own problems as Labour leader. He often appeared aloof from the party, undecided about issues; his deliberative and consensual style of decision-making was often taken as a sign of weakness. At times, he was actually weak. Moreover, his limitations as a communicator, and his unwillingness to play the media game of photo-ops and slick media performances, did not contribute to creating the image of the authoritative and natural-born leader, which, for good or evil, is the type of political leadership that is still valued in contemporary British politics.

The media also contributed to Miliband's woes. Throughout his leadership he faced a very hostile media that was determined to portray him as an inadequate politician who was totally unqualified to govern the country. Unfortunately for Miliband, the media had an important role in defining him as a leader and, in the process, in deciding his electoral prospects. By using particular frames, the media constructs the reputations of politicians by deciding the benchmarks against which their leadership skills and their agendas should be assessed. In the process, the media influences the way the public perceives politicians and political parties.

Because the British media was overly hostile to the Labour leader and devoted considerable energy to undermining his authority and ideas, his image and reputation have suffered as a result. Typically, Miliband was portrayed as 'Red Ed', and his policy proposals were often compared to those of the 'loony' left or, occasionally, to the Venezuela of Hugo Chávez. In other words, his programme was seen as lacking credibility because it was portrayed as too radical. The fact that so many backbenchers were ready to attack and openly criticise Miliband also enabled the media to frame him as a weak leader.

When some of Miliband's ideas were actually popular with voters (for example, the proposals to freeze energy prices), the media used other methods to discredit him. He was regularly 'framed' in media discourses as 'geeky', 'nerdy', and 'weird'. His style, voice, and body language were scrutinised in great detail and were generally assumed to lack authority or to be 'un-prime-ministerial'. Even his inability to eat a bacon sandwich with dignity was presented as the definite proof that he was not fit to enter Downing Street. Indeed, on the eve of the election, the image of Miliband eating a bacon sandwich was used by the *Sun* newspaper as a narrative device to persuade its readers to vote against the Labour Party.

The constraints outlined here undermined Miliband's ability to form a coalition of support for his ideas. As a result, he had to compromise, and some of those compromises led to some intellectual incoherence and vagueness. For example, his proposals to reform British capitalism (which, incidentally were completely ignored by the mainstream media) were undermined by Labour's endorsement of austerity and its approach to the financial services industry. Similarly, his critique of the unresponsive and centralised State resulted in timid proposals for power devolution from Whitehall to English towns and cities.

Last but not least, Miliband's programme was also influenced by electoral considerations. His programme of government had to be sanctioned by British voters and therefore it had to pass the electoral test. But to develop a popular programme was easier said than done. In an age of multiparty politics and of growing political disengagement it is increasingly difficult for political parties – and not only the Labour Party – to decide which coalitions of supporters they need to target in order to secure an electoral victory. For Labour the challenge was particularly difficult as it faced challenges from the left (Greens, Plaid Cymru, and most importantly the Scottish National Party (SNP), the centre (the Liberal Democrats), and the populist right (UKIP).

A word or two about ideologies

Thus far I have explained how I will map out the development of Miliband's programme; however, I have not yet explained which analytical tools will be used to determine whether Miliband's agenda constituted a renewal of social democracy. In order to do so, I will base my analysis on Freeden's morphological approach to the study of ideologies and also (loosely) on his morphology of socialism. As Finlayson pointed out,[42] Freeden's morphological approach dovetails nicely with Schmidt's methodology, in particular with her concepts of programmatic beliefs and political philosophies.

For Freeden, 'ideologies are distinctive configurations of political concepts, and they create specific conceptual patterns from a pool of indeterminate and unlimited combinations'.[43] These concepts can play core, adjacent, or peripheral roles in an ideology.[44] What then defines an ideology is the morphology – that is, the way (or the order) in which those concepts are grouped, but also the meaning ascribed to the different concepts. It is then the way whereby these concepts and their conceptions are arranged that distinguishes one ideology from another.[45] As Freeden explained using a fitting metaphor, an ideology is defined by particular concepts in its morphology as a kitchen differs from a living room by accommodating cookers and sinks.[46] It follows from here that though the morphology of an ideology is in constant mutation (in the same way that we can re-organise the furniture in a room), the structure of an ideology 'may snap' if 'completely alien meanings of concepts are hastily injected into a particular ideology'.[47] Using again Freeden's metaphor, this means that a kitchen stops being one when a cooker is removed and a desk is added. Thus, a political party that so far was defined as socialist will stop being so if it rejects equality or community as morphological concepts. When that happens what emerges is an ideological hybrid. By hybrid, Freeden means groups of concepts that 'cut across overbearing ideological families that have become inadequate categories in their inability to satisfy current comprehensions'.[48]

Freeden's morphological approach to the analysis of ideologies has been criticised for its essentialist assumptions. Andrew Vincent challenged the idea that ideologies are 'concepts bunched together'. Instead they are 'internally complex, intermixed and overlapping',[49] he argued. But despite his reservations, he too accepted the inevitability of a typology.[50] In similar vein, Mark Bevir considered Freeden's conceptual approach problematic because it assumed that ideologies were sets of concepts. According to him, 'ideologies are not constructs combining static, albeit contested concepts or debates'; instead they are 'contingent, changing traditions that people produce through their utterances and actions'.[51] Because ideologies are non-reified, they can only be analysed by tracing how they develop over time and as their 'exponents inherit beliefs and actions, modify them and pass them on to others'.[52] Thus, Bevir prefers to talk about 'traditions', but they are not so radically different from Freeden's morphologies.

Bevir rightly stresses the importance of contextualising ideologies and ideological change, but Freeden's morphological approach does not prevent that contextualisation. Indeed, he argues that the meaning of concepts and the way concepts are prioritised change through time and in reaction to specific contexts. He also assumes that concepts take on different conceptions depending on the context in which they are being used.

Moreover, political parties as carriers of ideologies and as historical institutions are limited in their ability to innovate. Their identity and distinctiveness rely on the understanding of the party's historical commitment to specific values, ends, and sometimes means. The implication of this is that the essentialism that Bevir and Vincent complain about can be, as Buckler and Dolowitz put it, 'a focus of loyalty and a means of rhetorical strategies in the context of party competition'.[53] In other words, the morphology of an ideology can both constrain political parties but also offer opportunities for party change.

The morphology of social democracy

Freeden's morphological approach enables us to make qualitative judgements about the way political parties use and develop ideologies. As Buckler and Dolowitz argued, as historical and ideational institutions political parties are judged on how they follow or deviate from their ideological traditions. Party leaders are acutely aware of this constraint, as party changes tend to be presented as a way of renewing the ideological roots of the party.[54] Thus, in order to make sense of how political parties understand their ideational trajectories it is important to recall the main concepts and values – that is, the morphology of the ideological traditions they claim allegiance to.

The Labour Party defines itself as a socialist party. But this definition is not as straightforward and simple as it seems, because the morphology of democratic socialism and social democracy is highly contested.[55] For a long time they meant different things. As Rafal Soborski said, whereas democratic socialists 'encourage a gradual pursuit of socialism', social democrats 'limit themselves to ensuring an equitable provision of social welfare in the capitalist system', and maintain a critical attitude towards capitalism.[56]

Despite the diversity of socialisms there are concepts that are common to all varieties of democratic socialism and social democracy: namely a concept of human nature rooted in social life and as essentially productive, a belief in the equality of human beings, a conception of history, a conception of welfare and happiness, a critical attitude towards capitalism and the free market, and a belief in democracy and liberty.[57] Across time and space, these concepts have been arranged and re-arranged in a myriad of ways and each arrangement of the socialist morphology has been bitterly contested. For example, the Labour Party has been debating since its foundation whether equality or community is the core concept of socialism. These debates have offered (and continue to do so) wonderful insights about the way political parties understand the world around them, how they prioritise the policy puzzles of the day, and how they see their role in British politics.

This deliberately loose morphology of socialism will enable me to make comparisons between New Labour and the Labour Party under Ed Miliband. Whereas New Labour's ideology was closer to a hybrid[58] than to social democracy because of its uncritical embrace of market capitalism and its acceptance of inequality, the Labour Party under Ed Miliband seemed to be closer to a social democratic morphology because it adopted a critical stance towards capitalism, and placed equality, democracy, and community as core concepts of the party. The party has also adopted localism as a peripheral concept upon which the promotion of equality and democracy rely.

The book identifies four areas where the Labour Party under Ed Miliband departed from New Labour. First, it articulated a critique of capitalism that sought to correct New Labour's uncritical embrace of globalisation and acceptance of neo-liberal orthodoxies. Second, it identified rising inequalities and unequal access to power as major policy puzzles that the party attempted to address. Third, it defended a conception of an active but relational State that simultaneously tried to correct the centralisation that characterised New Labour's statecraft and to revive the party's traditions of ethical and guild socialisms. Fourth, it developed a concept of patriotism that sought to correct New Labour's embrace of globalisation and that reformulated the party's approach to immigration.

This being said, there were some interesting continuities with New Labour, in particular with its earlier years. Like New Labour, the Labour Party under Ed Miliband placed community as a core value of the party. More importantly, the break with the neoliberal orthodoxies of New Labour was not as decisive as the Labour leader intended.

The plan of the book

As a book that seeks to map out the ideological and ideational trajectory of the Labour Party under Ed Miliband it will not offer an exhaustive analysis of all the policy proposals and public policy areas in which the party intervened. Thus, it will not analyse the party's stances on foreign and defence policy, education, law and order, or cultural policies. Indeed, in most of these policy areas, the party's programme was undeveloped. Instead, it will analyse the policy areas that defined Milibandism. By the same token, it will not offer a detailed analysis of the electoral strategy and challenges faced by the Labour Party during Miliband's leadership. Indeed, Tim Bale's *Five Year Mission: The Labour Party under Ed Miliband* offers such a comprehensive and pertinent account of those challenges that there is little left to say about them.[59] Finally, this book does not aim to offer a post-mortem analysis of why Labour lost the 2015 general election in such a catastrophic manner. Indeed, it is going to take some time until the party, observers, and political scientists can come up with a full explanation for that unexpected result. However, by explaining the ideational process that led to the drafting of Labour's 2015 manifesto it will be possible to identify some of the factors that can partly explain Labour's electoral defeat.

Chapter 1 discusses the state of European social democracy in the aftermath of the global financial crisis and ongoing European sovereign debt crisis. The chapter analyses how the process of European integration has weakened the position of social democratic parties in Europe and how it can partly explain their confused answers to the debt crisis of the Eurozone. The purpose of the chapter is to emphasise an important ideational constraint faced by the Labour leader. When Miliband was developing Labour's political programme, Europe was in turmoil and European social democratic parties were in no position to offer either inspiration or institutional support to the type of policies he sought to adopt.

Chapter 2 offers an overview of Miliband's broad agenda and identifies the main themes and ideas of his programme. The chapter also examines the institutional constraints he faced: namely the Labour Party, the media, and the party's relationship with the trade unions.

Whilst Chapters 1 and 2 work as background chapters that will help to understand the ideational, political, and institutional constraints Miliband faced when developing Labour's electoral manifesto, the following four chapters will examine his approach to specific policy areas that defined his agenda and will be similar in format. All these chapters will map out the normative and cognitive ideas that were debated by the Labour leadership, how they were adopted and adapted in the party's narrative and discourse, and how they were transformed into policy proposals. While explaining the process of adoption and adaptation of ideas, the specific political and institutional constraints associated with that policy area will be identified and discussed. There is some artificiality in the division of chapters by policy areas given that there are often overlaps between them; however, this separation will make the analysis clearer.

Thus, Chapter 3 deals with Miliband's economic agenda, Chapter 4 explains Miliband's equality and social justice agenda, Chapter 5 concentrates on Miliband's programme of democratic renewal and public services reform, and Chapter 6 focuses on Miliband's politics of belonging. Finally, the Conclusion brings all the different pieces of Labour's programme together and considers whether its programme constituted a renewal of social democracy. The Conclusion also reflects on the role of ideas in politics and on the constraints political leaders face when committed to a process of political change.

Notes

1 Ed Miliband, 'The New Generation: Speech to the 2010 Labour Party Annual Conference', 28 September 2010, www.labour.org.uk/ed-miliband–a-new-generation,2010-09-28 (accessed 10 January 2012).

2 Miliband, 'The New Generation'.

3 Mark Blyth, *Great Transformations: Economic Ideas and Institutional Change in the Twentieth Century* (Cambridge: Cambridge University Press 2002).

4 Alan Greenspan, quoted in Steve Coll, 'The Whole Intellectual Edifice', *New Yorker*, 23 October 2008, http://www.newyorker.com/news/steve-coll/the-whole-intellectual-edifice (accessed 20 August 2014).

5 The exact quote was: 'You never want a serious crisis to go to waste'; Rahm Emanuel, 'You never want a serious crisis to go to waste', 18 November 2008, https://www.youtube.com/watch?v=1yeA_kHHLow (accessed 22 August 2014).

6	Colin Hay, 'Treating the Symptom Not the Condition: Crisis Definition, Deficit Reduction and the Search for a New British Growth Model', *British Journal of Politics and International Relations* 15:1 (February 2013): 23–37 (p. 24).

7	In this study I use Daniel Béland and Robert Henry Cox's concept of ideas. For them, 'ideas are causal beliefs', and as such they 'posit connections between things and between people in the world' and they can 'provide guides for actions'. In Daniel Béland and Robert Henry Cox, 'Introduction: Ideas and Politics', in Daniel Béland and Robert Henry Cox (eds), *Ideas and Politics in Social Science Research* (Oxford: Oxford University Press, 2011), pp. 1–26 (pp. 10–11).

8	Sheri Berman, *The Primacy of Politics: Social Democracy and the Making of Europe's Twentieth Century* (Cambridge: Cambridge University Press, 2010), p. 11.

9	Blyth, *Great Transformations*, p. 37.

10	Blyth, *Great Transformations*, p. 44. See also Daniel Béland, 'The Idea of Power and the Role of Ideas', *Political Studies* 8 (2010): 145–154 (p. 145).

11	Blyth, *Great Transformations*, p. 37.

12	Richard Heffernan, *New Labour and Thatcherism: Political Change in Britain* (Houndmills: Palgrave Macmillan, 2001), p. 14.

13	Kathleen Thelen, 'Historical Institutionalism in Comparative Politics', *Annual Review of Political Science* 2 (1999): 369–404 (p. 380).

14	Vivien A. Schmidt, 'Taking Ideas and Discourse Seriously: Explaining Change through Discursive Institutionalism as the Fourth "New Institutionalism"', *European Political Science Review* 2:1 (2010): 1–25 (p. 4).

15	Alan Finlayson, 'Rhetoric and the Political Theory of Ideologies', *Political Studies* 60:4 (2012): 751–767 (p. 765).

16	Vivien A. Schmidt, 'Discursive Institutionalism: The Explanatory Power of Ideas and Discourse', *Annual Review of Political Science Review* 11 (2008): 303–326 (p. 314).

17	Schmidt, 'Discursive Institutionalism', p. 322.

18	Schmidt, 'Taking Ideas and Discourse Seriously', p. 4.

19	Schmidt, 'Discursive Institutionalism', p. 309.

20	Schmidt, 'Discursive Institutionalism', p. 309.

21	Schmidt, 'Discursive Institutionalism', pp. 305–307.

22	Alan Finlayson, 'From Blue to Green and Everything in Between: Ideational Change and Left Political Economy after New Labour', *British Journal of Politics and International Relations* 15 (2013): 70–88 (p. 71).

23	I am using Peter M. Haas's concept of epistemic community, which he described in the following manner: 'an epistemic community may consist of professionals from a variety of disciplines and backgrounds, they have (1) a shared set of normative and principled beliefs, which provide a value-based rationale for the social action of community members; (2) shared causal beliefs, which are derived from their analysis of practices leading or contributing to a central set of problems in their domain and which then serve as the basis for elucidating the multiple linkages between possible policy options and desired outcomes; (3) shared notions of validity – that is, intersubjective, internally defined criteria for weighing and validating knowledge in the domain of their expertise; and (4) a common policy enterprise – that is, a set of common practices associated with a set of problems to which their professional competence is directed, presumably out of the conviction that human welfare will be enhanced as a result'. Peter M. Haas, 'Introduction: Epistemic Communities and International Policy Coordination', *International Organization* 46:1 (Winter 1992): 1–35 (p. 3).

24 Finlayson, 'From Blue to Green', p. 74.

25 Schmidt, 'Discursive Institutionalism', p. 311.

26 Margaret Weir, 'Ideas and Politics: The Acceptance of Keynesianism in Britain and the United States', in Peter A. Hall (ed.), *The Political Power of Economic Ideas: Keynesianism across Nations* (Princeton: Princeton University Press, 1989), pp. 53–86 (pp. 54–59). ·

27 Peter A. Hall, 'Conclusion: The Politics of Keynesian Ideas', in Hall, *The Political Power of Economic Ideas*, pp. 361–391 (p. 367). See also Peter A. Hall, 'Policy Paradigms, Social Learning, and the State: The Case of Economic Policymaking in Britain', *Comparative Politics* 25:3 (April 1993): 275–296.

28 Hall, 'Conclusion', p. 367. See also Hall, 'Policy Paradigms'.

29 Hall, 'Conclusion', p. 370.

30 Hall, 'Conclusion', pp. 369–370. See also Jal Mehta, 'The Varied Roles of Ideas in Politics: From "Whether" to "How"', in Béland and Cox, *Ideas and Politics*, pp. 23–46 (pp. 28–29). Dobbin, Simmons, and Garrett add a further condition to Hall's approach. In order to gain political ascendancy ideas need also to be theorised and promoted by epistemic communities or policy entrepreneurs. For the purposes of this book, I will not explore this condition, as many of Miliband's ideas had been theorised by epistemic communities. Frank Dobbin, Beth Simmons, and Geoffrey Garrett, 'The Global Diffusion of Public Policies: Social Construction, Coercion, Competition, or Learning?', *Annual Review of Sociology* 33 (2007): 449–472 (p. 454).

31 Hall, 'Policy Paradigms', p. 280.

32 Finlayson, 'From Blue to Green', p. 75.

33 Hans-Dieter Kingemann, Richard I. Hofferbert, and Ian Budge, *Parties, Policies and Democracy* (Oxford: Westview Press, 1994), p. 24. See also Ian Budge, 'A New Spatial Theory of Party Competition: Uncertainty, Ideology and Policy Equilibria Viewed Comparatively and Temporally', *British Journal of Political Science* 24:4 (October 1994): 443–467 (p. 448).

34 Michael Freeden, 'Ideology and Political Theory', *Journal of Political Ideologies* 11:1 (February 2006): 3–22 (p. 18).

35 Richard Heffernan, 'Labour's New Labour Legacy: Politics after Blair and Brown', *Political Studies Review* 9 (2011): 163–177 (p. 169).

36 Schmidt, 'Discursive Institutionalism', p. 310.

37 Colin Crouch, *The Strange Non-Death of Neoliberalism* (Cambridge: Polity Press, 2011). Andrew Gamble, *The Spectre at the Feast: Capitalist Crisis and the Politics of Recession* (Houndmills: Palgrave Macmillan, 2009). Andrew Gamble, *Crisis without End? The Unravelling of Western Prosperity* (Houndmills: Palgrave Macmillan, 2014). Mark Blyth, *Austerity: The History of a Dangerous Idea* (Oxford: Oxford University Press, 2013).

38 Gamble, *Crisis without End?*; Blyth, *Austerity*.

39 Dobbin, Simmons, and Garrett, 'The Global Diffusion of Public Policies', p. 456.

40 Blyth, *Austerity*, p. 10.

41 Polly Toynbee, 'Tories at Half-Time: Cruel and Inept, with Worse to Come', *Guardian*, 3 December 2012.

42 Finlayson, 'From Blue to Green', p. 74.

43 Michael Freeden, *Ideologies and Political Theory: A Conceptual Approach* (Oxford: Clarendon Press, 1998), p. 4.

44 Freeden, *Ideologies and Political Theory*, p. 77.

45 Michael Freeden, 'Practising Ideology and Ideological Practices', *Political Studies*, special issue, 48:2 (2000): 302–322 (p. 304).

46 Freeden, *Ideologies and Political Theory: A Conceptual Approach*, p. 62.

47 Freeden, *Ideologies and Political Theory*, p. 82.

48 Michael Freeden, 'Conclusion: Ideology – Balances and Projections', in Michael Freeden (ed.), *Reassessing Political Ideologies: The Durability of Dissent* (London: Routledge, 2001), pp. 193–208 (pp. 195–196).

49 Andrew Vincent, *Modern Political Ideologies*, 2nd edn (Oxford: Blackwell, 1998), p. 19.

50 Vincent, *Modern Political Ideologies*, p. 91.

51 Mark Bevir, 'New Labour: A Study in Ideology', *British Journal of Politics and International Relations* 2:3 (2000): 277–301 (p. 281).

52 Bevir, 'New Labour', p. 280.

53 Steve Buckler and David P. Dolowitz, 'Ideology, Party Identity and Renewal', *Journal of Political Ideologies* 14:1 (February 2009): 11–30 (p. 13).

54 Buckler and Dolowitz, 'Ideology, Party Identity and Renewal', p. 13.

55 Rafal Soborski, *Ideology in a Global Age: Continuity and Change* (Houndmills: Palgrave Macmillan, 2013), p. 89.

56 Soborski, *Ideology in a Global Age*, p. 90.

57 Vincent, *Modern Political Ideologies*, pp. 91–95. Freeden, *Ideologies and Political Theory*, pp. 420–433.

58 Eunice Goes, *A era Blair em exame* (Lisbon: Quimera, 2003).

59 Tim Bale, *Five Year Mission: The Labour Party under Ed Miliband* (Oxford: Oxford University Press, 2015).

1

Social democracy at a time of crisis

I think this is a centre-left moment ... But for me it's a centre-left moment because people think there's something unfair and unjust about our society. You've got to bring the vested interests to heel; you've got to change the way the economy works. That's our opportunity.

Ed Miliband[1]

Eight years have passed since the beginning of the global financial crisis but its impact still reverberates across Europe. Levels of public debt are still high, the stability of European banks is questioned by rating agencies, economic growth is anaemic, and millions of people are still feeling the impact of unemployment and falling living standards. In fact, at the time of writing the spectre of permanent economic stagnation haunts Europe.

The global financial crisis that metamorphosed into a debt crisis and deep economic recession has also had a profound political impact. For those few social democratic parties that were in power when the crisis hit Europe, the impact was devastating. As they were forced to implement draconian public spending cuts in response to ballooning public deficits, voters blamed them for the economic recession that followed those austerity measures and condemned them to the opposition. In the process, these parties lost their credibility as efficient and safe managers of the economy.

But European social democracy is not merely suffering from a crisis of credibility. It is also suffering from an identity and ideological crisis. What had been social democracy's economic paradigm for over a decade was reduced to smithereens with the collapse of Lehman Brothers on Wall Street. As the old certainties floundered on Wall Street and in the City of London, and the State was left to pick up the pieces, European social democrats had no coherent response to those dramatic events. Some talked about a new 'social democratic moment', but few offered concrete ideas about how to create it, and most succumbed to austerity policies.

Their state of intellectual and ideological confusion was somewhat understand-able. On the one hand the magnitude of what was happening was too big to be fully comprehensible. On the other, the right, supported by the institutions of the EU, transformed what was a crisis of capitalism into a crisis of the State, which could only be cured by drastic public spending cuts and structural reforms. Thus, as Mark Blyth aptly put it, 'austerity became and remains the default policy response to the financial crisis in the Eurozone for both material and ideological reasons':[2] material because there have been few other easily available policy options, and ideological because the programme of reducing the size of the State matched the programmatic aims of the centre-right governments that governed most countries of the Eurozone at the time.

The crisis in European social democracy had a direct impact on the Labour Party. First, because Labour in Britain faced very similar challenges, and second, because there were few examples from which Ed Miliband could draw inspiration to develop his own response to the deficit crisis and deep economic recession that affected Britain. In other words, there were no social democratic parties in government or in opposition with plausible ideas and policy responses that offered an alternative to austerity.

In the countries of the Eurozone, the social democratic left was too absorbed by the intricacies of the requirements of the monetary union even to consider big-picture questions about models of capitalism. The absence of real alternatives is important because the first condition to effect transformative change is to have new, plausible, and coherent ideas that can offer some guidance on how to respond to specific political puzzles. If those ideas are missing, then there is little chance that a programme of political change can be developed.[3]

As Miliband's difficulties in developing a successful programme of political change cannot be properly understood without reference to current debates about the future of European social democracy, this chapter examines the ideational cri-sis of European social democracy in the post-global economic crisis period. To do so, it focuses on the institutional (in particular, the policy requirements of the Single Market and of the monetary union) and ideational constraints (the prevailing neoliberalism/ordoliberal[4] approach informing EU policy) that European social democratic parties faced whilst trying to find an ideologically coherent response to the sovereign debt crisis. Next, the chapter explains the impact of the Eurozone crisis on European social democratic parties. It also analyses how the radical left and the populist or extreme right are benefiting from the intellectual and ideological turmoil of European social democracy. The final section of the chapter assesses the failed attempts to develop a social democratic alternative to austerity politics.

Social democracy and European integration

The confused and incoherent response of European social democratic parties to the global financial and economic crisis and the Eurozone sovereign debt crisis is partly the result of the ambiguous relationship European social democracy has developed with the project of European integration. It is important to note that this ambiguous relationship is not uniform across the different social democratic parties. Instead, European social democrats developed a variety of reactions and approaches to the project of European integration. For instance, the German Sozialdemokratische Partei Deutschlands (SPD) maintained until the 1990s a sceptical attitude to European integration, mistrusting the 'market-making' nature of its project whilst at the domestic level it did not challenge the ordoliberal assumptions that had shaped Germany's postwar economic policy. A similar sceptical attitude could be found in the British Labour Party and in the French Parti socialiste (PS). Likewise, in Scandinavian countries, social democrats feared that the deepening of European integration could undermine their generous welfare states. But for the socialist parties of Southern Europe the European project inspired an altogether different response. For these parties the project was a guarantor of both democracy and economic prosperity. But with time, as argued by Dionyssis Dimitrakopoulos, most, if not all, European social democratic parties 'came to lend their – often critical – support to it'.[5]

From the late 1980s the diversity of positions on the European project became blurred and less relevant as the EU demanded greater uniformity from its member states in important policy areas such as macroeconomics, trade, and environmental policies, as well as in all the policy areas covered by the Single Market. With time, the internal dynamics of the European Single Market and of the monetary union became the accepted mould from which national policies had to be adopted and adapted.

The Single Market's four freedoms – workers, goods, services, and capital – were predicated on programmes of privatisation of public services and on economic and financial liberalisation, as well as on the erosion of labour and social rights that the freedom of movement of workers across the EU de facto provoked. As Gerassimos Moschonas showed, 'the politicisation of integration through a dense, rigid, institutional apparatus has consolidated and solidified the liberalisation of Europe'.[6] It turns out that in the medium-to-long term this development was detrimental to social democratic aims and means.

The first socialist or social democrat government to fall victim to this dynamic was François Mitterrand's PS in 1983. After two years of radical policies – which included nationalisations, the rise of the minimum wage, an interventionist industrial policy, the reduction of the working week to thirty-nine hours, and the strengthening of labour rights – Mitterrand was forced to implement drastic public spending cuts in order to fight inflation but also to remain within the then European Monetary System, the precursor of the monetary union.[7] Mitterrand's U-turn, called 'le tournant de la rigueur' (the shift to austerity), was conceived with two goals in mind. First, it aimed to pursue a *franc fort* policy; second, it aimed to neutralise the re-emergence of Germany as a dominant power in Europe. Interestingly, this U-turn was perceived in French socialist circles as

'Mitterrand's choice for Europe rather than socialism' and was defined as the PS's 'Bad Godesberg moment'.[8] However, Mitterrand's choice came with a price tag. A strong-franc approach led to the dramatic rise of unemployment, which has persisted for over three decades.

This path was then set in stone for all EU member states with the signing of the Treaty of Maastricht in 1992. As Perry Anderson said, after Maastricht, the 'historical commitments of both Social and Christian Democracy to full employment or social services of the traditional welfare state, already scaled down or cut back, would cease to have any further institutional purchase'.[9] The convergence criteria set in the Maastricht Treaty (public debt no higher than 60 per cent and public deficit no higher than 3 per cent of GDP, inflation within 1.5 per cent) not only drastically reduced the ability of member states to decide macroeconomic policy, but also reflected a small-state, or, in the words of Perry Anderson, a '*less* state', vision of Europe.[10] This neoliberal/ordoliberal logic was later on reinforced by the Stability and Growth Pact imposed by Germany as a way of ensuring that members of the monetary union complied with the convergence criteria and maintained fiscal discipline. In the process, European social democrats became active contributors to the construction of an 'ordoliberal' Europe.[11]

The macroeconomic approach underpinning the Single Market and the monetary union was consistent with the monetarist/ordoliberal approach promoted by centre-right governments in Europe; however, it was problematic for social democrats. As Moschonas argued, 'granting autonomy to central banks and to the European Central Bank – conservative, "inflation averse" institutions – at the national and European levels respectively constitutes an institutional constraint which significantly limits social-democratic freedom of manoeuvre'.[12] Indeed, for the members of the Eurozone it is next to impossible to invest in ambitious programmes of infrastructure building or to deepen the levels of social protection without violating the governing rules of the monetary union.

European social democrats tried to neutralise the monetarist effects of the Maastricht Treaty by making calls for a 'social Europe'. For example, the then president of the European Commission, Jacques Delors (himself a socialist) convinced some reluctant social democrats that 'more Europe' was the only way to secure the European social model. To a certain extent, the Social Chapter of the Maastricht Treaty tried to harmonise labour rights and social protection; however, the harmonisation of certain aspects of the welfare state was never on the cards.[13] Those countries that had weak welfare states did not have incentives to develop them further. More importantly, these developments signalled the impossibility of pursuing social democratic policies at the national level but also at the EU level. As social democratic governments have a limited scope to deliver social democratic policies to their voters, the national level then becomes irrelevant.[14] However, and as Moschonas claimed, 'the European level is neither sufficiently structured and unified, nor sufficiently flexible, to facilitate the implementation of a European social democratic strategy'.[15] In other words, European social democrats found themselves in an ideological cul-de-sac. Their embrace of the European project left them unable to deliver the type of vision and policies that were inscribed in their ideological and historical DNA.

For one reason or another, socialists and social democrats across Europe accepted this logic. Interestingly enough, it was only the Scandinavian countries who rejected the membership of the single currency on social democratic grounds. Indeed, they did not want to erode their welfare states. By contrast, in Southern Europe, membership of the single currency was presented as the 'only game in town', with centre-right and centre-left parties pursuing it as a 'patriotic cause'. Moreover, socialists in Portugal, Spain, and Greece believed that the Single Market and later the monetary union would enable them to launch the market-corrective policies that they could no longer implement nationally. In Germany and in the Netherlands, the social democratic left, which had been in opposition for most of the 1980s, came to accept the idea that the return to power required the acceptance of the agenda of their opponents. By the early 1990s, the British Labour Party endorsed the values of the Single Market and of the European Social Chapter, and advocated Britain's membership of the European Exchange Rate Mechanism (which set the path to EMU membership).[16]

Though the Single Market established strict rules and monitoring mechanisms to ensure that liberalisation and privatisation processes would proceed according to plan, the endorsement of this neoliberal/ordoliberal agenda was more acutely felt in the countries that joined the single currency. Indeed, in order to meet the convergence criteria set in Maastricht, the members of the monetary union introduced drastic public spending cuts to reduce public deficits but which had the side effect of negatively affecting their economic growth rates. Indeed, for the poorer countries of the Eurozone which had relatively open economies and relied on exports, joining the single currency had an immediate negative impact on their balance-of-trade figures. If before joining the single currency the low costs of their exports gave them a competitive edge in international markets, when the euro was launched that advantage disappeared almost overnight. In addition, the acceptance of this agenda had important consequences for social democratic parties. By agreeing to a monetarist approach they were subscribing to an economic model of growth that imposed significant constraints on the ability of national governments to respond to economic crisis or to invest in public infrastructures and in public services. In some cases, it led to the enactment of reforms that had the effect of eroding social rights and undermining the welfare state.

Third-way politics and neo-revisionism

As we saw in the previous section, the logic of European integration imposed severe constraints upon European social democracy. But there were other contributing factors to the electoral decline of European social democrats. The stagflation of the 1970s demonstrated to many the shortcomings of Keynesian economics, robbing social democrats of an economic narrative with which to sway voters. Moreover, citizens started to question the key achievements of European social democracy, in particular the universality values underpinning the welfare state and the level of bureaucratic control that accompanied it.[17]

Another important factor explaining the electoral decline of social democratic parties was the economic transformation that led to the drastic reduction of the industrial working class and to the decline of trade unions. If we link these demographic changes in the composition of the electorate to the decline of partisan identification and subsequent partisan de-alignment, we have a potent combination that has contributed to a substantial reduction in the share of the vote held by social democratic parties across Europe. Simply put, the traditional coalitions of supporters that historically had voted for social democratic parties were substantially diminished.

But social democrats also lost faith in their own solutions. As Donald Sassoon argued, by the mid-1990s social democrats 'were not optimistic about their own future' and 'mentioned socialism less and less'.[18] By contrast, the New Right was in a triumphalist mood as it saw its vision vindicated in the policies implemented by the EU, and in the United States and Britain. This intellectual and political confidence led to a relentless attack on statist solutions (and in particular on the welfare state), to a celebration of markets and consumer choice as liberators of human potential, and to the praise of private initiative as the engine of economic innovation and prosperity for all.

The new confidence of the right, which was reinforced by the defeatism of the left, changed the terms of the political debate and created what Andrew Gamble called 'a new economic morality', based on market values.[19] This 'new economic morality' became the orthodox thinking adopted by most social democratic parties. Indeed, they accepted a neo-revisionism that postulated that the goal of socialism was no longer to transform capitalism, but to accommodate it even if that meant dismissing the egalitarian ethos that had hitherto characterised social democracy.[20] Consequently, social democrats accepted the neoliberal axiom about the unsustainability of the welfare state and became enthusiastic advocates of privatisations – labour market reforms that effectively hollowed out the welfare state. They also promoted the marketisation and privatisation of public services and fiscal discipline, turned a blind eye to the financialisation of European economies, and became keen promoters of individualist and entrepreneurial values.

The neo-revisionism implied as well that social democrats accepted the limits of State socialism. That is, social democrats accepted that the regulation of the market could only be achieved through supranational means, which implied that 'the concept of national roads to socialism should be abandoned'.[21] Thus, social democrats stopped promoting Keynesian economics, started to endorse fiscal discipline and low inflation as the macroeconomic panaceas to achieve the holy grail of economic growth and job creation. In the process they surrendered – without hesitation – the ability of national governments to decide their macroeconomic policies to a supra-national body. As we saw, this acceptance of neoliberalism was set in motion at different times for different social democratic parties, but by the late 1990s social democratic neo-revisionism was the only game in town.

This strategy paid off electorally, at least in the short term. In the late 1990s there was a revival of social democratic parties in Europe. In the short period from 1995 to 1999, twelve countries of the European Union were led by social democratic parties (some in coalition governments). This electoral revival coincided with the strategy of the ideological accommodation to neoliberalism. From Lisbon to London, European social democrats talked incessantly about having found the formula to generate economic growth *and* social justice. Social democrats believed that redistributionist policies as well as a commitment to some vague idea of social justice could only be delivered by high rates of economic growth, and these could only be achieved through economic de-regulation, and greater reliance on the financialisation of the economy and on the erosion of workers' rights.[22]

In most cases, the process of European integration was the vehicle for the social democratic neo-revisionism. This being said, Tony Blair's 'Third Way' offered an intellectual and ideological justification for the policies that centre-left parties were now pursuing. With the exception of the French socialist prime minister Lionel Jospin, who insisted that markets should be subordinate to politics, most European social democratic governments participated enthusiastically in the debates about the Third Way.

This Euro-enthusiasm for the Third Way generated a lot of intellectual froth, but it also produced a policy agenda. Its most visible result was the Lisbon Agenda of 2000, which aimed to turn the EU into the 'most competitive and dynamic knowledge-based economy in the world capable of sustainable economic growth with more and better jobs and greater social cohesion' by 2010. Thus far, the Lisbon Agenda has failed in its stated goals, but it is revealing of the intellectual mindset of European social democrats at the time.

Underpinning the Lisbon Agenda were proposals to reform the welfare state, which combined active labour market policies with conditional social rights, and the adoption of means-testing criteria to decide access to welfare benefits. The implicit logic of the Lisbon Agenda was that full employment could only be achieved at the expense of security in the labour market. Interestingly, the Lisbon Agenda did not propose either to regulate globalisation or to mitigate its adverse effects. Instead, financial and economic globalisation was seen as a force of nature that could not be challenged.

In the early 2000s the European social democratic wave collapsed. One by one, those social democratic parties that had been in power (heading majority governments or in coalition) in the golden era of the Third Way found themselves on the opposition benches. The demise of Third Way politics can be explained in part by its electoral outcomes. In the 1990s most of these parties secured parliamentary majorities, however their share of the vote was becoming smaller. The reality was that the electoral base of European social democratic parties has been in steady decline for the past decades. As Marlière reminds us, in the 1990s, European social democratic parties attracted only 29.7 per cent of the vote (in the EU12), which was below the 1980s average (31.1 per cent), and well below the 1950s average (33.2 per cent).[23]

By 2005, most EU countries, including France and Germany, were led by centre-right governments. The few social democratic parties in government across the EU had very little room for manoeuvre. Indeed, they faced the double-whammy of having to implement the fiscal discipline required by the Stability and Growth Pact whilst they dealt with the political consequences of slow economic growth and rising unemployment that resulted from the membership of the single currency.

The impact of the financial crisis in Europe

When the 2007–08 credit crunch hit the United States, and soon after the United Kingdom, European leaders were alarmed, but overall they felt that the crisis was primarily American in nature and in its origins. In short, Europe had no reasons to be too worried because European capitalism was allegedly more robust. But this state of denial did not last long. Those German and French leaders who thought that Europe could be insulated from the problems of Anglo-American capitalism were soon reminded of how the financial sector was internationally integrated. Moreover, and as Andrew Gamble argued, German and French banks were as enamoured of 'casino capitalism' as their American or British counterparts.[24]

The initial response to the global financial crisis was one that used the power of the State to save capitalism from itself. In the United States, the Bush administration bailed out the banks that were deemed too big to fail, and Barack Obama was elected president in 2008 on a pro-stimulus and anti-Wall Street platform. In Europe, the picture was somewhat similar. European Institutions instructed all governments of the Eurozone to bail out the failing banks, whilst several European governments started stimulus programmes. Under the stewardship of the then prime minister Gordon Brown, the G-7 countries agreed in 2009 to implement a large programme of economic stimulus that sought to save the financial sector and to prevent a global recession.

However, the approach defended by the EU proved to be too minimalist and inadequate. As Moschonas put it, 'Europe was seeking Keynesian-type solutions to the crisis while at the same time striving to maintain a neo-liberal status quo to preserve the Stability and Growth Pact.'[25] The leader of the German SPD, Peer Steinbrück, identified this contradiction when he labelled Gordon Brown's 2009 stimulus package as an example of 'crass Keynesianism.'[26] Unsurprisingly, this approach led to the exponential rise of public deficits across the EU.[27] Most European countries, including those that had budgetary surpluses before the crisis – such as Spain and Ireland – saw their public deficits rise dramatically.

The rise of public deficits was particularly problematic to the Eurozone countries. As saving the single currency was the priority of EU institutions, European governments were under pressure to tackle their public deficits by implementing programmes of drastic public spending cuts and tax rises. But these public spending cuts soon plunged Eurozone countries (in particular the countries of the periphery) into deep economic recessions and achieved only modest results as deficit reduction strategies.

Not all Eurozone countries were able to convince the financial markets about their ability to pay their national debts and to reduce their budget deficits. The bond markets, aided by the rating agencies, soon started to exploit this inequality by speculating heavily on the weakest links of the Eurozone area. Soon the bailouts that the austerity measures sought to avoid became inevitable.

Greece was the first casualty of this logic. The Greek situation was made worse by the revelations of the then prime minister, George Papandreou, about the true state of Greece's public finances. In 2010, a candid Papandreou decided to tell the truth: the previous Government (with the help of Goldman Sachs) had lied about the real size of the public deficit and of its public debt–GDP ratio. It turned out that in 2009 Greece's public deficit was at 13.6 per cent of GDP and its debt was 115 per cent of the GDP. This revelation provoked an immediate response from the bond markets, whose speculative interventions raised the cost of borrowing to prohibitive heights.

Prevented from devaluing its currency or from defaulting, the Greek Government had to wait for a response from the European Central Bank (ECB) and from its Eurozone partners, whilst it implemented round after round of public spending cuts and tax rises. But Papandreou's promise to 'put the house in order' did nothing to assuage the financial markets. The economy contracted, unemployment rose dramatically, and the waves of strikes and popular discontent were a real threat to political stability.

But the EU still did not know how to respond, and the dithering had dramatic consequences for Greece. Northern European countries, led by Germany and the ECB, debated moral hazard issues. They feared that giving bailouts to weaker European economies would reward fiscal irresponsibility. Whilst this debate was going on, the continued speculation in the financial markets led to unaffordable borrowing costs that made a bailout inevitable. Finally, in May 2010, the ECB, the European Commission (EC), and the IMF (known as the troika) proposed what the Nobel prize-winning economist Joseph Stiglitz defined as a 'shock and awe' bailout programme.[28] In exchange for a bailout of €110 billion Greece had to implement a draconian programme of public sector cuts, privatisations, and substantial structural reforms. The austerity measures brought Greece almost to bankruptcy and caused unprecedented levels of popular unrest that eventually led to Papandreou's resignation. In the meantime the party system imploded. The EU orchestrated the appointment of the former head of Greece's Central Bank, Lucas Papademos, to lead a 'technocratic government' in November 2011, which lasted until the 2012 parliamentary elections. The unclear electoral results of these elections resulted in a coalition government between the centre-right party New Democracy, and the centre-left Panhellenic Socialist Movement (PASOK).

After the Greek bailout, financial speculators shifted their attentions to Ireland and Portugal, which were perceived as the next vulnerable Eurozone countries. The sequence of events followed to the letter the script applied to Greece. Financial speculation resulted in the dramatic rise in interest rates in the bond markets, making the cost of borrowing unaffordable to these countries. In December 2010, the Irish prime minister Brian Cowen was forced to ask the ECB–IMF–EC troika for a rescue package of €85 billion. The troika approved the loan on the condition that the Irish Government would implement a programme of spending cuts and structural reforms, and commit itself to reducing the budget deficit to 3 per cent of the GDP in a four-year period.

Three months after the Irish bailout, it was the time for the socialist Portuguese Government to ask the troika for a €78 billion rescue plan. As in the case of Greece and Ireland the conditions attached to the Portuguese bailout were draconian public spending cuts; tax rises; and privatisations and structural reforms to the labour market, to the health-care system, and to unemployment protection. The implementation of these structural adjustment programmes plunged these three countries into deep economic recessions from which they have yet not recovered.

As Spain and Italy were the next targets of financial speculators, the Spanish and Italian governments tried to pre-empt a financial rescue plan (and all the social and political implications such plans entailed) by implementing successive waves of public spending cuts, and labour market and welfare reforms. Fearing contagion, most, if not all, governments of the Eurozone started to pursue austerity measures. The purpose of these punitive policies was to reassure the financial markets; to prevent new troika bailouts; and to protect the integrity of the single currency, whose future was at that time uncertain.

The effects of austerity in the Eurozone countries have been devastating. The contraction of the economies of the 'rescued' countries has led to a dramatic rise in unemployment, in particular amongst the young; poverty has made a comeback to Southern Europe. Crucially, the bailed-out countries failed the public deficits targets set out by the troika. In fact, the austerity measures had such a negligible effect on Greek debt that Greece's withdrawal from the monetary union is, at the time of writing, a real possibility. Both Ireland and Portugal fared slightly better, but they were given more time to meet their public deficit and public debt targets. In the summer of 2014, the troika declared 'mission accomplished', and as a result Ireland and Portugal exited from their perspective bailout programmes; however, their public deficits and public debt are still above the level required by the Stability and Growth Pact, and the size of their economies has markedly shrunk.

Social democrats and the sovereign debt crisis

In the midst of these dramatic events, social democrats had very little to say about the causes of the Eurozone debt crisis and even less about solutions to address it. At the time, social democratic parties were still attached to the economic paradigm upon which the 1990s social democratic revival had been based. If some sought to resuscitate Keynesianism and 'bring back the State', they did it with little conviction.

In fairness, most social democratic parties were in opposition at that time, thus they lacked the institutional and popular support to promote these ideas vigorously. In particular, the two largest European social democratic parties – the French PS and the German SPD – were in opposition and were therefore unable to offer a coordinated response. Whereas the French PS tried to articulate a Keynesian response, the German SPD did not question the ordoliberal/monetarist logic at the heart of the monetary union. In fact, for the SPD, the solution for the Eurozone crisis was 'more Europe'[29] in the shape of a fiscal union.

Those social democratic parties that were in power, like those in Greece, Spain, and Portugal, were equally powerless. They had little or no ability to challenge the full force of the financial and currency markets, the diktats of the Stability and Growth Pact and of the German Government. Most had accepted the requirements of the single currency and, in the words of Jürgen Habermas, had elevated the Stability and Growth Path to the status of a 'fetish'.[30] As a result, a commitment to reducing the public deficit through severe public spending cuts was the main priority. Apart from some isolated voices, European social democrats only demanded some minor adjustments to the Stability and Growth Pact, tighter financial regulation, the introduction of a financial transactions tax, and some piecemeal reforms to keep the credit rating agencies and the financial markets off their backs. Still today, the social democratic parties of the Eurozone are committed to maintaining the integrity of the monetary union with all its original neoliberal/ordoliberal accoutrements.

In policy terms this meant that most accepted the logic of austerity. In 2011, the Irish Labour Party entered a coalition with Fine Gael and is implementing the austerity policies imposed by the troika. In Portugal, the socialist Government, which imposed two years of public spending cuts before negotiating the bailout deal with the troika, was defeated in 2012 and now defends a softer version of austerity (though an important faction of the party wants to reconsider Portugal's membership of the single currency). In Spain, the socialist Government of José Luis Rodríguez Zapatero was decimated at the 2011 elections, following two years of eye-watering spending cuts, tax rises, and a dramatic rise in the unemployment rate.[31] In Greece, PASOK faced a similar fate. At the 2015 legislative elections, the party was relegated to the league of small parties, obtaining only 4.7 per cent of the vote.

The few social democratic parties that were in power in the EU during this period accepted austerity too. After a period in opposition, the Dutch Labour Party joined a pro-austerity coalition government in 2012 with the centre-right People's Party for Freedom and Democracy. In Denmark, the social democrats have led the Coalition Government in the period of 2011–5, but they offered no alternative to austerity. The prime minister, Helle Thorning-Schmidt, has pursued fiscal discipline, which resulted in a substantial number of redundancies in the public sector and wide-ranging spending cuts to welfare programmes.

The demise of European social democracy was also visible in European institutions. The size of the group of European Socialists in the European Parliament (EP), following the 2009 elections, was reduced to 25 per cent of the seats, and this had an impact on their ability to influence the overall direction of the EU. This trend was confirmed in 2014 when the group of European Socialists and Democrats obtained only a 21 per cent share of the vote at the EP elections. This paltry electoral record enables us to conclude that European social democratic parties have paid a heavy political price for their confused and timid response to the global economic crisis and ultimately for succumbing to austerity policies as the only solution to Europe's sovereign debt crisis. Indeed, they are either deeply unpopular opposition parties, or they are deeply unpopular Government parties.[32]

This outcome should not come as a surprise. Andrew Gamble reminds us that, historically in times of recession, 'parties and leaders of the right have generally been much more adept at seizing the initiative, and framing the narrative in ways which favour them'.[33] In the three big crises of capitalism of the last seventy years, the left has always lost political ground. It was the case in the 1930s, where, with the exception of the United States, the left was punished at the ballot box for the Great Depression. And again, during the stagflation of the 1970s, the left was accused of profligacy with public finances and blamed for the economic crisis. This scenario was repeated in 2008. The social democratic left was blamed for the crisis, and was accused of borrowing too much and of being irresponsible with public finances.

The steady rise of the radical left ...

As social democratic parties find themselves entangled in the politics of austerity and without a coherent and plausible alternative to it, their traditional, but also potential, supporters are looking for answers elsewhere. Many disillusioned centre-left and left-wing voters, who want an alternative to the austerity policies demanded by Brussels, have been seeking ideological succour in radical left parties. These parties are often described in the media as 'far-left' parties, but in effect they are far less dogmatic and committed to a revolutionary agenda than a typical far-left political party. Therefore it is more correct to define them as parties of the radical left.

Across Europe, radical left parties are on the rise. Since 2008 the vote share for these parties has increased on average by 30 per cent.[34] This phenomenon is most pronounced in Greece, where Syriza, a movement that aggregates several radical left parties and associations, won the 2015 parliamentary election, effectively relegating PASOK to the position of seventh place in the Greek party system. Syriza's electoral rise is directly related to the austerity policies imposed by the troika, given that before the crisis this party would routinely obtain no more than 5 per cent of the vote. This spectacular rise was obtained mostly at the expense of the centre-left party PASOK. To understand the magnitude of the decline of mainstream social democracy in Greece it is important to bear in mind that PASOK has been a party of government for the past four decades.

A similar phenomenon is taking place in Spain. At the 2011 parliamentary elections, the coalition United Left–The Greens secured a third place by winning 6.97 per cent of the vote. Since then, PSOE has made little progress at the ballot box. Similarly, at the 2014 EP elections, PSOE lost nine seats, obtaining only 23 per cent of the vote. By contrast, the recently formed movement Podemos was the fourth most voted-for party, obtaining 7.98 per cent of the vote and electing five MEPs;[35] polls suggested that it could be one of the most voted-for parties at the December 2015 parliamentary elections.[36]

In France, Jean-Luc Mélenchon's Left Front has been a thorn in the PS's side, though its results in the first round of the 2012 French presidential election were below the party's expectations. In Germany, Die Linke (or the Left Party), founded in 2007 but with origins in East Germany's Party of Democratic Socialism, became the third-largest political party in the Bundestag following the 2013 elections, winning 8.2 per cent of the vote.[37] As a result of these pressures, the SPD had been unable to secure a majority or even a plurality of votes. At the 2013 election, the SPD marginally increased its share of the vote by only 2.7 per cent to 25.7 per cent, and is now the junior partner of a Christian Democratic Union-led coalition government. Similarly, in Italy, the populist (and difficult to categorise) Five Star Movement led by Beppe Grillo robbed the Democratic Party of a majority at the 2013 general elections, and in Portugal the Left Bloc Party obtained 10.19 per cent of the vote while the Communist/Green Party obtained 8.25 per cent at last year's legislative elections.

In Britain, there is no credible radical left party, but parties that are to the left of the Labour Party have been making an impact. Indeed, the Green Party, and in particular the SNP, were successful at winning centre-left voters who were disillusioned with Labour's embrace of austerity. At the 2015 general election, the SNP won fifty-six of Scotland's fifty-nine seats, and the Green Party obtained 3.8 per cent of the vote.

? UKIP
(see next page)

Similarly, in the Netherlands, the Dutch Labour Party is challenged by the Green Left, whereas in Ireland, Sinn Fein is making electoral inroads into the territory traditionally fought by Labour. Finally, in Finland, Denmark, Norway, and Iceland, radical left parties have participated in coalition governments, and in Cyprus they have governed alone. Rather unsurprisingly, anti-austerity parties are obtaining better electoral results than those mainstream social democratic parties that accepted the austerity policies of the Eurozone.

Several factors explain the popularity of these parties. First, it is clear that the radical left is benefiting from the crisis of social democracy. Indeed, over a quarter of their supporters are disillusioned social democratic voters, and another significant portion come from green supporters.[38] Second, these parties are able to recruit mainstream socialist voters because they have recently undergone an ideological transformation of their own.

The collapse of State Communism in the Soviet Union and in Eastern Europe in the 1990s led many orthodox Leninist parties in Europe to revise their programmes. These parties still present themselves as anti-capitalist, but they are committed to democracy and they do not advocate a planned economy. Instead, they attack neoliberal and globalised capitalism, and defend a mixed economy and the welfare state.[39] The electoral focus of these parties has also changed. Instead of focusing on endless doctrinal debates about the future of socialism, they concentrate on finding pragmatic solutions to current political, economic, and social problems.[40] They are also innovative parties in terms of organisation. Their preference for informal and more horizontal forms of decision-making has attracted many young voters who thus far had refused to get involved in traditional political parties.

The radical left was also able to absorb popular discontent, and thanks to their grassroots campaigns on concrete themes such as home evictions, or health-care provision, have managed to nurture the support of large numbers of voters. As a result of these changes, but also of new campaigning techniques and of a new approach to party organisation, they have de facto become the defenders of the social democratic Keynesian settlement. Moreover, many of their long-standing policies, such as the proposal to introduce a financial transactions tax, have become quite mainstream. Finally, many of these parties, though not all, are ready to enter dialogues and participate in governments with social democratic parties. In other words, radical left parties are in the process of becoming office-seeking, rather than just policy-seeking, political parties.

That being said, the popularity of these parties should not be overstated. In most European countries, the electoral salience of the radical left is negligible. France, Greece, Portugal, and Spain are the only countries where their support reaches over 10 per cent of the electorate. Moreover, the ideological pragmatism of these parties has come at a cost. Because they have become the repositories of the anger and frustration felt by disillusioned voters, who used to vote for social democratic parties, their electoral base is more volatile.[41] Finally, the power-strategies of some (though not all) of these radical left parties can be defined as risky. Indeed, whenever they have joined coalition governments their share of the vote has suffered significant losses at the following elections. Research by Jonathan Olsen, Dan Hough, and Michael Koß has shown that 'when they have participated in government, left parties on average have lost about 25 per cent of their vote'.[42]

But for the moment the weaknesses of radical left parties offer little comfort to the European social democratic left. For as long as austerity policies are pursued (and accepted by European social democrats), and the economic and financial crisis continues to hit voters across Europe, it is likely that the radical left will continue to benefit from the disillusion of progressive voters.

... and the meteoric rise of the populist right

The challenge to social democratic parties does not come merely from the radical left. Rising unemployment, wage stagnation, rising prices, and a sense of insecurity led many working-class voters to seek solace in the messages of populist and extreme-right parties, which claim that Europe and immigration are too blame for their woes. This phenomenon – of shifting allegiances of working-class voters from the left to the populist or far right – is not new. In France, the demise of the Communist Party in the 1980s led many former Communist supporters to defect to the National Front (NF).

In truth, the NF has pursued a deliberate policy of targeting the frustrations of working class voters since 2012 by defending republican values and public services. This strategy has paid off. The NF has become a force to be reckoned with in French politics.[43] At the 2014 EP elections, Marine Le Pen's NF was the most voted-for party, winning 24.86 per cent of votes. However, the electoral strength of the NF should not be overstated. It has only two seats in the National Assembly (out of 577) and two seats in the Senate (out of 348). It is also a party with a weak organisational structure and few cadres, which means that its ability to capitalise on voters' discontent is not unlimited.

In austerity Europe, this phenomenon of *gaucho-lepénisme* is again on the rise. The most significant examples can be found in Greece, where Golden Dawn made impressive electoral gains. At the 2015 general elections it became the third largest party, attracting 6.28 per cent of the vote. In the Netherlands, the Freedom Party has been gaining ground for over a decade, mostly at the expense of the Labour Party. In Denmark, the People's Party has made significant electoral gains, winning 21.1 per cent of the vote at the 2015 legislative elections, and in Sweden the antics of the populist right-wing party Sweden Democrats led to the collapse of the two-month-old Social Democrat-led Government in December 2014. In Hungary the Jobbik Party gained popularity by targeting the Roma population, and obtained 12.18 per cent at the 2012 parliamentary elections. In Britain, UKIP started to target working-class voters and traditional Labour Party supporters, and won 27.5 per cent of the vote at the 2014 EP elections,[44] causing substantial damage to the Labour Party at the 2015 general election.

In different ways, the rise of both radical left and far-right/populist-right parties poses considerable electoral challenges and dilemmas to social democratic parties. In effect, these parties are pushed in opposite directions. Whereas the challenge that comes from the radical left pressures social democratic parties to defend the welfare state, and to promote greater equality, and libertarian and cosmopolitan values, the challenge that comes from the populist and extreme right pushes them to endorse immigration controls, anti-EU policies, anti-equality policies, and the erosion of the welfare state.

But whichever direction they choose to follow it will have electoral costs. If they target the voters of radical left parties, they risk losing mainstream voters, and will be unable to address the concerns of those who are voting for the populist right. If they target the voters of the populist right, they will alienate centrist and radical left voters. Finally, if they pursue centrist voters, as they did in the 1990s, they will fail to win the votes of the radical left and of the populist right sympathisers, and maybe those of centrist and volatile voters who prefer to put their economic futures in the hands of centre-right parties.

Searching for alternatives to austerity

The fortunes of European social democracy started to turn, but only moment-arily, in June 2012, with the election of the socialist candidate François Hollande to the French presidency. Thus far, the other social democratic prime minister in Europe had been Helle Thorning-Schmidt, who had led a coalition government in Denmark until last summer. However, the Government of Thorning-Schmidt rejected Keynesian solutions and instead put in place substantial public spending cuts (also affecting welfare policies) and public sector job losses, with the purpose of tackling the economic recession. This course of action is surprising considering that Denmark is not a member of the single currency, and as a result is not subject to the straitjacket of the Stability and Growth Pact, but it is yet another example of how European social democrats have acquiesced to the austerity policies promoted by the institutions of the EU.

François Hollande was thus the first weighty European social democrat to chal-lenge the austerity consensus prevailing in Europe since the start of the Eurozone crisis in 2009. It was by then evident that the austerity policies were having a neg-ligible effect in the reduction of public deficits and public debt; however, it was also clear that they were leaving a trail of social destruction across Europe. The draconian public spending cuts led to a substantial slowdown of economic activity, and to a dramatic rise in unemployment, in particular in the countries that were bailed out by the troika. According to figures released by Eurostat, the countries with the highest unemployment rates in the spring of 2015 were Greece (25.7 per cent) and Spain (23 per cent),[45] whilst in countries like Portugal, where unemploy-ment affected 13.5 per cent of the active population, the Government persuaded the young to emigrate.

During the French presidential electoral campaign, Hollande tried to go against the European austerian current. He centred his campaign on the promise to offer an alternative to the austerity policies defended by the EU institutions and the Government in Berlin. That promise was forcefully explained when he said he rejected a 'Europe that condemns countries to austerity without end'. In place of public spending cuts, Hollande defended an economic stimulus programme as a solution for France's and Europe's deficit problems. Whilst he claimed that he would reduce the deficit, he said he would do it via a Keynesian pro-growth strategy that included some public spending cuts and tax rises for higher-income tax-payers (namely the now infamous 75 per cent tax on incomes over €1 million euros, which was rejected by the French Constitutional Court).

Hollande's economic programme also stressed the need to regulate the financial sector and to conduct an active industrial policy. In terms of solutions for the sovereign debt crisis in the Eurozone, he proposed the emission of Eurobonds, which would have pooled Eurozone countries' debts. However, Hollande did not address the design flaws of the Stability and Growth Pact, which were at the root of the crisis, and limited himself to arguing for the addition of a Growth Pact to the Treaty on Stability, Coordination and Governance in the EMU (colloquially known as the fiscal compact), which commits Eurozone governments to even stricter budgetary rules than those outlined in the Stability and Growth Pact.

As the first European leader who was ready to challenge the austerity dogma of the EU, Hollande's won a few plaudits for his pro-growth strategy in Europe, namely in Southern Europe. For example, the Portuguese Socialist Party demanded the renegotiation of Portugal's memorandum of understanding with the troika. Similarly, the Spanish and Italian centre-right governments relied on the support of Hollande to press for a flexible interpretation of the Stability and Growth Pact, and to ask for more time to reduce their countries' public deficits. In Britain, the Labour Party saw in Hollande a *compagnon de route* for its anti-austerity agenda, but this enthusiasm did not last long.

Hollande's anti-austerity drive took place at a time when other European social democrats started to look for alternatives not only to austerity, but also to the democratic deficit that had been exposed and widened by the EU response to the sovereign debt crisis in Europe. To counter the effect of this tendency, Hollande and other European social democrats have discussed the need to deepen democratic accountability within the EU but also within member states. Indeed, the document *Building the Good Society*, written by Jon Cruddas (from the Labour Party) and Andrea Nahles (from the German SPD), called for the 'restoring of the primacy of politics', 'rejecting the subordination of political to economic interests', and 'creating a democratic state that is accountable and more transparent, strengthening our institutions of democracy at all levels, including the economy'.[46] The Party of European Socialists, which aggregates the socialist and social democratic parties in the EP, has echoed this sentiment by calling, in different statements, for greater social dialogue and for the greater democratisation of EU institutions. These ideas have galvanised the circles of European social democratic elites, however they have been pursued with timidity.

This timidity magnified Hollande's isolation in Europe. As he failed to reduce France's public deficit, and the French economy entered recession in 2013, his Government succumbed too to austerity. Henceforth, Hollande was forced by the ECB and the EC to introduce drastic public spending cuts, and to introduce labour market reforms that facilitated layoffs and enabled companies to reduce workers' pay and working hours during economic downturns.

The French president signalled his endorsement of a *politique de rigueur* (just like Mitterrand's in 1981) in the spring of 2014 by appointing as French prime minister Manuel Valls, a politician with weak socialist leanings. Hollande also dismissed the more left-wing and abrasive ministers Arnaud de Montebourg and Benoît Hamon, who were famous for their defiant anti-austerity and anti-Merkel rhetoric. But Hollande's *politique de rigueur* made him the most unpopular president of the French Fifth Republic. It has also considerably weakened the unity and the electoral standing of the PS. At the 2014 EP elections the PS was humiliated by voters, winning only 14 per cent of the vote. More worryingly, the NF, which came first in the French EP elections, not only seemed to have attracted a substantial number of former PS voters and sympathisers, but signalled as well the rise of Euroscepticism in France.

Hollande's response to his electorally weak position has been one of capitulation – with some timid signs of resistance – to the austerity ideology. The French prime minister, Manuel Valls, signalled that his Government would not introduce more public spending cuts despite the fact that France was in breach of the deficit rules of the Stability and Growth Pact. Perhaps more importantly, he warned that the EU's 'absurd' austerity policies were endangering the stability of Europe.[47] However, he was under pressure from Brussels and Berlin to reduce France's public deficit and to comply with the rules of the Stability and Growth Pact.

Hollande's endorsement of austerity is symbolic of the failure of European social democrats to find an alternative to it. Though there is a growing number of European governments that contest the monetarist logic of the Stability and Growth Pact, the direction of policy across the Eurozone is still the one imposed by the German Government and the EU institutions. Despite the weaknesses of the German economy and the manifest need for investments in public infrastructure, the German chancellor Angela Merkel continues to defend austerity to the detriment of an economic growth strategy.

In the Eurozone countries, the sovereign debt crisis has led to a deficit obsession to the exclusion of everything else. The incremental alternatives proposed by different European social democrats – such as the emission of Eurobonds, tighter regulation of the financial services industry, or the further deepening of European integration – failed to unify the European social democratic family. More importantly, none of the proposals offered a coherent and comprehensive response to the crisis. None addressed the complexities of policy-making in a transnational space like the EU or sought to tackle the structural flaws of the EMU. To do so would question the commitment of European social democrats to the project of European integration, and it would also threaten the viability of the monetary union to which they remain committed. But as social democrats ponder solutions to the economic crisis and assess their commitment to the European project, they may risk, as Lavelle suggested, 'death by a thousand cuts'.[48]

Concluding remarks: social democracy and paradigm shifts

For a very brief moment, the global financial crisis led many social democrats to believe that their moment had come. In Europe, the Party of European Socialists grouped in the EP clearly nurtured that ambition. As the near collapse of the global economy exposed the flaws of turbo-capitalism, it was believed that the solutions for the crisis could only be social democratic in flavour.

In the early days and months that followed the collapse of Lehman Brothers, proposals to regulate the financial sector and to nationalise the banks, as well as ideas to implement quantitative easing and Keynesian-inspired stimulus programmes aimed at preventing an economic recession, abounded. Some of these discussions were ambitious in scope as they went beyond immediate socio-economic factors. As the Cruddas and Nahles document showed, there was an attempt to reflect upon quality-of-life issues, and to engage in a debate about the state of health of European democracies. These ideas had a clear social democratic tinge, but they were too limited in scope. None of them tackled the problems raised by the design flaws of the monetary union, and as a result, their impact was quite modest. At best, social democrats asked for a more flexible interpretation of the Stability and Growth Pact, or in the case of the German SPD, for 'more Europe'.

But as the global financial crisis reached Europe and metamorphosed into a sovereign debt crisis, the 'social democratic moment' quickly evaporated. Over the past eight years, European social democrats have been unable to articulate – let alone implement – a coherent response to the global financial and economic crisis. Instead, austerity, defended with great vigour by Berlin, the ECB, and the EC, but which has so far delivered meagre results, quickly became the only game in town.

The triumph of the austerity doctrine had a disastrous impact on European social democratic parties' electoral fortunes. Their share of the vote at the national level has declined, and for some, permanent opposition is a realistic prospect. For parties such as Spain's PSOE and Greece's PASOK, which implemented stringent structural adjustment programmes, that period in opposition can be very long. Their economic credibility is in tatters and the radical left is reaping the benefits of their electoral fallout.

For the few European social democratic parties that were elected after the crisis, their prospects are not very different. After a brief period of resistance to the austerity paradigm, the French socialist Government was forced by the European institutions to implement drastic public spending cuts and structural reforms to its labour market and pensions system. This U-turn provoked huge turmoil in the PS, and has turned François Hollande into the most unpopular president of the French Fifth Republic. In Italy, Matteo Renzi started his term in office with a promise of compliance with Europe's demands for fiscal rigour, but his reformist zeal has cooled down in the face of party, institutional, and popular opposition to more economic pain. Finally, in Denmark, the public spending cuts imposed by the centre-left Government of Helle Thorning-Schmidt resulted in electoral defeat for her party at last summer's elections.

The current predicament of European social democracy should not surprise us. In fact, it has been looming for several decades and it is directly linked to social democratic support for the project of European integration. This project, and in particular support for the Single Market and for the EMU, led social democratic parties gradually to water down their programmatic and ideological goals.

In the early stages of the creation of the Single Market, the European neoliberal/ordoliberal order was reluctantly accepted by European social democratic parties. But by the 1990s, the embrace of the neoliberal order was no longer reluctant. With a few notable exceptions, most European social democrats enthusiastically embraced the neo-revisionism encapsulated in New Labour's Third Way. The erosion of social rights and the undermining of public services were considered inevitable, globalisation was seen as an uncontrollable force of nature, and the market economy was seen as an irresistible force, whereas the ideology of the small state was sacralised in the convergence criteria and in the Stability and Growth Pact that bind the members of the EMU.

Today European social democrats face impossible challenges. Their commitment to the project of European integration and their endorsement of social democratic neo-revisionism left them unable to respond in an ideologically coherent manner to the current challenges. Not only has the global financial crisis challenged the assumptions that had guided them in the past twenty years, but the requirements of EU (and in particular of EMU) membership also imply that they do not have the institutional capacity to implement the social democratic policies their national supporters desire. To do so would endanger the process of European integration and in particular the integrity of the single currency. But to follow the diktats of Brussels, Frankfurt, and Berlin condemns them to electoral oblivion.

For Ed Miliband the crisis of European social democracy was extremely relevant as it mirrored the predicament of the Labour Party. It has also offered instructive – though also discouraging – lessons. Though Labour has barely discussed the Eurozone crisis, it has followed closely how it unfolded and the impact it had on its sister parties. Miliband and his team have also participated in European debates about the future direction of social democracy but these debates have been more demoralising than inspiring. After a brief period of enthusiasm for the anti-austerity drive of Hollande, the Labour leader became acutely aware of the political and institutional constraints that hamper the development of a social democratic alternative to austerity, and to the challenges posed by the global financial crisis. In fact, the only lesson that the Labour leader was able to learn was offered by Hollande's failed attempts to swim against the austerian current. Like Hollande, Miliband found himself isolated, under pressure from the right, from his party, from the neoliberal conventional wisdom that prevails in the British media, and with a limited horizon from where he could draw support and inspiration.

Notes

1 Jason Cowley, 'Ed Miliband Interview: He's Not for Turning', *New Statesman*, 5 September 2012.

2 Mark Blyth, 'The Austerity Delusion: Why a Bad Idea Won Over the West', *Foreign Affairs* 92:3 (May/June 2013): 41–56.

3 Margaret Weir, 'Ideas and Politics: The Acceptance of Keynesianism in Britain and the United States', in Peter A. Hall (ed.), *The Political Power of Economic Ideas: Keynesianism across Nations* (Princeton: Princeton University Press, 1989), pp. 53–86 (pp. 54–55).

4 I will be using the terms 'neoliberal' and 'ordoliberal' interchangeably but there are differences between the two concepts. Whereas neoliberalism has become the catch-all term to define free-market and small-state policies, ordoliberalism was, as Andrew Gamble explained, the first form of neoliberalism. It is also a German-inspired neoliberalism. As such, ordoliberalism defended a free market economy but an equally strong state that would ensure the proper and effective functioning of markets. For a more detailed and enlightened explanation of the typology and variants of neoliberalisms (including ordoliberalism) please see Andrew Gamble, 'Neo-Liberalism and Fiscal Conservatism', in Vivian A. Schmidt and Mark Thatcher (eds), *Resilient Liberalism in Europe's Political Economy* (Cambridge: Cambridge University Press, 2013), pp. 53–76. See also Mark Blyth, *Austerity: The History of a Dangerous Idea* (Oxford: Oxford University Press, 2013).

5 Dionyssis G. Dimitrakapoulos, 'Introduction: Social Democracy, European Integration and Preference Formation', in Dionyssis G. Dimitrakapoulos (ed.), *Social Democracy and European Integration: The Politics of Preference Formation* (Abingdon: Routledge, 2011), pp. 1–22 (p. 1).

6 Gerassimos Moschonas, 'Reforming Europe, Renewing Social Democracy? The PES, the Debt Crisis and the Euro-Parties', in David J. Bailey, Jean-Michel de Waele, Fabien Escalona, and Mathieu Vieira (eds), *European Social Democracy during the Global Economic Crisis: Renovation or Resignation?* (Manchester: Manchester University Press, 2014), pp. 252–269 (p. 253).

7 Jeffrey Sachs, Charles Wyplosz, Willem Buiter, Gerhard Fels, and George de Menil, 'The Economic Consequences of President Mitterrand', *Economic Policy* 1:2 (April 1986): 261–322 (p. 294).

8 Philippe Marlière, 'The French Socialist Party and European Integration: Faltering Europeanism', in Dimitrakapoulos, *Social Democracy and European Integration*, pp. 51–82 (p. 64).

9 Perry Anderson, 'The Europe to Come', in Peter Gowan and Perry Anderson (eds), *The Question of Europe* (London: Verso, 1997), p. 130.

10   Anderson, 'The Europe to Come', p. 130.

11   Fabien Escalona and Mathieu Vieira, '"It Does Not Happen Here Either": Why Social Democrats Fail in the Context of the Great Economic Crisis', in Bailey, De Waele, Escalona, and Vieira, *European Social Democracy*, pp. 19–41 (p. 24).

12   Gerassimos Moschonas, *In the Name of Social Democracy: The Great Transformation. 1945 to the Present* (London: Verso, 2002), p. 263.

13   Philippe Marlière, 'The Decline of Europe's Social Democratic Parties', 16 March 2010, https://www.opendemocracy.net/philippe-marliere/decline-of-europes-social-democratic-parties (accessed 4 August 2015).

14   James Sloam and Isabelle Hertner, 'The Europeanization of Social Democracy: Politics without Policy and Policy without Politics', in Henning Meyer and Jonathan Rutherford (eds), *The Future of European Social Democracy: Building the Good Society* (Houndmills: Palgrave Macmillan, 2012), pp. 27–38 (p. 36).

15   Moschonas, 'Reforming Europe', p. 253.

16   Donald Sassoon, *One Hundred Years of Socialism: The West European Left in the Twentieth Century* (London: Fontana Press, 1997), p. 739.

17   Herbert Kitschelt, *The Transformation of European Social Democracy* (Cambridge: Cambridge University Press, 1994), p. 280.

18   Sassoon, *One Hundred Years of Socialism*, p. 733.

19   Andrew Gamble, 'The Legacy of Thatcherism', in Mark Perryman (ed.), *The Blair Agenda* (London: Lawrence and Wishart, 1996), pp. 18–38 (pp. 25–26).

20   Gamble, 'The Legacy of Thatcherism', p. 734.

21   Gamble, 'The Legacy of Thatcherism', p. 734.

22   Mark Mazower, 'The Great Reckoning: Why the European Ideal Is under Threat', *New Statesman*, 15–25 April 2013.

23   Marlière, 'The Decline of Europe's Social Democratic Parties'.

24   Andrew Gamble, *The Spectre at the Feast: Capitalist Crisis and the Politics of Recession* (Houndmills: Palgrave Macmillan, 2009), p. 124.

25   Gerassimos Moschonas, 'When Institutions Matter: The EU and the Identity of Social Democracy', *Renewal* 17:2 (Summer 2009): 11–20 (p. 16).

26   Stefan Theil, 'Peer Steinbrück on the Global Economic Crisis', *Newsweek*, 5 December 2008.

27   Costas Lapavitsas, Annina Kaltenbrunner, Duncan Lindo, J. Mitchell, Juan Pablo Painceira, Eugenia Pires, et al., 'Eurozone Crisis: Begga Thyself and Thy Neignbour', *Journal of Balkan and Near Eastern Studies* 12:4 (December 2010): 321–373 (p. 349).

28   Joseph Stiglitz, *Freefall: Free Markets and the Sinking of the Global Economy* (London: Penguin Books, 2010), p. 324.

29   Ingo Schmidt, 'German Social Democracy: A Popular Project and an Unpopular Party', in Bailey, De Waele, Escalona, and Vieira, *European Social Democracy*, pp. 132–152 (pp. 144–145).

30   Jürgen Habermas, 'Germany and the Euro-Crisis', *The Nation*, 28 June 2010.

31   Paul Kennedy contends that the sovereign debt crisis is not the only reason why the Spanish Socialist Workers' Party (Partido Socialista Obrero Español (PSOE)) is unpopular. He argues that Zapatero's leadership style, which stifled internal dissent, as well as his misguided economic priorities before the crisis, help to explain the downfall of PSOE. Paul Kennedy, 'Back

to the Drawing Board: The PSOE after the 2011 Elections', in Bailey, De Waele, Escalona, and Vieira, *European Social Democracy*, pp. 176–192 (p. 188).

32 Sloam and Hertner, 'The Europeanization of Social Democracy', p. 33.

33 Gamble, *The Spectre at the Feast*, p. 109.

34 Luke March, 'The European Radical Left and the International Economic Crisis: Opportunity Wasted?', 5 March 2013, https://www.opendemocracy.net/luke-march/european-radical-left-and-international-economic-crisis-opportunity-wasted (accessed 4 August 2015).

35 Cristina Flesher Fominaya, ' "Spain Is Different": Podemos and 15-M', 29 May 2014, https://www.opendemocracy.net/can-europe-make-it/cristina-flesher-fominaya/%E2%80%9Cspain-is-different%E22%80%9D-podemos-and-15m (accessed 3 August 2015).

36 Mike Pope, 'The Rise of Podemos and Its People's Assembly', 7 November 2014, https://www.opendemocracy.net/can-europe-make-it/mike-pope/rise-of-podemos-and-its-people%27s-assembly (accessed 30 November 2014).

37 Dan Hough, 'From Pariah to Prospective Partner? The German Left Party's Winding Path towards Government', in Jonathan Olsen, Dan Hough, and Michael Koß (eds), *Left Parties in National Governments* (Houndmills: Palgrave Macmillan, 2010), pp. 138–154 (p. 144).

38 Luke March, 'Os partidos radicais da esquerda radical após a crise: Marxismo, mainstream ou marginalidade', in Luke March and Andre Freire, *A esquerda radical em Portugal e na Europa* (Vila do Conde: Quidnovi, 2012), pp. 25–104 (p. 75).

39 March, 'Os partidos radicais', pp. 27–30.

40 March, 'Os partidos radicais', p. 37.

41 March, 'The European Radical Left'.

42 Jonathan Olsen, Dan Hough, and Michael Koß, 'Conclusion: Left Parties in National Governments', in Olsen, Hough, and Koß, *Left Parties in National Governments*, pp. 173–205 (p. 182).

43 Michelle Hale Williams, 'A New Era for French Far Right Politics? Comparing the FN under the Two Le Pens', *Análise social* 46:201 (2011): 679–695 (p. 682).

44 Robert Ford and Matthew Goodwin, 'Now UKIP Is Gunning for Labour, What's Ed Miliband Going to Do about It?', *Guardian*, 30 May 2013. See also Robert Ford and Matthew Goodwin, *Revolt on the Right: Explaining Support for the Radical Right in Britain* (London: Routledge, 2014).

45 'Unemployment Statistics', March 2015, Eurostat, http://ec.europa.eu/eurostat/statistics-explained/index.php/Unemployment_statistics (accessed 21 May 2015).

46 Jon Cruddas and Andrea Nahles, *Building the Good Society: The Project of the Democratic Left* (London: Compass, 2009), p. 2.

47 Ambrose Evans-Pritchard, 'France Cautions Germany Not to Push Europe Too Far on Austerity', *Daily Telegraph*, 6 October 2014, http://www.telegraph.co.uk/finance/economics/11144769/France-cautions-Germany-not-to-push-Europe-too-far-on-austerity.html (accessed 9 August 2015).

48 Ashley Lavelle, 'Postface: Death by a Thousand Cuts?', in Bailey, D e Waele, Escalona, and Vieira, *European Social Democracy*, pp. 270–283 (p. 271).

2

The road to somewhere

Yes, friends, to come through the storm, to overcome the challenges we face, we must rediscover that spirit. That spirit the British people never forgot. That spirit of One Nation. A country where everyone plays a part. A country we rebuild together.

Ed Miliband[1]

In his first speech as Labour leader, Ed Miliband announced that he did not plan to lead the opposition for longer than necessary. Instead, his goal was to bring Labour back to power by 2015. But his words sounded hollow in the central hall of Manchester's conference centre, where the 2010 Labour Party Annual Conference took place.

The Labour delegates were still licking their wounds from the disastrous electoral defeat suffered a few months earlier. Above all, for the many Labour delegates sitting in that conference hall, Ed Miliband's election as leader was not the uplifting moment the party needed. Some were unconvinced by his leadership skills, ideas, and party credentials, whilst others were unimpressed by the ruthlessness with which he had decided to compete against his brother David.

Ed Miliband tried to make the most out of this inauspicious beginning as leader of the Labour Party by pressing with his message of transformative change. In those early days, many of what later became known as the flagship themes and proposals of 'Milibandism' were still vague, but their foundations were already visible. Underpinning Miliband's vision was an ideologically cogent, if undeveloped, analysis of what went wrong with New Labour and with the British economy, and the beginnings of an answer to those problems could be glimpsed.

In politics, the development of recipes to tackle particular policy problems almost always starts with ideas. Indeed, ideas often guide a political actor through the complex and messy process of understanding difficult policy puzzles, and developing political blueprints that simultaneously offer credible solutions to the problems of the day and reflect that actor's historical and intellectual trajectory. This is particularly true for political parties that seek to govern.

However, political programmes are rarely – if ever – exclusively the outcome of theoretical and doctrinarian debates about political ideologies, zeitgeist ideas, and policy instruments. Ideas interplay with electoral considerations and context, as well as with institutional, political, and competing ideational factors. The implication of this is that political programmes are the product of a complex process of negotiation and accommodation among all these factors.

This chapter identifies the main institutional constraints Ed Miliband faced throughout his leadership of the Labour Party, and explains how they influenced his behaviour, transformed his initial vision, and impacted his chances of winnning the 2015 general election. In order to do so, the chapter starts by contextualising the election of Ed Miliband as Labour leader. Next, it outlines very briefly the main planks of his vision, and maps out the main ideas that influenced the Labour leader's agenda. From here the chapter identifies the two main institutional factors – the party and the media – that influenced the development of Miliband's programme of party renewal. It will become clear that these two institutional factors worked as a constraint to the development of his programme in a variety of ways. However, they have also led to a change to the party's relationship with the trade unions and to its approach to the media.

The leadership election

The 2010 general election was disastrous for Labour. The party only won 29 per cent of the vote, its second lowest share of the vote since 1918. Steven Fielding contends that Labour's results were 'not the wipe-out many members feared',[2] considering the impact of the economic recession and Gordon Brown's unpopularity; nonetheless it was still a very heavy defeat from which it would be extremely difficult to recover in only five years. That, at least, was the feeling amongst many Labour MPs. For example, Jon Cruddas admitted that 'in the history of the party it is unheard of' to recover so quickly from an electoral defeat.[3] Similarly, John Denham acknowledged that the task of winning the 2015 election was considerable because 'no one has ever come back from a defeat as big as we have and then won' the election.[4] Both Cruddas and Denham were correct in their diagnosis. Labour suffered a disastrous defeat in 2015 and the flaws of Milibandism were not the only cause. To understand the electoral plight of Labour it is important to look back at what happened in 2010.

Voters did not abandon Labour in 2010 only because of Gordon Brown's unpopularity as a prime minister, or as a result of the global financial crisis. Labour's unpopularity had deeper roots. Between 1997 and 2010 the party lost almost five million voters.[5] Amongst those five million voters there were many middle-aged, white, working-class men who were worried about immigration, economic security, and employment prospects, but there were also many middle-class left-liberals, who had stopped supporting the party because of New Labour's participation in the invasion of Iraq, and/or its stances on civil liberties.[6] Winning back those five million voters – and some more to guarantee a parliamentary majority – was seen as the main task of the new Labour leader.

But in order to do so, the party had to understand why it had lost their support. That also proved to be a difficult task, as the party was divided about the causes of the 2010 electoral defeat. Whilst some thought the global financial crisis and the 2010 electoral defeat demanded a serious rethinking of the party's strategy, many others felt that it could recover quickly. According to Cruddas, the party had under-estimated how voters, and in particular working-class voters, were detached from Labour.[7]

But this gloomy and challenging prospect did not deter six Labour MPs – four of them with a background in the previous New Labour governments – from standing for the leadership of the party. David Miliband was the first contender to announce his bid. Two days later, his brother Ed announced that he too wanted to become leader. Aware that his bid would be seen as a ruthless move by too ambitious a politician, Ed Miliband justified his decision by saying he was the 'only person who can decisively move the Labour Party from the Blair–Brown era'.[8]

In the following two weeks, Andy Burnham, Ed Balls, Diane Abbott, and John McDonnell (who failed to be nominated) announced their intentions to run for the leadership. All the contenders tried to offer distinct visions of change, but only Diane Abbott could do so with credibility, given that she had played no role in the New Labour governments. David Miliband's campaign focused on changing the party's culture through the type of bottom-up, community politics promoted by the grassroots movement Citizens UK. Ed Miliband, on the other hand, made the living wage (a successful campaign also promoted by Citizens UK) the centre of his bid. The remaining three candidates centred their campaigns on themes that played on their strengths or areas of expertise and interests. Ed Balls focused on austerity, though he also addressed the problem of immigration; Andy Burnham proposed a radical reform of the social care system; and Diane Abbott's campaign attacked the Coalition's public spending cuts.

The leadership campaign lasted all summer, with the different candidates participating in televised debates and party hustings around the country, but from an early stage it became clear that it would be dominated by the Miliband brothers. The reasons for this were simple. Not only were they the stronger contenders, but the biblical undertones of two brothers fighting in public for the same position had pathos, and as a result, it attracted substantial media attention.

The format of the campaign, and in particular its media coverage, was problematic for Ed Miliband. The decision to run for the leadership against his brother was not well seen by some Labour backbenchers and activists. He was perceived as a ruthless individual, whose personal ambition seemed to be more important than his family. For example, the Dagenham MP who later chaired the party's Policy Review, Jon Cruddas, could not understand why Ed Miliband 'went against his brother'.[9]

Because he was seen as a victim of his younger brother's scheming, David Miliband attracted some sympathy; however, he faced problems of a different nature. In the televised debates and in some of the party hustings he seemed to be tense and distracted, and did not come across as a confident contender. But his main problem was the fact that he was associated with New Labour, and with Tony Blair in particular. Throughout the campaign he was outspoken in his criticism of New Labour, and his stances on different policy issues were to the left of Tony Blair, but his support for the Iraq invasion, and the fact that the 'Blairite' wing of the party supported his leadership bid, helped to define him as a 'Blairite'.

By contrast, and though Ed Miliband was as deeply embedded in the New Labour project as his brother, he was more successful at positioning himself as an alternative to it. The crucial difference between the Miliband brothers was their stance on the Iraq war. Whilst David, as a cabinet minister in the Blair Government, had supported the invasion of Iraq, Ed was against it. However, it must be said that he never publicly voiced his opposition to it (and in 2003 he was not constrained by the principle of collective responsibility that binds members of the Government) until the party's leadership election.

But this difference helped to present Ed Miliband as the Labour figure who could move the party a few steps leftwards from New Labour. And that is exactly what he did. Ed Miliband made a deliberate effort to present himself as the post-New Labour candidate. He went further than his rivals in his critique of New Labour, and this stance became the defining feature of his bid for the leadership.[10] For example, in a speech delivered during the leadership campaign, Ed Miliband spoke of the need to change the party ideologically, electorally, and organisationally, and to move it from 'New Labour's comfort zone'.[11] It is also noteworthy that he identified New Labour as the tradition from which the party should depart: 'Traditional New Labour solutions won't work, and that is why I am the modernising candidate in this election.'[12]

Ed Miliband also had something distinct to say about the party's electoral challenges. If in 1997 New Labour's targeting of middle-class voters was the right approach from an electoral viewpoint, in the post-2010 political landscape the Labour Party faced different challenges, and as a result it had to target both middle- and low-income voters. He was particularly concerned with 'the poorest and the low paid', who 'felt we had nothing to say to them about the challenges in their lives'.[13] This message was repeated continuously throughout the leadership election in speeches and in interviews.

With his focus on the living wage, equality, a critique of capitalism, and the unproblematic use of words that had been banned from the New Labour lexicon – such as socialism and equality – Miliband gave a clear indication of the direction in which he wanted to take the Labour Party. Moreover, the fact that his leadership bid was supported by Neil Kinnock, Roy Hattersley, Elizabeth Smith (the widow of John Smith), and most trade unions offered more signs about his desired direction of travel.

As a strategy it was an effective galvanising tool for a party exhausted by New Labour's triangulation and internal in-fighting, but it was less successful as a presentational device. Miliband's ideas were seen as too radical by many media commentators, and he was therefore perceived as un-prime-ministerial. In fact, Miliband faced media hostility from the very beginning. He was framed either as an unreconstructed socialist – hence the sobriquets 'Red Ed' and 'Bennite' – or as not fit to become prime minister. Critics called him 'Ed the Unready', 'Wallace' from the Aardman cartoon's Wallace and Gromit, or simply 'weird'.

Despite his image problems, Miliband was elected Labour leader with the support of 50.6 per cent of Labour's Electoral College, narrowly defeating his brother by only 1.3 per cent of the vote. But more than the narrow victory it was the distribution of votes that proved to be controversial. Whilst David Miliband won the majority of votes from MPs, MEPs, and the constituency sections of the Electoral College, Ed won thanks to the votes of the trade unions and affiliated organisations (19.93 per cent). Among the MPs, MEPs, and constituency party section he came second with 15.20 per cent of the votes (whilst David had secured 18.14 per cent of support). It soon became apparent that such a slender victory – made possible thanks to the support of the trade unions – was the wrong way to win. As Ed Miliband's biographers recognised, 'the intensity and breath of hostility that greeted Ed's victory was astonishing, if perhaps inevitable after the dubious and problematic breakdown of the result'.[14]

Several media commentators and Labour backbenchers felt that Ed Miliband stole the leadership from his older brother. Some even felt that a victory based on the vote of trade unions was not totally legitimate. There were allegations that the trade unions had helped his campaign team by giving them access to membership lists, whilst they had withheld them from the other candidates,[15] and that some trade unions distributed 'vote-for-Ed' leaflets together with the ballot papers.

The sense of outrage felt by David Miliband's supporters in the party and in the media made them overlook the shortcomings of his campaign. Yet those shortcomings also contributed to his defeat. His leadership campaign suffered from a lack of focus and from a sense of entitlement. Some Labour backbenchers felt manhandled by David Miliband's team, while others thought 'he didn't make an effort to court them in the House of Commons tearooms.'[16]

Miliband's vision

Despite his controversial victory, Ed Miliband used his first speech as Labour leader to set out a new course for the party, and that implied jettisoning many of the assumptions that had informed New Labour whilst in government. So what did this ambitious vision of change entail? What answers did it offer to the policy puzzles of the day? Miliband's starting point was the 2007–08 global financial crisis. He argued that finding a credible response to the challenges and problems created by the global financial crisis, which was followed by the deficit crisis, and by a deep economic recession, was conditional on understanding its causes.

For him those were clear. The 2007–08 global financial crisis exposed an economy that was not working for the interests of the majority. Indeed, the economic model that New Labour had endorsed was posited on promoting greater economic growth, but at the expense of an unbalanced economy that concentrated wealth and power at the top of society. In Miliband's view, the global financial crisis had exposed the fallacies of unregulated capitalism, which New Labour had wholeheartedly embraced.

For Miliband, 'big change' could only happen if the party was ready to challenge 'established thinking' and 'stale failed ideas'. He was particularly disparaging of New Labour's uncritical acceptance of the neoliberal consensus. For instance, he argued that 'globalisation is not an untameable force of nature to which we must adapt or die'.[17] In other words, the State could and should intervene in markets to ensure that they work efficiently, fairly, and without endangering again the world economy. Likewise, he did not share New Labour's endorsement of flexible labour markets, and believed that life was about more than just work and the bottom line.

Instead of New Labour's embrace of neoliberalism, Miliband proposed, in the words of Stewart Wood, 'a fundamental rejection of the post-1979 settlement'.[18] Similarly, Cruddas argued that the purpose of the party's policy renewal was about 're-imagining social democracy'.[19] This fundamental rejection of neoliberalism would be characterised by an agenda focused on tackling social and economic inequalities, promoting sustainable economic growth, and promoting community renewal. But tackling inequality would require two fundamental reforms. First, Labour would intervene and reform markets with a view to producing a fairer and more balanced economy. Second, Miliband would reform what he saw as an excessively managerial and hierarchical State. In place of the centralised and unresponsive State, Miliband argued for the devolution of power to local communities, but also to individuals. His overall aim was to redistribute power in society by giving individuals a greater control of their lives, and by promoting the 'good life', where work plays a part but 'it is not all that matters'.[20]

Ideas: old and new

Miliband's vision was ambitious but he was not alone in developing it. Indeed, there was a strong epistemic community of scholars, think-tank experts, policy advisers, and party activists who helped him develop his programme. His team had solid academic credentials. Lord (Stewart) Wood, a former Oxford academic, was Miliband's main policy adviser throughout his leadership; Marc Stears, a political theorist also from Oxford, was Miliband's speech-writer, but also friend and adviser (his influence is visible in Miliband's approach to the State); Jon Cruddas, a maverick parliamentarian with a vast intellectual hinterland, chaired Labour's Policy Review and drafted the manifesto (together with Marc Stears and the academic Jonathan Rutherford). These three important advisers nurtured networks, circles of debate, and policy discussions with academics, think-tanks, other Labour backbenchers, sympathetic public intellectuals, and journalists. Despite the fact that there were different tendencies vying to influence Miliband, there was also a substantial amount of fluidity and dialogue among the different factions, as the numerous reports published by the IPPR, the Resolution Foundation, Policy Network, and the Fabian Society, and by the journals *Soundings, Renewal,* and *Juncture* demonstrate. Different party factions also sought to influence the debate by publishing books and pamphlets such as *The Purple Book, The Red Book, After the Third Way,* and *The Labour Tradition and the Politics of Paradox,* to name just a few.[21] These debates were academic in tone and invited criticism from Labour backbenchers who were outside Miliband's tent. But the media enjoyed them and gave ample coverage to Miliband's gurus and 'buzzwords'.

From the different tendencies that competed for the leader's attention, the Blue Labour group, founded by the academic and social activist Maurice Glasman (now Baron Glasman), stood out. Indeed, Labour figures as different as Jon Cruddas, James Purnell, Marc Stears, Stewart Wood, Jonathan Rutherford, and Anthony Painter were active participants in Blue Labour debates. Moreover, many of Blue Labour's themes and ideas were embraced by other tendencies in the party. For instance, Blue Labour's critique of Labour's traditional statecraft was a rallying call for the different factions within the party, from the soft left like Compass to the centre-right Labour thinkers from Policy Network. Above all, and according to Jon Cruddas, Blue Labour forced Labour into some 'difficult conversations' whilst testing the party's 'liberal and cosmopolitan disposition'.[22]

More than a detailed and coherent political programme, Blue Labour can be described as an intellectual tendency that offered a particular reading of the post-crisis political settlement, and highlighted the main themes of Labour's programme of renewal. Roughly put, Blue Labour proponents argued that the solutions for Labour's predicaments in 2010 could be found in the historical roots of the party, in particular in the legacy of the Independent Labour Party, guild socialism, and the cooperative movement, but also in the ideas of Karl Polanyi (widely quoted in Labour's policy renewal document), and of the New Left.[23] For Blue Labour thinkers such as Maurice Glasman, Jonathan Rutherford, and Graeme Cooke, only local communities, grassroots associations, families, and individuals could counter the powers of both the unregulated market and the unresponsive State. Glasman's take on the economy reflected a Polanyian view of the market, in the sense that he was particularly concerned with the effects of capitalism on communities. Like Polanyi,

Glasman believed that capitalism was unstable, prone to speculative bubbles, inefficient, had a destructive effect on communities and families, and undermined the value of reciprocity and relationships.

But equally, he believed that the State could be almost as nefarious in its impact on society. Indeed, Glasman was consistently critical of Labour's postwar legacy (which, incidentally, most Labour members tend to see as the party's finest hour), and in particular of its statecraft, which he saw as too blunt, elitist, and undemocratic. For Glasman, Labour's postwar legacy represented an undesirable departure from a traditional Labour commitment to what he called the 'Common Good', which was associated with the earlier democratic and pluralist traditions of the party.[24] For Glasman and those around Blue Labour, these traditions were Labour's *raison d'être*. A third strand of Blue Labour's thinking was a focus on questions of belonging, nationhood, and patriotism. Glasman and other Blue Labour thinkers were particularly concerned with the impact of New Labour's neglect of its traditional working-class English supporters.

To wrap these different strands, Glasman, Rutherford, and others used sometimes provocative language and ideas. For example, they defined Blue Labour as a 'conservative' tradition and were open in their admiration for David Cameron's 'Big Society' ideas. They were critical of Labour's egalitarian and feminist values and seemed nostalgic for a world where men were valued in the workplace and women at home. More controversially, Glasman's critique of multiculturalism and cosmopolitan values led him to defend immigration controls. This proved to be fatal for the prospects of Blue Labour. Figures like Jon Cruddas, Marc Stears, and even his academic partner Jonathan Rutherford were quick to distance themselves from him and to declare the death of Blue Labour.

But if Glasman's controversial statements and policy suggestions on immigration put an official end to Blue Labour, many of its concerns, themes, and even ideas were shared by other Labour tendencies, and were visible in Miliband's agenda and in the party's 2015 electoral manifesto. The first signs of that influence were in the Labour traditions he invoked. Like Blue Labour thinkers, Miliband sought to renew the Labour traditions of ethical socialism, mutualism, and the guild socialism of G. D. H. Cole. By invoking these traditions Miliband was signalling a particular approach to the State – more decentralised and democratic – that was clearly distinct from New Labour's managerial style and indicated an ambition to tackle what he called the 'inequalities of power'. It suggested as well a desire to develop a politics of the Common Good. Blue Labour also offered Miliband a particular way of talking about patriotism that was congruent with Labour's values and traditions.

But there were significant parts of Miliband's agenda that departed quite radically from Blue Labour. For example, whereas egalitarian concerns were absent from Blue Labour's agenda (the focus was instead on poverty and on the power of democratic mobilisation to overcome deprivation and lack of freedom), they played a central role in the Labour leader's agenda. Indeed, throughout his leadership he claimed

2.   that fighting inequality was the reason why he was in politics. Second, Miliband's
     approach to the State was somewhat ambivalent. If on the one hand he argued for
     decentralisation, for the relational State, and for the devolution of power to local
     communities, on the other he still believed in the power of the State to transform
3.   society and in particular to reform capitalism. Thus, if he argued for regional banks
     and cooperative companies, he also knew that they were not enough to bring the
     radical transformations he advocated.

Miliband's agenda for change was composed of four main planks (each one of
them will be analysed in separate chapters in this book). The first plank sought to
respond to the challenges created by the global financial crisis and the deficit crisis. Starting from a social democratic analysis of the failings of modern capitalism,
 Miliband's agenda revolved around ideas about reforming capitalism with a view to
promoting competition, developing an active industrial policy that aimed to generate sustainable economic growth.

The second plank of his agenda was directly linked to the first. If one of the features of modern capitalism was its tendency to distribute in an unequal manner
 the proceeds of economic growth, then at the heart of Labour's agenda was a commitment to tackle social inequality. The third plank focused on the distribution of
power in society and was based on a thick concept of equality. Indeed, Miliband's
power to the people agenda went beyond addressing social inequalities, and sought
to empower individuals through reform of public services and devolution of power.
This agenda also included proposals to reform representative institutions with a
view to deepening democracy. Finally, the fourth plank of Miliband's agenda was
a politics of belonging, centred on a particular understanding of nationhood and
citizenship, which sought to address the sense of cultural and economic insecurity
promoted by economic globalisation and immigration.

The politics of the 'One Nation' narrative

Miliband's agenda chimed with the party's ethos and ideological traditions; however, it seemed disjointed. In particular, voters had difficulty in understanding how
fighting predator capitalism was linked to ideas about devolution of power to cities
and towns, or how the campaign for the living wage was linked to creating a more
balanced and productive economy. To many, these proposals looked more like a
 shopping list than a coherent and wholesome electoral offer. To sew together all
these different pieces, Ed Miliband developed the 'One Nation' narrative thread.

From the start, 'One Nation' aimed to be more than just a narrative device that
united the different components of Labour's electoral programme. Indeed, the 'One
Nation' narrative served two other purposes. First, the 'One Nation' vision presented Miliband as a Labour politician committed to regaining the centre ground
of politics and to unifying the nation. By invoking the Victorian Conservative prime
minister Benjamin Disraeli, 'One Nation' helped him to downplay the radicalism of

his programme. Indeed, it is noteworthy that he used Disraeli to talk about values that were dear to Labour in a fairly radical language. By quoting Disraeli, Miliband was saying that his focus on inequality was not necessarily a social democratic concern because a Conservative like Disraeli had been equally exercised by it.

But his language was quite radical. By using the narrative device of 'One Nation' he was able to talk about the widening gap between rich and poor, and about the unfairness of a government that offered 'a tax cut for millionaires' and 'rip-off for everyone else', delivering 'a recovery for the top' and 'a recession for everyone else'.[25] Miliband's 'One Nation' vision contrasted with the Coalition's approach. In Miliband's One Nation everyone played their part, everyone had responsibilities, and prosperity was widely shared. The unemployed on benefits had the responsibility to take on job offers and the millionaires the responsibility to pay their fair due in taxes.

But Disraeli was not the only reference in the 'One Nation' narrative. Clement Attlee was the other politician that Miliband quoted as another worthy example of 'One Nation' politics. As he put it, Attlee's Government 'rebuilt Britain after the war'. By referring to Attlee in those terms, Miliband signalled that he wanted to be seen as a transformative leader but in a way that unified the nation. Indeed, it was in these terms that Marc Stears (the main contributor to the 'One Nation' speech) explained it. According to him, One Nation was 'a vision of a nation that comes together but that comes together to change things'.[26] He elaborated further on this explanation: 'Attlee really tried to use the energy and national unity of coming out of the war to change our society with the welfare state and to effectively protect people in vulnerable moments. I think the way Ed thinks about this is in terms of moments in history where you had that combination of national unity and effective and incredible change.'[27]

Miliband's desire to be seen as a transformative leader was suggested a second time in his tribute speech to Margaret Thatcher. In this speech, he praised Thatcher's deep convictions, her belief in the power of ideas, and the fact that she had been a prime minister 'who defined her age'.[28] Again, Marc Stears offered an interesting reading of Miliband's interest in Thatcher: 'Obviously he has deep ideological disagreements with Thatcherism and with what Mrs Thatcher's government did, but there is a part of him who thinks that there was a kind of national spirit about it; she was committed about changing the country. She believed in what she was trying to do.'[29]

The references to Clement Attlee revealed other interesting aspects of Miliband's vision. In particular, they shed light on the type of patriotism he wanted to promote. As Ben Jackson argued, Labour under Attlee laid claim 'to a social patriotism that focused on the growth of liberty, democratic government and social justice as the most important British traditions'. As such, it portrayed 'British history as a story about the long struggle for democracy and the gradual improvement of the condition of the people'.[30] This progressive patriotism was anchored in the labour movement and was not based on a nostalgic vision of the past. Instead, as Jackson noted, it was conflictual because 'social reform was opposed by a powerful minority pursuing its own sectarian agenda'.[31]

The 'One Nation' narrative was extremely well received in the media, and for a while the party tried to develop the concept. Any new policy, no matter how small, was presented as part of a 'One Nation' vision. But by the end of 2013 the 'One Nation' narrative faded. It was mentioned in fewer speeches and there was a general feeling that it had been 'a good starting point' but that it needed some fleshing out. Perhaps more importantly, 'One Nation' was an idea that was difficult to explain to voters. As Judi Atkins argued, the 'One Nation' narrative 'failed to gain traction with the electorate'.[32] In fact, as she put it, it muddied the ideological commitments of the party and alienated voters with its constant sloganeering.

In addition, the narrative failed to present Miliband and his team as post-New Labour.[33] Miliband seemed to be aware of this effect because by the second half of 2014 he stopped referring to 'One Nation'. Instead he talked about togetherness. In his speech to the 2014 Labour Party conference he did not mention 'One Nation', but referred to the principle of 'together' forty-one times.[34]

Miliband's attempt to develop a narrative of national unity and togetherness points to a distinctive feature of his style of leadership. Indeed, his desire to be a unifying leader suggests that he was above all a cautious politician who could only take decisions after building a consensus around him. This cautiousness was well described by Marc Stears: 'Ed was always keen to build the broadest possible consensus before taking an action.' But he was also 'uneasy about dramatic political risks, preferring to hold back an action until he was fully persuaded that effective support could be mobilised'.[35] This personality trait has been noted by others. According to an activist close to the leadership, Miliband was 'good at nudging people in a particular direction and at creating a sense of inevitability about issues'.[36] The downside of this character trait was that it could create a sense of paralysis. Indeed, his chronic indecisiveness brought many in the party close to despair.

Moreover, Miliband's cautious and deliberative style of leadership was not always an asset, though for the first three to four years of his leadership it was more a necessity than an attribute. As Peter Hall's and Margaret Weir's insights on the power of ideas suggest, the Labour leader needed to convince his party about the credibility and soundness of his political agenda. As will become clearer in the following pages, the absence of support from the party and, more importantly, Miliband's standing and reputation as a leader proved to be important institutional constraints to the development of his political agenda of change, and therefore to its success.

Controlling the party

The fact that Ed Miliband won the 'wrong kind of victory' meant that he devoted more time to trying to build a coalition of support within the party and to appeasing different warring factions than to developing and fleshing out his vision. Though he knew where he wanted to take the party, he lacked the necessary institutional and political support to develop his agenda. Some ideas – like those about 'responsible capitalism', the 'squeezed middle' – had been well received but there had been no follow-up to them. More often than not, Miliband's policy proposals looked like he was still undecided about the direction he wanted to follow. However, this apparent dithering was not a sign of vagueness of purpose, but of isolation and of lack of authority. Because he lacked internal support, Miliband was unable to present concrete policy proposals that matched his vision. In the process, he sacrificed clarity and radicalism for the sake of unity.

Ed Miliband's difficulties in persuading his party to rally around his vision have a variety of causes, but perhaps the most important one is the fact that he lacked a basis in the party. Miliband had little experience as a rank-and-file Labour politician. His meteoric rise through the ranks of the party followed the well-trodden path of the new generation of professional politicians. From being an adviser he was parachuted to a safe seat and quickly into a cabinet post, having spent hardly any time on the backbenches. As a result, many Labour activists felt he had 'not earned his medals'. At best, trade unionists and ordinary party members saw him as an interesting proposition.

Within the parliamentary party his standing and authority were even weaker. Several Labour backbenchers, in particular those who had supported his brother David, questioned the legitimacy of his victory and the soundness of his ideas. Even amongst Ed's supporters there were those who took his style of leadership for indecision and weakness. The academic and Labour peer Maurice Glasman was not the only one to say that there was 'no strategy, no narrative and little energy' in Miliband's approach.[37] Others doubted his leadership skills, or feared that the country and the media were not ready for his type of politics, and tried (unsuccessfully) to plot a few leadership challenges.

The strongest challenge to Miliband's leadership came from the Blairite wing of the party, which benefited from important supporters in the media. The most stinging attacks came from the architects of New Labour, the former prime minister Tony Blair and Lord (Peter) Mandelson. Blair rarely intervened, but when he did the impact was extremely damaging. For example, in April 2013 Blair advised Miliband to resist being 'the repository for people's anger' by shifting to the left on the economy and welfare and to the right on Europe and immigration.[38] In case somebody missed the meaning of Blair's intervention, Lord Mandelson offered some clarification: 'Tony is saying what he has always thought – that the old dividing lines between the uncaring Conservative cuts and Labour spending has [*sic*] got to be redrawn for new times', he said in an interview.[39] It was also clear that Mandelson did not trust the Labour leader's leadership skills. Indeed, he personally blamed Miliband for Labour's electoral defeat in 2010,[40] believed that that his vision would take 'Labour backwards',[41] and never missed an opportunity to attack him.

When he finally came round to offer qualified support to the Labour leader a lot of damage had been done.

The right's objections to Miliband's agenda stemmed from the belief that any deviation from the New Labour rule book would result in a heavy electoral defeat. Hence, Miliband was under pressure to regain electoral credibility by endorsing austerity, developing a pro-business agenda, and pursuing a 'tough' approach to welfare reform. Observers associated with the centre-right think-tank Policy Network and with party group Progress argued that Labour could not win the 2015 general election by concentrating solely on a core voter strategy. In order to win, Miliband had to 'avoid the comforting, but fundamentally illusory assumption that the electorate is shifting irrevocably to the left'.[42]

But it was not only the right of the party who attacked the Labour leader. Across the party many backbenchers were worried about the party's standing in the opinion polls. Labour had consistently led the polls since 2011, but as the general election approached the gap narrowed significantly (the results of the 2015 general election showed that most opinion polls had been misleading). There were also concerns with the party's difficulty in convincing voters about its economic credibility. Poll after poll showed that on the issue that normally decides general elections – the economy – Labour lagged behind the Conservatives. More worryingly, Ed Miliband's personal ratings were abysmal. In fact, they were so abysmal that members of the shadow cabinet were not allowed to talk about them.[43]

The left and the soft left of the party (represented in organisations such as Tribune and Compass), if initially encouraged by Miliband's attacks on austerity and commitment to an egalitarian agenda, mistrusted a politician who had spent most of his political career working for New Labour first as an adviser, second as an MP parachuted to a safe seat, third as a cabinet minister, and finally as a Labour leader who promoted to prominent shadow cabinet posts so many figures associated with New Labour. Many on the soft left of the party thought he was too cautious, and pushed him to develop a more radical political agenda. For example, Neal Lawson from Compass argued that Miliband 'had some good ideas but they were not sufficiently fleshed-out'. Lawson also thought that Labour's agenda did not go far enough and as a result could lead to disastrous electoral consequences in 2015.[44]

Ed Miliband was mindful of his capital within the party and made strenuous efforts to mend fences. His appointments to the shadow cabinet recognised all the contenders for the leadership of the party (with the exception of his brother David, who ruled himself out) but he initially appointed them to surprising portfolios. For example, Ed Balls was given the post of shadow home secretary and Andy Burnham was given the shadow education post. Failing to convince his brother to take a post in the shadow cabinet, Ed Miliband appointed David's supporters Jim Murphy as shadow defence secretary and Douglas Alexander as shadow work and pensions secretary (all these positions changed at a later stage).

As an initial attempt at unifying the party, his first shadow cabinet was far from being successful. Blairite grandees and members of the shadow cabinet often briefed against him, attacking his leadership skills. At regular intervals, 'well-placed sources' would brief the media on how Miliband's leadership was hanging by a thread. There were also Labour frontbenchers who openly challenged the authority of the leader. Alan Johnson, who did not last more than three months as shadow chancellor (he resigned for personal reasons), openly challenged the party leader on three important policy issues. The first one was the graduate tax – which Miliband supported and Johnson opposed – and the second and third were about fiscal policy. Whilst the Labour leader was a strong defender of the 50p tax rate for high-income earners, Johnson said he was not an enthusiast. Finally, he was critical of the leader's stance on austerity and defined himself as an 'instinctive cutter'.[45] The fact that Johnson was able to challenge him in such an open way illustrates Miliband's difficulties in establishing himself as an authoritative leader.

This open in-fighting also showed how the party was deeply divided about its future. Though Miliband and those around him acknowledged the scale of the party's defeat, there were many who had underestimated it. This meant that Labour was divided between those who believed that the party could scrape through a parliamentary majority in 2015 with just minimum changes to its programme, and those who thought that victory could only be achieved if the party was ambitious in its plans for reform.[46]

In the shadow cabinet that schism was visible. Miliband's circle of advisers (and in particular Stewart Wood), supported by Jon Cruddas and some young frontbenchers, were pushing for radical reform, but the shadow chancellor Ed Balls and figures such as Douglas Alexander, Jim Murphy, and even Chuka Ummuna defended a more cautious approach that was closer to a New Labour blueprint. Indeed, they were particularly concerned with Miliband's anti-business reputation.

It was an open secret in Westminster that Miliband had a tense though professional relationship with Ed Balls. But if they worked together with relative effectiveness there was no great meeting of minds between them. This fracture had personal and ideological contours. Both men had worked for Gordon Brown, but Balls had been senior to Miliband. In addition, Balls was sceptical of Miliband's take on 'predator capitalism' and of reforms that would harm the interests of the banking industry. He was also – like his former boss, Gordon Brown – an instinctive centraliser. Hence, he was sceptical of Miliband's plans for devolution of fiscal powers to local councils.

The constant in-fighting, negative briefings, and occasional public debates about leadership challenges meant that for most of the time the Labour Party under Ed Miliband looked like a one-man band. There were no loyal backbenchers fighting his corner in the media or on the backbenches themselves. As Mehdi Hasan argued, the Labour Leader was 'his own outrider, making a lonely case for change'.[47] The appointment of Jon Cruddas in 2012 as chair of the party's Policy Review helped him to develop a base within the party, but it was still not enough to rally the party around his agenda. The 2013 shadow cabinet reshuffle marked the moment from which Miliband could show he had the party behind him.

The removal and/or demotion of Jim Murphy, Stephen Twigg, and Liam Byrne from their shadow cabinet posts to give way to a younger generation of Labour MPs was seen by many media commentators as the 'culling of the Blairites',[48] but others, like Rafael Behr, saw the reshuffle in a different way. According to Behr, the reshuffle was about Miliband taking control of the party. 'One principal motive behind the reshuffle is to accelerate the process of re-branding Labour as neither old nor new; neither Blair nor Brown – but wholly Milibandist', he wrote.[49]

But if by then it looked as though Ed Miliband finally had the party behind him, this apparent unity of purpose did not mark the end of his woes. He was still isolated and he trusted few of his colleagues in the shadow cabinet. Moreover, his negative poll ratings and constant media hostility were a permanent worry and distraction. The lacklustre 2014 Labour Party Annual Conference showed a party that was over-cautious, nervous, and still uncertain about how to approach the 2015 general election. The fact that Miliband omitted from his speech references to the 'deficit' and 'immigration' and emphasised the themes of the cost-of-living crisis was strongly criticised. Many Labour supporters and media commentators saw Miliband's speech as the moment where the party abandoned 'One Nation' politics to focus on a core vote strategy that could have disastrous electoral consequences. Finally, the result of the Heywood and Middleton by-election in the autumn of 2014, where the Labour candidate won by a very small margin, reflected the electoral challenges that Labour still faced. The fact that some Labour backbenchers plotted a leadership challenge without securing a candidate for the post is revealing of the degree of panic felt on the Labour benches.

Miliband's problems were also self-inflicted. He may have had a clear and bold agenda (which he had not been able to develop fully), but he struggled to come across as an authoritative and credible future prime minister. In other words, Miliband suffered from an image problem. Though he often delivered robust performances at Prime Minister's Questions against a very skilful David Cameron, he was not a natural orator. His delivery rarely galvanised his audience and was often flat. He also tended to tackle Prime Minister's Questions as an academic seminar, seeking to refute the Government's policies on a point-by-point basis, when what was required was a more visceral and populist approach to the occasion.

In the early days of his leadership, there were complaints about the tone of his voice, deemed too nasal for a potential prime minister. Similarly, his media performances on television and radio failed to impress. His image problems were also associated with his lack of visibility. His set-speeches were highly publicised in the media, but there was little follow-up after them. In fact, he jumped from theme to theme, creating the impression that his agenda was not fixed and lacked a core.

In a speech in the summer of 2014, Miliband admitted to his image problem but tried to suggest that his ideas were more important than photo-ops:

> I am not from central casting. You can find people who are more square-jawed. More chiselled. Look less like Wallace. You could probably even find people who look better eating a bacon sandwich. If you want the politician from central casting, it's just not me, it's the other guy … But here's the thing: I believe that people would quite like somebody to stand up and say there is more to politics than the photo-op.[50]

This speech was important because it marked the moment when the leadership of the party openly admitted that the leader had an image problem. But as Miliband suggested in the speech, there was not much the party or him could do about it. It was only when the electoral campaign started that the public's perception of the Labour leader started (marginally) to change.

His image problems were also the result of media hostility, which intensified during the six-week electoral campaign. As Peter Hain argued, the media hostility faced by Miliband rendered the task of developing a transformative agenda, and in particular of breaking the 'neoliberal consensus', more difficult.[51] With an overwhelmingly hostile press, who felt and explored his weakness in the party, it was particularly difficult for the Labour leader to rally supporters around his programme.

Fighting the Murdoch empire

Miliband was not the first Labour leader to face a hostile media. Indeed, dealing with a hostile press seems to have been a perennial problem for most Labour leaders since the foundation of the party. After all, the Labour Party's ideology and agenda are anathema to the politics of the right-wing press barons who control most of the media outlets in Britain. In this war of attrition, the right-wing media owners managed almost always to be on the winning side, contributing to most of Labour's electoral defeats in the twentieth century. On some occasions, even the Labour-supporting press turned against the party. In the 1960s Harold Wilson lost (temporarily) the support of the *Mirror*, and in 2010 Gordon Brown did not obtain the support of the *Guardian*. Tony Blair was the only Labour leader who was able to win the support of the right-wing press, and in particular of the Murdoch papers. Between 1995 and 2009, the Murdoch press supported the Labour Party, thanks in large part to Tony Blair's and Gordon Brown's willingness to court the 'Murdoch empire'. It also helped that New Labour pursued a business-friendly agenda and even promised to hold referendums on Britain's membership of the single currency and on the European constitution. However, in 2009 Gordon Brown lost that support to the Conservative Party.

This legacy meant that Miliband had to accept, as Tim Bale argued, the 'withering fire from a print media dedicated to keeping Labour out of office'.[52] The fact that he seemed to have no problem in defining his politics as socialist, as he did several times in public events and in media interviews,[53] was an open invitation to attacks from Fleet Street.

From the first moments of his leadership, Ed Miliband faced daily attacks from the media, and some of them were quite vicious. He was often accused of being 'in the pockets of the trade unions', and his policy proposals were defined as either Stalinist or inspired by Hugo Chávez's Venezuela. He was also seen as 'wonky', 'nerdy', 'weird', and a 'Hampstead socialist'. In short, Miliband was presented as being completely out of touch with voters. In his first media interview as Labour leader, on the BBC's *Andrew Marr Show*, he was forced to respond to these critics by insisting that his leadership was 'not about some lurch to the left'.[54] Even the Labour-supporting *Guardian* argued that Miliband 'must make clear that he will give no special favours to the unions'.[55]

The most vicious attack came from the right-wing *Daily Mail* in the autumn of 2013.[56] The paper published an article about the Labour leader's father, the Marxist intellectual Ralph Miliband, entitled 'Ralph Miliband: The Man who Hated Britain'. The purpose was twofold. First, the editor of the *Mail* wanted to show that Ralph Miliband was unpatriotic, and second, he wanted to discredit the Labour leader by claiming that he aimed to 'achieve his father's vision'.[57]

But the media's opposition to Miliband was not restricted to the right-wing press. His image problems were amply discussed across all media outlets. One typically used media frame was the idea that the Labour leader was 'weird'. He did not know how to relate to normal people; he used academic jargon that voters could not relate to on the doorstep; and even John Humphrys, one of the presenters of the *Today* programme, wondered whether the Labour leader was 'too ugly' to be the next prime minister. Above all, the media felt that Miliband was weak because he was unable to command the loyalty of his own party.

But the hostile media coverage also had a liberating effect on the Labour leader. When the 'hacking scandal', involving the newspaper *News of the World*, broke in 2011, he took the opportunity to attack Rupert Murdoch's News International. The timing was problematic for Rupert Murdoch, who had bid to acquire two-thirds of BSkyB, and was waiting for a response from the Coalition Government.

The revelations that the *News of the World* had hacked the mobile phone of the teenager Milly Dowler, while her parents were still searching for her, caused public revulsion against the Murdoch newspapers. As a result, an official inquiry led by Lord Leveson started to investigate the case, and this fact had a spill-over effect on to News International's bid for BSkyB. Not losing any time, the Labour leader demanded that News International withdraw their bid to acquire BSkyB on the grounds that such concentrations of power were 'quite dangerous' because they led to abuses of that power.[58]

This attack on Murdoch surprised both Miliband's critics and his allies. After all, historically the Labour Party had paid a heavy price every time it did not play the press barons' game. But Miliband seemed determined to pursue this campaign and by doing so he strengthened his position as a Labour leader. Instead of looking undecided, ineffective, and overly cautious, his stance against Rupert Murdoch was seen as a bold and courageous move.

As the Leveson Inquiry gathered evidence on the murky reporting practices of the tabloid press, the Labour leader pursued his anti-Murdoch (and anti-tabloid press) crusade by pushing for press regulation. For Miliband, the purpose of independent regulation was to create a new system that would provide 'independent protection and redress for citizens' and 'safeguards to ensure press freedom'.[59] He was careful to avoid presenting his proposals in a way that could be interpreted as anti-press freedom. Thus, he insisted that he was in favour of 'a press that can expose abuse of power without abusing its own'.[60]

When the Leveson Inquiry presented its recommendations in November 2012, Miliband was immediately supportive. Later, he joined the prime minister David Cameron and the deputy prime minister Nick Clegg in cross-party talks that sought to transform the Leveson recommendations into a draft bill. But in March 2013 both Labour and the Liberal Democrats accused the Conservatives of watering down the draft bill, and presented their own proposals for the statutory underpinning of the press regulator.

Miliband's offensive against Murdoch's news empire struck a chord with public opinion and enhanced his credibility as Labour leader, but had little or no effect on the way he was treated by the media. Indeed, the 2015 electoral campaign was marked by vicious attacks by the right-wing media. Miliband was presented as a dangerous leader who, if elected, would break and ruin the country.

During the electoral campaign, he challenged the media narrative about his leadership skills with a more confident demeanour. His media appearances were no longer the wooden performances of previous years. In the televised debates he was articulate and direct, and exuded passion and a sense of purpose. His combative style in interviews with broadcasters, or even revelations about his musical taste or former girlfriends, challenged the prevailing idea that the Labour leader was 'weird'.

To many viewers, he looked very different from the caricature the media had painted so far. Interviews with non-mainstream broadcasters circulated in the social media and showed a more personable, relaxed, and even witty Labour leader. The height of his popularity happened in the fourth week of campaign when a teenager's 'Milifandom' Twitter account went viral. Suddenly, commentators were describing their astonishment at Miliband's transformation from 'Wallace to Poldark'. But by then it was too late dramatically to change voters' perceptions about Miliband's suitability to become prime minister. His difficulties in communicating with the public and in coming across as an authoritative leader are one of the reasons why the party lost so badly in the 2015 general election.

Miliband and the trade unions

Another major constraint to Ed Miliband's standing as a party leader was his perceived closeness to the trade unions. The perception, promoted by the media and by
the opposition parties, that he was a puppet of the trade unions was problematic. It
assisted the media in portraying him either as a radical or as a member of the 'loony'
left – that is, as someone who was not fit to run the country.

Miliband was acutely aware of this perception and as a result he was very strategic
in his dealings with the trade unions. For instance, he was vocal in his criticisms of
public sector strikes at a time when those 'squeezed-middle' voters he claimed to
represent were experiencing a decline in their living standards as a result of public
sector pay freezes. This stance disappointed many Labour supporters, but the party
presented it as a traditional Labour stance. As Stewart Wood put it, 'the Labour
Party has never supported a strike. Never has done, never will do.'[61]

In the early days of his leadership, he had signalled a desire to reform the party's
links to the trade unions. He was particularly interested in reviewing their role in
policy-making and in the election of the leader. However, his plans for reform were
unclear. Apart from vague proposals to cap donations to political parties and some
allusions to the need to reform the system of party funding nothing concrete was
spelled out before the end of 2013. In truth, Miliband simply avoided addressing
the controversial link to the trade unions because this would draw attention to his
own problematic relationship with them and to Labour's funding problems. Given
Labour's dependence on the financial and logistical support of the trade unions,
especially during electoral campaigns,[62] those reforms could not lead to the break of
their historical link.

Miliband avoided the issue whilst he could, but the Falkirk scandal of 2013, about
the alleged vote-rigging by the trade union Unite, forced him to take action. In
the summer of 2013, Unite was accused of manipulating the recruitment of party
members in order to secure the election of Karie Murphy as a Labour candidate
for the Falkirk West constituency.[63] It was alleged that in order to boost the number
of supporters, Unite officials had forged signatures and coerced Unite union members into signing direct debit forms. Following these allegations, the Labour leader
announced both police and party inquiries into the recruitment practices of Falkirk
West's party office, as well as reforms to the role of trade unions in the Labour Party.

Miliband's reaction to the Falkirk West scandal outraged some trade unions,
including, of course, Unite, who denied the allegations. If some accepted that
vote-rigging was unacceptable they also knew that Labour's selection practices were
not exactly stellar examples of democracy.[64] Indeed, the practice of 'parachuting'
former advisers of cabinet ministers or protégés of the leadership to safe seats had
been a point of contention with constituency party branches for some years.

In February 2014, the party's inquiry into voting irregularities in Falkirk West
concluded that there was evidence that members had been recruited without their

knowledge and that some were pressured to complete direct debit forms. There was also evidence that signatures had been forged.[65] These damning conclusions created the platform for Miliband's sweeping reforms to the role of trade unions in the party's policy-making and to the introduction of the one-member-one-vote principle in the leadership elections of the Labour Party.

The reforms proposed by Miliband and drafted by Lord (Ray) Collins, to be implemented in two stages over a period of five years, will bring greater transparency to Labour's relationship with the trade unions and will make the party's voting procedures more democratic. That transparency will be achieved by changing the way trade union members are affiliated to the Labour Party. The *Collins Review into Labour Party Reform* proposed a simple but radical idea: trade union members should be given the opportunity to decide whether they want to become party members or supporters. Following some heated debates, the party reform proposals were approved with 82.29 per cent of the votes.

Miliband's party reforms also affect how the party's conference operates in terms of the balance of power between the trade unions and the constituency parties. More controversially, he proposed an electoral system whereby the votes of ordinary members count as much as those of MPs (though MPs will have the power to choose the shortlist of candidates to the leadership of the party). He proposed as well conducting open primaries for the selection of Labour's London mayoral candidate as a way to engage a broader range of supporters.

But Miliband's reforms go beyond the party's relation with the trade unions. He also sought to transform Labour into a mass party by inviting the participation of 'supporters' (as opposed to members) of the party in future leadership elections. These reforms complement other initiatives implemented by Labour's general secretary Ian McNicol and by Angela Eagle, the chair of the National Policy Forum, which sought to open and democratise the party and to invite the input of members to its policy-making process.

Interestingly, the way Miliband negotiated, formulated, and secured the approval of these reforms was quite revealing of his deliberative and consensual style of leadership. He devoted considerable time to the quiet diplomacy of persuading trade unionists, recalcitrant backbenchers, and constituency parties to support his reforms. From the start he was clear in his intentions, but he was not abrasive and his criticisms to particular trade union leaders were made in private. He also insisted on saying that his reforms were about letting 'people back into our politics', and about transforming the party into a movement that was able to attract new supporters. This aim chimed with his pluralist approach to politics.

By getting these reforms approved, Ed Miliband showed his growing authority over the party. Convincing Labour – and in particular the trade unions – to support his sweeping party reforms allowed him to demonstrate that his often criticised personality traits – his caution and his deliberative style of decision-making – were actually important assets. He also gained the respect of sceptical media commentators who disagreed with his politics but who were forced to accept that Miliband had demonstrated himself to be an effective party leader.

Concluding remarks

This chapter has sought to explain the political and institutional constraints the Labour leader faced whilst developing his vision of political change. To do so, it started with the contextualisation of Ed Miliband's election as Labour leader and with an analysis of the main planks of his agenda. The purpose of these initial sections was to show that Ed Miliband became Labour leader at a particularly inauspicious time. Labour had suffered its heaviest electoral defeats since 1918 and was blamed for the deficit crisis that afflicted the country. The Labour Party was also intellectually exhausted after thirteen years in power. Moreover, the state of intellectual confusion and powerlessness amongst European social democrats (addressed in the previous chapter) meant that the Labour leader had few political friends from whom he could draw inspiration and political support.

The contextualisation of Miliband's election to Labour's leadership helps to explain the main obstacles he faced when developing his political agenda. His difficulties in gathering support for his political project came from two main sources: the party and the media. As we now know, both had an impact on how the Labour leader and his agenda were perceived by voters.

His isolation in the party was all too apparent. The constant whispering on the Labour backbenches about his leadership skills, the occasional plot to oust him from the leadership, and the lack of support from his frontbench team whenever he made a new announcement hindered the development of his agenda. He did not enjoy the support of the party or of the majority of the shadow cabinet, nor did he command strong personal ratings, which would have enabled him to impose his vision. In fact, for the duration of his leadership, his personal poll ratings were negative. Even when his image slightly improved during the electoral campaign, the leader of the Conservative Party, David Cameron, was seen as a more authoritative figure. To use Richard Heffernan's framework to analyse leaders of the opposition, Ed Miliband may have been 'preeminent' but he was definitely not 'predominant'. Indeed, he did not have the reputation for being leadership material; he was not associated with actual or anticipated political success; he was not electorally popular and he did not enjoy a high standing in his parliamentary party.[66]

Because of his vulnerabilities as a party leader, he spent more than half of his time as Labour leader fighting the different factions and trying to unite the party around his One Nation vision than developing a strong, coherent, and detailed programme of transformative change. It took him almost four years to gain the support of important sections of the party and to fully develop and present his vision.

However, the party never gave him unwavering support. That support was always conditional, temporary, and contingent on the fact that there were no obvious alternative candidates for the leadership of the party. The media was also an important constraint. For ideological reasons, some sections of the right-wing media, in particular the *Daily Mail* and the Murdoch newspapers, seemed determined to undermine his authority.

He managed to transform some of these constraints into opportunities. For instance, his 'zen' attitude to media hostility led him openly to confront News International, and to campaign for the regulation of the press. None of these interventions had the effect of winning him new friends in Fleet Street but they marginally enhanced his credibility as leader. He also turned on its head the accusation that he was in the pockets of the trade unions by enacting sweeping reforms to the party's policy-making structures.

But the fact that it took him so long to secure the party's tenuous and reluctant backing had an impact on his agenda. He was forced not only to make concessions, but also to remain silent over a number of policy issues that were important to him. A case in point was Miliband's devolution agenda, which he was only fully able to develop and unveil after he secured the support of Ed Balls. As a result, what he proposed to voters was often less than the sum of its parts. There was a considerable gap between the rhetoric and the policies he proposed to enact his vision.

He was also extremely cautious in his pronouncements. Every step he took, every policy announcement he made was carefully calibrated with a view to acquiring that elusive yet crucial quality in politics: credibility. The following chapters will show how Ed Miliband pursued the dual goals of credibility and radicalism in different policy areas: namely in the economy, social justice, the people-power agenda, and the politics of belonging.

Notes

1 Ed Miliband, 'Speech to the Labour Party Annual Conference 2012', 2 October 2012, http://www.labour.org.uk/ed-miliband-speech-conf-2012,2012-10-02 (accessed 4 October 2012).

2 Steven Fielding, 'Labour's Campaign: Things Can Only Get …Worse?', *Parliamentary Affairs* 63:4 (2010): 653–666 (p. 653).

3 John Cruddas, private interview, 2 September 2013.

4 John Denham, private interview, 2 June 2013.

5 Fielding, 'Labour's Campaign', p. 653.

6 Richard Heffernan, 'Labour's New Labour Legacy: Politics after Blair and Brown', *Political Studies Review* 9 (2011): 163–177 (p. 164).

7 Jon Cruddas, private interviews, 2 September 2013 and 4 March 2015.

8 Quoted in Mehdi Hasan and James Macintyre, *Ed: The Milibands and the Making of a Labour Leader* (London: Biteback Publishing, 2011), p. 177.

9 Jon Cruddas, quoted in Hasan and Macintyre, *Ed*, p. 210.

10 Richard Jobson and Mark Wickham-Jones, 'Gripped by the Past: Nostalgia and the 2010 Labour Party Leadership Contest', *British Politics* 5:4 (2010): 525–548 (p. 526).

11 Ed Miliband, 'A Mandate for Change', 30 August 2010, http://www.labourincoventry/org.uk/index.php?option=com_content&view=article&id (accessed 24 January 2014).

12 Miliband, 'A Mandate for Change'.

13 Miliband, 'A Mandate for Change'.

14 Hasan and Macintyre, *Ed*, p. 262.

15 Andrew Rawnsley, 'Ed Miliband Boldly Goes where Even Tony Blair Feared to Tread', *Observer*, 2 February 2014.

16 Hasan and Macintyre, *Ed*, p. 208.

17 Ed Miliband, 'Why I Want to Lead the Labour Party', *Guardian*, 15 May 2010.

18 Stewart Wood, private interview, 17 January 2003.

19 Cruddas, private interview, 4 March 2015.

20 Ed Miliband, 'The New Generation: Speech to the 2010 Labour Party Annual Conference', 28 September 2010, www.labour.org.uk/ed-miliband–a-new-generation,2010-09-28 (accessed 10 January 2012).

21 Robert Philpot (ed.), *The Purple Book: A Progressive Future for Labour* (London: Biteback Publishing, 2011); Eoin Clarke and Owain Gardner (eds), *The Red Book: Labour Left* (Cambridge: Searching Finance, 2012); Olaf Cramme and Patrick Diamond (eds), *After the Third Way: The Future of Social Democracy in Europe* (London: I.B. Tauris, 2012); Maurice Glasman, Jonathan Rutherford, Marc Stears, and Stuart White (eds), *The Labour Tradition and the Politics of Paradox: The Oxford London Seminars 2010–11* (n.p.: Oxford London Seminars, 2011).

22 Cruddas, private interview, 2 September 2013.

23 Jonathan Rutherford, 'The Labour Party and the New Left: The First New Left, Blue Labour and English Modernity', *Renewal* 21:1 (2013): 9–14.

24 Maurice Glasman, 'Labour as a Radical Tradition', in Glasman, Rutherford, Stears, and White, *The Labour Tradition*, pp. 14–34 (pp. 24–25).

25 Ed Miliband, 'Speech to the Labour Party Annual Conference 2012'.

26 Marc Stears, private interview, 18 June 2013.

27 Stears, private interview, 18 June 2013.

28 Ed Miliband, 'Margaret Thatcher Tribute', 10 April 2013, http://www.labour.org.uk/ed-milibands-statement-on-margaret-thatcher,2013-04-10 (accessed 7 May 2013).

29 Stears, private interview, 18 June 2013.

30 Ben Jackson, 'The Masses against the Classes', *Public Policy Research* 19:3 (2012): 160–165 (p. 163).

31 Jackson, 'The Masses against the Classes', p. 163.

32 Judi Atkins, 'Narrating One Nation: The Ideology and Rhetoric of the Miliband Labour Party', *Politics* 35:1 (February 2015): 19–31 (p. 29).

33 Atkins, 'Narrating One Nation', p. 29.

34 Ed Miliband, '2014 Labour Conference Speech', 23 September 2014, http://www.labour.org.uk/blog/entry/2014-labour-conference-speech (accessed 24 September 2014).

35 Marc Stears, 'The Personal Politics of Ed Miliband', in John Denham (ed.), *The Shape of Things to Come: Labour's New Thinking* (London: Fabian Society, 2012), pp. 123–132 (p. 127).

36 Private interview, 9 July 2014.

37 Maurice Glasman, 'Ed Miliband Must Trust His Instincts and Stand Up for Real Change', *New Statesman*, 5 January 2012.

38 Tony Blair, 'Labour Must Search for Answers and Not Merely Aspire to Be a Repository for People's Anger', *New Statesman*, 1 April 2013.

39 Andrew Grice, 'New Labour, New Danger: Tony Blair Leads Party Grandees in Attack on Ed Miliband', *Independent*, 12 April 2013, http://www.independent.co.uk/news/uk/politics/new-labour-new-danger-tony-blair-leads-party-grandees-in-attack-on-ed-miliband-8568148.html (accessed 11 August 2015).

40 Peter Mandelson, quoted in Nicholas Watt, 'Peter Mandelson Hits Out at Ed Miliband's "Crowd-Pleasing" Election Manifesto', *Guardian*, 19 September 2010, http://www.theguardian.com/politics/2010/sep/19/peter-mandelson-ed-miliband-manifesto (accessed 7 February 2014).

41 'Lord Mandelson Attacks Ed Miliband for "Taking Labour Backwards"', *Huffington Post UK*, 26 September 2013, http://www.huffingtonpost.co.uk/2013/09/26/mandelson-miliband-taking-labour-backwards_n_3993694.html (accessed 7 February 2014).

42 Patrick Diamond, 'Labour Must Wise Up to What Voters Really Want', *Guardian*, 24 January 2014.

43 Tim Bale, 'Four Reasons Ed Miliband Is Still a Good Opposition Leader', *Guardian*, 16 October 2014.

44 Neal Lawson, private interview, 10 May 2014.

45 Hasan and Macintyre, *Ed*, p. 266.

46 Cruddas, private interview, 2 September 2013.

47 Mehdi Hasan, 'Miliband's Vision Is Bold – But Now It's Time to Convince the Country', *New Statesman*, 3 October 2011.

48 Dan Hodges, 'Miliband Has Told the Blairites: There's No Place for You in This Party. He'd Better Watch His Back', *Daily Telegraph*, 7 October 2013 http://blogs.telegraph.co.uk/news/danhodges/100240240/ed-miliband-has-told-the-blairites-theres-no-place-for-you-in-this-party-hed-better-watch-his-back/ (accessed 3 August 2015).

49 Rafael Behr, 'Miliband's Reshuffle Was Post-Blairite, Not Anti-Blairite', *New Statesman*, 8 October 2013, http://www.newstatesman.com/politics/2013/10/milibands-reshuffle-was-post-blairite-not-anti-blairite (accessed 1 August 2015).

50 Ed Miliband, 'The Choice: Leadership. Speech by Ed Miliband MP', 25 July 2014, http://press.labour.org.uk/post/92819342334/the-choice-leadership-speech-by-ed-miliband-mp (accessed 28 July 2014).

51 Peter Hain, private interview, 25 March 2015.

52 Tim Bale, 'Concede and Move On? One Nation and the Welfare State', *Political Quarterly* 84:3 (2013): 342–352 (p. 342).

53 'Ed Miliband: Yes, I Am Socialist', Channel4.com, 26 November 2010, http://www.channel4.com/news/ed-miliband-yes-i-am-a-socialist (accessed 7 February 2014).

54 Hasan and Macintyre, *Ed*, p. 244.

55 'Labour's New Leader: Ed Miliband's Moment', *Guardian*, 27 September 2010, http://www.theguardian.com/commentisfree/2010/sep/27/labours-new-leader-ed-miliband-editorial (accessed 11 August 2015).

56 Ivor Gaber offers an enlightening analysis of how the *Daily Mail* framed Ed Miliband. Ivor Gaber, 'The "Othering" of "Red Ed", or How the *Daily Mail* "Framed" the British Labour Leader', *Political Quarterly* 85:4 (October–December 2014): 471–479.

57 Geoffrey Levy, 'The Man who Hated Britain: Red Ed's Pledge to Bring Back Socialism Is a Homage to His Marxist Father …', *Mail Online*, 27 September 2013, http://www.dailymail. co.uk/news/article-2435751/Red-Eds-pledge-bring-socialism-homage-Marxist-father-Ralph-Miliband-says-GEOFFREY-LEVY.html (accessed 11 August 2015).

58 Toby Helm, Jamie Doward, and Daniel Boffey, 'Murdoch's Empire Must Be Dismantled – Ed Miliband', *Observer*, 16 November 2011, http://www.theguardian.com/politics/2011/jul/16/ rupert-murdoch-ed-miliband-phone-hacking (accessed 3 August 2015).

59 Ed Miliband, 'When Leveson Reports, Parliament Must Act Swiftly', *Guardian*, 25 November 2012, http://www.guardian.co.uk/commentisfree/2012/nov/25/leveson-reports-parliament-act-swiftly (accessed 8 July 2013).

60 Ed Miliband, 'Statement on the Leveson Inquiry', 29 November 2012, http://www.labour.org. uk/statement-on-the-leveson-inquiry,2012-11-29 (accessed 11 January 2013).

61 Wood, private interview, 17 January 2013.

62 George Eaton, 'Who Will Pay for Labour's Next Election Campaign?', *New Statesman*, 12 September 2013, http://www.newstatesman.com/politics/2013/09/who-will-pay-labours-n ext-election-campaign (accessed 21 February 2014).

63 Ed Miliband, 'One Nation Politics', 9 July 2013, http://www.labour.org.uk/one-nation-politics-speech (accessed 10 July 2013).

64 Email exchanges between Ed Miliband's office and Unite representatives that were published in the press revealed that Ed Miliband was aware of the unorthodox recruiting practices of Unite.

65 Rajeev Syal, 'Labour Party's Falkirk Membership Inquiry Report – Analysis', *Guardian*, 3 February 2014. However, there are claims that these conclusions are not supported by evidence.

66 Richard Heffernan, 'UK Party Leaders Are "Preeminent", but Can Also Be "Predominant": Cameron and the Conservatives, 2005–2010', *British Politics* 9:1 (April 2014): 51–67 (p. 51).

3

Labour and the economy

Reforming capitalism

As we emerge from the global economic crisis we face a choice: we can return to business as usual or we can challenge old thinking to build the new economy we need.

Ed Miliband[1]

For a brief moment the global financial crisis offered European social democrats the opportunity to reframe the political debate about the state of the global economy and refashion a new 'social democratic moment'. Like other European social democratic parties, Labour under Ed Miliband tried to develop an alternative to neoliberalism and austerity policies but faced formidable obstacles. Ultimately, Labour reluctantly succumbed to the prevailing neoliberal views – on the grounds that it was the only way to regain economic credibility – by accepting public spending cuts as the only acceptable recipe to eliminate the public deficit and public debt.

This chapter examines the Labour Party's approach to the economy with a special focus on its response to the 2008 global financial crisis and to the subsequent deficit crisis. It will argue that under Ed Miliband the Labour Party sought to develop an alternative to the neoliberal orthodoxies of New Labour and to the austerity policies of the Coalition. This alternative was based on a new understanding of the market, on an active role for the State in the development of industrial capacity, and in ensuring that the proceeds of growth would be equitably shared. However, the Labour Party faced ideational, institutional, and political constraints that had the effect of making the break with neoliberalism and austerity policies less clear-cut than was perhaps intended.

Using Vivien Schmidt's analytical framework, the chapter maps the context and the ideas (and their sponsors) that have informed Labour's economic agenda. Next, it explains how those ideas and context influenced Ed Miliband's approach to the economy at the level of narrative but also at the level of policy proposals. Along the way, the different ideational, political, and institutional constraints that influenced

Labour's development of a new economic approach are identified and discussed. In the final section, the chapter discusses the interplay among ideas, interests, and institutional constraints, and uses Hall's criteria to assess the influence of specific ideas over Labour's approach to the economy.

Labour's economic approach is directly linked to its equality agenda. For example, Labour's diagnosis of the causes of the global financial crisis focuses on the social impact of neoliberal economic policies. Moreover, its plans to diversify the British economy were predicated on the promotion of new apprenticeship schemes and a high-wage economy. But as these schemes also fit into Labour's equality agenda, they are analysed in the next chapter.

Context and the legacy of New Labour

The Labour Party's search for an alternative to austerity policies and for a new approach to the economy took place in the context of a deficit crisis and deep recession that followed the credit crunch of 2007 and the financial crisis of 2008. The global financial crisis provoked a healthy and vigorous debate about the nature of capitalism in political and financial circles. Books about the financial crisis and the crisis of capitalism sold like airport best-sellers. Keynesian economists such as Thomas Piketty, Paul Krugman, and Joseph Stiglitz gained substantial visibility in media debates. The American philosopher Michael J. Sandel filled lecture halls with his reflections on the moral limits of markets, whilst economics students at prominent British universities demanded new approaches to the teaching of the 'dismal science' which had failed to predict the crisis.

But if the intellectual apparatus of neoliberalism had collapsed, its death was prematurely announced.[2] Indeed, neoliberalism was still the model favoured by the leading economic and financial institutions of Europe, by the IMF, and by centre-right politicians, and as a result the policy paradigm of austerity was unassailable in British and European politics.[3] The parties of the Coalition Government, influential commentators, and even important sections of the Labour Party fully subscribed to austerity as the only plausible solution that could eliminate the public deficit. According to the prevailing narrative, the growth of the public deficit was not caused by the failures of the financial sector, but by irresponsible Government spending. The Labour Party under Ed Miliband failed to dispel this perception. The fact that a large number of voters believed that the previous Labour Government had overspent and that that had caused the economic crisis is one of the main reasons the party lost the 2015 general election.

But this was not the only difficulty that Labour faced. The Keynesian solutions favoured by social democrats were difficult to grasp. The idea that public deficits can be reduced and eliminated through programmes of public investment in infrastructure and project financing (which relied on borrowing) defied popular understandings of economics. To use one of Peter Hall's criteria to assess the success of ideas,

Keynesian approaches, and in particular the 'paradox of thrift' idea, failed the comprehensibility test. On the other hand, the idea that you eliminate debt by cutting public spending resonates with voters' personal experiences. As a result, the financial crisis that started as a credit crunch and that had exposed the fatal flaws of casino capitalism was refashioned as a debt crisis created by profligate governments that could only be cured with draconian public spending cuts and State retrenchment.

If dealing with this ideational context was not hard enough, the Labour Party under Ed Miliband had to address New Labour's economic legacy. This had to be done for two main reasons. First, because New Labour had contributed to the global financial crisis by embracing light-touch regulation, flexible labour markets, privatisations, and all the accoutrements of neoliberal economics.[4] An example of this embrace was Gordon Brown's uncritical support of the financial sector. Just a few months before the collapse of Northern Rock, he congratulated the financial services industry for its 'remarkable achievements', which demonstrated the heralding of a new golden age for the City of London.[5]

Second, New Labour's attempts to solve the financial crisis – in particular the bank bailouts and the millions spent in quantitative easing – left a huge hole in the public finances. In 2009, the United Kingdom's public deficit stood at 12.6 per cent the GDP. The precarious state of public finances, as well as the weak position of banks, had an immediate impact on the British economy. By 2009 Britain was officially in recession. Traditional high-street names were closing their doors, unemployment rose, and economic activity slowed down.

But New Labour's economic legacy was not limited to the damage created by the financial sector. It turned out that despite the sixty quarters of uninterrupted economic growth, New Labour economics also lacked the Midas touch. As Roger Liddle and Patrick Diamond remind us in sharp and succinct manner, New Labour's economic legacy was also

one of under-investment in key infrastructure, notably transport and energy; a continuing decline in manufacturing contributing to a structural balance of payments deficit; an accelerating regional economic divide; and a speculative property and construction boom financing public and private consumption through highly leveraged government and household debt.[6]

In short, this approach could not form the basis of Labour's economic approach for the post-crisis period. In truth, the economic credibility of the Labour Party was in tatters. If in 1997 voters had trusted New Labour as a competent manager of the economy, by 2010 that level of trust had completely evaporated. Voters blamed Labour for the financial and deficit crisis and for the ensuing economic recession.

Dealing with this context was difficult because both factors necessitated different – and even contradictory – responses. Addressing the intellectual and economic inconsistencies of neoliberalism required a new understanding about the role of the

State in market economies, in particular in the areas of financial regulation but also at the level of market reforms aimed at enhancing competition and protecting consumers. Moreover, the re-balancing of the economy also implied substantial public investments in education and in the development of economic infrastructure. However, advocating a new role for the State was problematic for Labour in terms of public perception, because the party had to recognise the very tangible legacy of the public deficit. But to do so was tantamount to accepting that, when in government, Labour had been profligate with the public finances, and the only way to tackle this economic misdemeanour was to embrace fiscal and financial probity. In short, Labour faced a difficult political dilemma. It would either have to choose to reform capitalism, with a view to preventing the emergence of a new crisis, or it would have to focus its energies on recovering its reputation as a credible manager of the economy, which would imply ditching or diluting its reformist proposals. As the next pages will show, the party tried to pursue these two goals, but the result of this approach raised important questions about the coherence of its programme.

Ideas: old and new

This ideational, political, and economic context framed the contours of Labour's search for an alternative to austerity, and to a certain extent limited the party's policy options. Nonetheless, a range of ideas about 'what went wrong' and about 'what should be done' was available, and many were appropriated and adapted by Miliband's team, but also by the different Labour factions that sought to influence the party's programme. Some of these ideas, debated and circulated in a variety of publications and seminars promoted by think-tanks, party groups, and grassroots organisations close to Labour, were overlapping and complementary, but there were also competing ideas about the role of the State, or about the rightful place of the market in promoting sustainable economic growth and tackling inequalities of wealth and of power.

Labour's search for new ideas had obviously to consider the impact of the global financial crisis but also to reassess New Labour's accommodation of neoliberalism and its response to that crisis. Here the debate was dominated by three main interpretations of the causes of the crisis and by three main prescriptions. The first approach was articulated by Blue Labour thinkers who brought Polanyian insights into their interpretation of what had led to the global financial crisis, but also into their recommendations about what Labour needed to do. For Blue Labour thinkers like Maurice Glasman, the global financial crisis offered an opportunity to rethink the social democratic embrace of neoliberalism. Reflecting Karl Polanyi's thinking, they argued that capitalism was inherently unstable.[7]

The second important Polanyian insight used by Blue Labour was about the power of the market to disrupt social relations and to promote an undesirable marketisation and commodification of society.[8] Blue Labour's response to the problem of commodification was to propose a 'democratic resistance to the commodification of human beings'.[9] As Alan Finlayson explained, this specific form of anti-capitalism was mostly concerned with how the market undermined 'embedded communities'.[10]

If Blue Labour was critical of unregulated capitalism it was equally critical of the State, and in particular of Labour's traditional statecraft. Thus, instead of advocating a larger role for the State in addressing the problem of commodification, or promoting economic growth and delivering wealth redistribution, they emphasised the role of communities, and the values and traditions of localism, of mutualism, of the cooperative movement, and of grassroots movements.[11] This particular reading was reflected in Labour's Policy Review document, where Jon Cruddas and Jonathan Rutherford argued that 'Polanyi's analysis offers a socialism that rejects the impersonal forces of laissez-faire capitalism and provides another model to the statism and central planning implied in Beveridge's report', and that the 'way to build a prosperous economy lies in social renewal'.[12]

The second dominant approach was informed by a Keynesian response to the deficit crisis, which advocated public investment to stimulate job creation and economic growth. The new Keynesians in and around Labour shared with Blue Labour the understanding that capitalism was unstable and prone to crisis, however they did not share its critical approach to the State. The central point of Keynesian economists was that the State should concentrate on creating employment, as the deficit, to misquote Keynes, would 'take care of itself'. In addition, they did not share Blue Labour's belief in the ability of mutualism to transform capitalism single-handedly. Indeed, Neal Lawson from Compass was very dismissive of that approach. As he put it, capitalism could not be transformed 'by holding hands on street corners'.[13]

The American economists Paul Krugman and Joseph Stiglitz were the strongest advocates of this diagnosis, and their arguments found some sympathetic ears in Labour circles, in particular around Compass. Indeed, both Miliband and Balls quoted these two economists in their speeches (though Balls was critical of 'naive versions of Keynesianism'). In response to the financial crisis, Keynesians within the party argued for a deficit reduction plan that focused on a fiscal stimulus and on job creation. It was the argument of Peter Hain, who used his book *Back to the Future of Socialism*, as well as countless articles published in the *Guardian*, to make the case for a 'growth by active government' approach that emphasised the importance of investing in housing and infrastructure projects.[14] The proponents of this approach advocated as well an active industrial policy with a view to re-balancing the British economy away from its overreliance on the financial services industry and towards a fiscal policy that would not harm the most vulnerable.

But the Keynesian approach was strongly resisted by those in the party who were worried about Labour's credibility as a trusted and efficient manager of the economy. Thus, a third approach, which I define as 'lite-austerian', forced its way into the debate. This tendency was popular amongst New Labour circles and think-tanks such as Policy Network, party groups such as Progress, the ginger group Black Labour, and a fair number of influential media commentators. Briefly put, 'lite-austerians' believed that the neoliberal model pursued by New Labour worked 'reasonably well' in Britain, and warned that 'social democrats must be careful not to throw out the baby [commitment to the market economy] with the New Labour bath water'.[15] The 'lite-austerians' argued that Labour's economic credibility could only be gained by a commitment to reducing the deficit through public spending cuts (and not through tax rises and a stimulus programme, as Keynesians advocated).[16] Moreover, the 'lite-austerian' tendency wanted Miliband to recognise the mistakes of the previous New Labour Government, in particular the fact that public spending had risen on its watch. 'Lite-austerians' tended to agree with Blue Labour on the critique of the State and shared their belief in the transformative attributes of mutualism.

In terms of proposals for economic reform, these three main approaches tended to agree that the British economy needed to be re-balanced through public invest-ment in infrastructure projects and via the promotion of new economic sectors, such as the green economy, the technology sector, or the cultural industries. They also agreed that economic growth depended on administrative decentralisation. Thus, the three tendencies advocated the devolution of fiscal and economic powers to cities, towns, and local communities. In some instances, they even endorsed simi-lar ideas. It was the case of 'pre-distribution', a concept developed by the Harvard academic Jacob S. Hacker that found a hearing within Blairite think-tanks, Compass, Blue Labour pamphlets, and all the other tendencies in between.

The advocates of pre-distribution shared many of the Keynesian and Polanyian insights about the instability of capitalism, but they focused on the role of income and wealth inequality in generating economic instability. Hacker and Pierson argued that the extraordinary concentration of wealth and stagnant social mobil-ity that took place in the last three decades of the twentieth century were directly related – via the expansion of cheap credit to poorer individuals – to the 2007 credit crunch, to the 2008 financial crisis, and to the 2009 deficit crisis.[17] Interestingly, they claimed that those wealth differentials were not related to skills or to technological change, but to a politically orchestrated 'winner-take-all' economy.[18] In other words, the 'winner-take-all' economy had been manufactured by governments. Over the years, tax reforms, labour legislation, and in particular legislation that restricted the activities of trade unions had the cumulative effect of increasing the wealth and power of the wealthy and powerful at the expense of everyone else. The implication of this reasoning was fairly straightforward. The 'winner-take-all' economy was nei-ther 'God-given' nor a force of nature. If the State had contributed to such an uneven distribution of economic power, it could as well intervene to fix and improve mar-kets.[19] Similarly, the French economist Thomas Piketty contended that economic growth was adversely affected by income inequality, and provided weighty statistical evidence to sustain his argument in the best-selling tome *Capital in the Twenty-First Century.*[20]

To counter these tendencies, Hacker proposed the idea of pre-distribution, which he defined as 'market reforms that encourage a more equal distribution of economic power and rewards even before government collects taxes or pays out benefits'.[21] Thus, pre-distribution ideas focused on intervening in markets to ensure that they are competitive and serve the public. A pre-distribution strategy would also include proposals such as a living wage, affordable childcare, and investment in training and skills, as well as the strengthening of democratic institutions (the social dimension of pre-distribution ideas will be analysed in the next chapter).

Another set of ideas that found support in different Labour circles concerned the German model of economic development which emphasised an active industrial policy, the role of apprenticeships and vocational training in developing a 'high skill, high pay economy', long-term investments, and a consensual style of economic management. Strangely enough, both Blue Labour and Keynesians were proponents of the German model, however they emphasised different aspects. Whilst Blue Labour thinkers like Maurice Glasman and Duncan Weldon praised the role of local institutions in enhancing private sector growth,[22] Keynesians emphasised the role of the State in spearheading investment in key sectors of the economy.

But perhaps the most knowledgeable and influential advocate of the German model was in Ed Miliband's team. Lord (Stewart) Wood, Miliband's chief policy adviser, had been an advocate of the German model for a long time. Wood had some reservations about Britain's ability to learn and transpose some of the practices that made the German model so effective and Germany's economy so strong. In particular, he claimed that governments are constrained by the different organisational capacities of employers in coordinated market economies and liberal market economies.[23] Nonetheless, he argued that Britain could learn a few lessons from Germany, namely its 'statecraft projects; its apprenticeship system; its consensual style of managing the economy and the labour market; its rules on corporate governance that incentivise companies to have a long-term approach to investment in research and development, and in the skills of their workers'.[24]

The German model fitted neatly with ideas about an active industrial policy advocated by the economists Mariana Mazzucato, Ha-Joon Chang, and Antonio Andreoni. These economists attacked austerity policies on the grounds that they did not work, and argued instead for a re-appraisal of the role of the State as a dynamic innovator.[25] In her book *The Entrepreneurial State*, Mazzucato argued for a different understanding of the role of the State in a market economy. The State, she argued, 'is neither a "meddler" nor a simple "facilitator" of economic growth', but 'is a key partner of the private sector – and often a more daring one, willing to take the risks that business won't'.[26] In this capacity, the role of the State goes beyond correcting market failures. Mazzucato also claimed that the State is in the business of shaping and creating markets[27] and investing in innovation, and argued that it should be rewarded for its risky investments.[28] In the same spirit, Ha-Joon Chang and Antonio Andreoni argued for a re-balancing of the British economy based on a new manufacturing renaissance. But for that to happen, a new Government would have to address the structural weaknesses of the British industrial sector and that would require, amongst other things, a substantial upgrading of Britain's 'physical infrastructure, technical infrastructure', and 'infrastructure-producing skills'.[29]

But if the ideas about the entrepreneurial State pleased the Keynesian-inclined Labour politicians, they did not find favour with those – like Blue Labour and New Labour – who saw the State as part of the problem. For these two tendencies mutualism seemed to offer the necessary solutions to the deficit crisis and to the structural weaknesses of the British economy. Blue Labour thinkers like Glasman and Weldon defended the role of civil society, in particular of employee-led companies (inspired by the guild socialism of G. D. H. Cole) such as those promoted by cooperative movement, in creating a different political economy.[30] From a New Labour perspective, Anthony Painter made a similar argument and presented mutualism as a 'beyond the state' alternative.[31]

Mutualism was thus seen as a tool to redistribute power and to create a new 'financial ecosystem'. In a chapter published in the Blairite *Purple Book*, Tristram Hunt claimed that mutualism could 'help to shake up the existing pre-distribution of power with the sector, and the economy more generally, but it could also help to create a more stable and secure financial sector'.[32] Likewise, Patrick Diamond argued that 'a financial sector that contains a variety of vibrant mutual entities such as building societies and community-based credit unions would be more balanced and resilient'.[33] It follows from here that a financial ecosystem that included mutual banks or building societies would be in a stronger position to reduce risk in the financial sector.

The thinkers associated with all these ideas were either actively courted by Labour or participated in debates taking place around Miliband's inner circle of advisers, think-tank experts, and academics. As we have seen, the expert on the German model, Lord Wood, was Miliband's chief policy adviser. Mariana Mazzucato addressed the Labour Party Policy Review in 2012 and was invited to contribute to the shadow business secretary Chuka Umunna's Policy Network's edited pamphlet on industrial policy. Jacob S. Hacker met Ed Miliband and several of his advisers, and was invited to give public lectures at think-tanks such as the IPPR and Policy Network, which had been heavily involved in developing policy ideas for the Labour Party. Finally, Thomas Piketty met Miliband, addressed the IPPR, and participated in a public discussion with Lord Wood, which was hosted by the think-tank Class.

Miliband's vision: reforming capitalism

Many of the ideas discussed above found their way into Miliband's narrative and economic agenda. But their endorsement and transformation had to accommodate the different political, economic, and institutional constraints he encountered whilst developing Labour's approach to the economy. In particular, Miliband was under pressure to develop 'credible' economic policies that would acknowledge the 'mistakes' made by New Labour whilst in government, but that would offer as well solutions to eliminate Britain's public deficit.

The difficulty in addressing these two requirements was that 'credibility' is a highly subjective notion that is entirely dependent on how the conventional wisdom of the time defines it. In other words, the notion of 'economic credibility' relies more on the public perception of what constitutes a credible approach to the economy than on policy proposals that might actually reduce the public deficit and generate economic growth. As Labour was unable to set the political debate on the deficit, this meant that it was under pressure to endorse austerity solutions to the deficit crisis that were perceived as examples of financial probity and fiscal responsibility. Whether these policies were effective in reducing the public deficit was an altogether different question.

To compound these difficulties, the new leader had difficulty in imposing his vision on the party. Several members of Labour's frontbench team had a different reading of the causes of the global financial crisis and consequently did not defend such a stark break with New Labour. Moreover, the Labour leader's desire to turn the page on New Labour was framed in media discourses as an undesirable 'lurch' to the left, and this worried several frontbenchers and many backbenchers.[34] In fact, many feared that some of Miliband's ideas and language could be interpreted as anti-business. As a result, it took time until the frontbench team supported Miliband's approach to the economy, and when they finally did it was never in a wholehearted manner.

Notwithstanding these difficulties, Miliband was clear about the direction in which he wanted to take the party. In several speeches made during the leadership campaign and in the early days of his leadership, he revealed his thinking. He was critical of New Labour's cosy accommodation of neoliberalism. He believed New Labour 'got stuck – defending flexible labour markets and not understanding the limits to markets at a time when the world had moved on',[35] and he rarely missed an opportunity to dismiss 'trickle-down economics'. He argued that 'globalisation is not an untameable force of nature to which we must adapt or die'.[36] But Miliband also indicated that he saw the global financial crisis as an opportunity to reform British capitalism with a view to making it more stable, productive, and fairer and insisted that 'old ideas won't work anymore'.[37]

In an article he co-signed with Douglas Alexander before the 2010 general election, he argued that the financial crisis was a demonstration of 'massive market failure' that showed the relevance of the State.[38] Echoing the arguments made by Hacker and Pierson, he linked the global financial crisis to the rise of inequality. As he put it in another article, where he explained in detail his approach to the economy, the global financial crisis and the crisis of living standards had 'their roots in the inability of our economy to generate stable prosperity for the many, at the same time as it created spectacular rewards for the few'.[39]

Miliband's analysis of the causes of the global financial crisis set the stage for his economic agenda. If the global financial crisis was a demonstration of 'massive market failure' the Labour Party under Ed Miliband would put in place measures that would prevent the emergence of a new crisis. That would involve the development of 'an economy that is more resilient, more genuinely competitive, more focused on the long term and that people feel is fairer'. In other words, he would create the foundations of 'an economy that works for working people'.[40]

One dominant theme of Miliband's agenda was the idea of 'reforming the market so that it works in the public interest'.[41] Echoing the thinking of Polanyi but also of Hacker, Pierson, and Mazzucato, he argued that governments play a crucial role in forming the rules of capitalism, and that therefore they should 'play a more active role in making markets work for working people'.[42] In this spirit, Miliband 'waged a war' on what he termed 'predator capitalism' or the 'zero-zero' economy, and sought to address what he defined as the 'cost-of-living crisis'. Proposals such as freezing energy prices, introducing a cap on train fares, intervening in the rentals market, imposing new rules on corporate takeover bids, regulating the banking sector, tackling tax evasion, or allowing the State to compete with the private sector in bids for contracts in the railway industry were presented as strategies to tackle predator capitalism and the cost-of-living crisis, and to promote pre-distribution.

Labour's alternative to 'predator capitalism' was 'responsible capitalism', which would rely on the 'producers' that 'train, invest, invent, sell',[43] and would place the creation of jobs and the tackling of inequality at the centre of its economic strategy.[44] In addition, this 'responsible capitalism could', according to Stewart Wood, become a 'platform for social democratic politics after the crisis' where responsibility is rewarded, ensuring that 'economic power and rewards are more evenly distributed'.[45]

Implicit in Miliband's concept of responsible capitalism was the desire to diversify the British economy, which thus far had been too dependent on the financial services industry, and which had produced very unequal outcomes. Thus, Labour's active industrial policy implied an active role for the State in championing and supporting strategic industrial sectors; in ensuring that those sectors received appropriate financing from the banks (through the creation of a British Investment Bank and a Green Investment Bank); and in developing a 'high-skilled and high-waged' workforce through a new emphasis on vocational training and apprenticeships, the promotion of the living wage, the rise of the minimum wage, and the enforcement of other social rights (this aspect of Labour's agenda will be analysed in the next chapter). Last but not least, Labour committed itself to an ambitious project of building 200,000 homes per year between 2015 and 2020 and to investing in the renewal of infrastructure.[46] Miliband also proposed the devolution of economic and financial powers to English cities and towns as a way of promoting regional growth and delivering Government savings.

This vision reflected many of the ideas discussed above. Indeed, Miliband argued for a British adaptation of the German model, but his proposals reflected as well the ideas of Mazzucato on the 'entrepreneurial State', Chang and Andreoni's proposals for investment in infrastructure, and Hacker's ideas on pre-distribution (in particular in the areas of competition policy in 'captured' markets), with a small nod to the mutualist and localist ideas defended by Blue Labour and New Labour advocates.

To fund this ambitious and long-term plan of economic renewal Labour committed itself to a temporary and vague rise in public borrowing to fund capital investment projects from 2020,[47] to a rise of income tax to top earners, to the creation of what is popularly known as the 'mansion tax', to a myriad of different taxes on bank profits and bank bonuses, and to tackling tax evasion by multinational companies. Some of these tax rises were ear-marked to fund specific projects. For example, the proposed mansion tax, the tax on the tobacco industry, and new (and unspecified) proposals to address tax evasion were designated to fund new investments in the National Health Service (NHS), whereas taxes on bankers' bonuses would fund free childcare. In other words, it was clear that Labour would 'tax and borrow' to fund its programme, however it was unclear whether the sums collected through the several tax rises would be sufficient to fund the ambitious programme of transforming British capitalism. There were also doubts about the calendar of implementation for this programme. At the 2014 Labour Party Annual Conference, both Miliband and Balls suggested that many of these big reforms would be implemented only in the post-2020 period – that is, only after Labour had demonstrated its fiscal responsibility by 'balancing the books'. But during the electoral campaign both Balls and Miliband announced that some of the proposed measures – namely those on housing and infrastructure-building – would be implemented from their first day in government.

Labour and the deficit

If transforming British capitalism was a long-term project, Miliband faced other more immediate challenges. The public deficit, which emerged during New Labour's last years in government, was a problem that Miliband could not evade. The Conservatives and the Liberal Democrats had successfully managed to convince the public that Labour's 'irresponsible' policies, in particular its alleged profligacy with public finances, were responsible for the country's public deficit and debt. Unable to convince the media and the public that the deficit was a result of the global financial crisis, the party's economic credibility depended on developing a programme of deficit reduction that was considered credible by the City and by the media. The problem for Labour was that credibility could only be acquired by accepting the Coalition's terms of the public debate on the public deficit. These terms dictated that the only viable deficit-reduction policies were drastic public spending cuts. As a result, instead of reducing the deficit through a pro-growth strategy based on an economic stimulus and tax rises – an approach favoured by many social democrats – the 'credible approach' dictated a deficit reduction programme based on such harsh public spending cuts.

Miliband's initial response was to follow his political instincts, and those were Keynesian. Though he admitted that some public spending cuts were necessary, he argued that 'economics teaches us that at times of recession governments run up deficits'.[48] He also said that Britain's 'problem of debt' could not be tackled 'without addressing our problems of growth'.[49] In other words, public spending cuts would increase the size of the public deficit. In similar Keynesian vein, Ed Balls argued that the best way to reduce and eliminate the deficit was by promoting economic growth and job creation. In 2011, both Balls and Miliband used a joint press conference to argue that 'the best way to get the deficit down' was to develop 'a plan that puts jobs and growth first'.[50] Thus, for a while, both resisted austerian arguments and policies.[51] Balls even tried to run against the austerian current that was so prevalent in political debates. For example, in his Bloomberg speech of 2010, he explained the logic behind his thinking but admitted as well to feeling frustrated with the reactions it provoked. In that speech he said:

> Interviewers look aghast when I tell them that cutting public spending this financial year and pre-announcing a rise in VAT is economically foolish, when growth and consumer confidence is so fragile. 'But what would you cut instead?' they demand.
>
> So strong and broad is this consensus that a special name has been given to those who take a different view – 'deficit deniers' – and some in the Labour Party believe our very credibility as a party depends on hitching ourselves to the consensus view.[52]

But the Keynesian approach to deficit reduction had few supporters in the Labour Party. The Blairite wing of the party was pressuring Miliband to develop a 'credible' approach to deficit reduction centred on public spending cuts, and also to concede to the prevailing narrative on the deficit and admit that Labour had overspent whilst in government. A group of authors claiming to represent 'Black Labour' argued that Labour's credibility on economic policy was conditional on Miliband's accepting the Coalition's terms on the economic debate. They also contended that 'Labour must put fiscal sustainability at the absolute core of its policy agenda'.[53] Implicit in this proposal was the idea that in order to be credible Labour had to accept austerity, rule out tax rises to higher-income earners, and articulate a pro-business agenda that would also rule out minimum-wage rises or extra costs to employers. This argument received further support from the heavy-weights of New Labour. For example, former Labour leader and prime minister Tony Blair attacked Labour for being the party that was against spending cuts.[54]

As a result of these pressures, neither Miliband nor Balls held his nerve for very long. Depending on the party's lead in the opinion polls, Labour's response to the public deficit zigzagged between Keynesianism and 'lite-austerianism'. After zigzagging for some time, Labour finally succumbed to austerity in the summer of 2013, albeit with little conviction. There had been inklings of this inclination before, in particular in early 2012 (when Miliband's leadership went through one of its many crises), but by the mid-2013 the party's endorsement of austerity was unequivocal.

Over the spring of 2013, when Labour's poll lead dropped (again), and the first signs of an economic recovery were starting to be visible, the leadership of the party was under pressure to deliver a 'tough' and 'credible' message on the economy. Labour was also under pressure to present 'pro-business' policies. Miliband's attack on predator capitalism and his promise to tax bankers' bonuses was seen as overly hostile to the business community. Indeed, many Labour frontbenchers worried about Miliband's apparent inability to attract the support of high-profile business people.

In addition, several Labour MPs and some frontbenchers were furious with Ed Balls's failure to capitalise on the Coalition's 'omnishambles' budget of 2012. Finally, the first signs of economic recovery – magnified by a sympathetic coverage in the conservative press – seemed to vindicate the Coalition's austerity approach, though the deficit and the levels of public borrowing were far from being under control. In fact, the chancellor of the exchequer, George Osborne, had changed its approach to deficit reduction by slowing down the pace of public spending cuts and by putting in place a mini-stimulus programme.

It was in these circumstances that Labour capitulated to the prevailing conventional wisdom about austerity. In a widely leaked speech in June 2013, Balls announced that Labour would follow a 'tough deficit reduction plan' and warned his 'Labour colleagues' about his 'tough message'. His choice of words – particularly the use of words such as 'tough' – was revealing of the party's mindset. Balls's argument was that once in government Labour would have to demonstrate an 'iron discipline' and to follow 'tough fiscal rules', because there would be 'less money around' as a result of the Coalition's deficit legacy.[55]

This 'iron discipline' was translated into a commitment to respecting the Coalition's public spending targets for 2015/16, and a commitment to stopping the payment of the winter fuel allowance to those Balls defined as 'rich' pensioners. Similarly, Balls announced that a Labour Government would 'cap structural social security spending', in particular child benefit, and would increase the age of retirement. Indeed, the cap on child benefit was presented as an example of Labour's commitment to fiscal probity. Balls's 'tough' approach to deficit reduction was confirmed and refined by Ed Miliband in two speeches delivered a few days later. In one speech, Miliband made the case for 'a cap on overall benefits',[56] whilst in the second he argued that in order to be credible the party had to accept fiscal discipline.[57]

These speeches were widely discussed in the media, and Labour's 'spin' presented them as the definite signs that Labour was a 'responsible' party ready to adopt a 'tough' approach to public spending. However, a close reading of those speeches tells a different story. Whilst accepting the need to impose public spending cuts, Labour also made the case for an expansionary policy. Indeed, Balls and Miliband defended tax rises, arguing for the boosting of capital spending to invest in housing and infrastructure projects. Moreover, Labour's commitment to reducing the public deficit contrasted with the Conservatives in terms of timeframe – Labour's programme was predicated on a longer timeframe to reduce the deficit – and also in terms of policy instruments. Labour's plans to reduce the deficit relied on ensuring that 'those with the broadest shoulders' would pay more taxes.

Labour's conversion to a lighter shade of austerity did not go down well with the trade unions, the left, and the soft centre of the party. From the Keynesian side, Peter Hain reluctantly accepted that Labour had to 'operate within a neoliberal consensus' that promoted austerity, but insisted that the way to deal with the deficit was 'through growth'.[58] From the soft centre, Patrick Diamond argued that such an approach would not be 'sustainable in the long-term', because it 'was inconsistent with voters' preferences for the continued universal provision of public services'.[59]

The trade unions, on the other hand, were more severe in their reactions. Mark Serwotka argued that 'austerity in a red rosette is no less brutal and damaging than in a blue one'.[60] In similar vein, Neal Lawson from Compass regretted Labour's acceptance of austerity: 'Labour has in effect capitulated to austerity. Yes, in the detail there will be nuance about some investment in housing, but the only message that matters is clear – economic credibility is now defined by austerity'.[61]

Indeed, parts of the media also interpreted Balls and Miliband's announcements as a capitulation to austerity. John Rentoul from the *Independent* wrote that Labour was abandoning its earlier Keynesianism: 'Thus protected by the amulet of the Sainted Clem [Clement Attlee], Miliband could go on to bury John Maynard Keynes'.[62] By contrast, the right represented by Black Labour greeted Miliband and Balls's conversion to austerity. Adam Lent, Hopi Sen, and Anthony Painter argued that their speeches had 'demonstrated that Labour understands a real need for fiscal responsibility in the coming decade'.[63] In true New Labour fashion, the authors argued for 'the pursuit of social justice, greater employment, [and] pay and growth at the heart of a fiscally responsible Labour agenda', though they failed to explain how all these goals could be achieved in the context of public spending cuts and anaemic slow growth.[64]

Labour's embrace of austerity was confirmed in 2014 when Balls committed a future Labour Government not only to 'balanc[ing] the books' – as he put it – but also to delivering a budgetary surplus during the next Parliament.[65] At the last Labour Party Annual Conference before the 2015 general election, Ed Balls defended Labour's approach on the grounds of 'economic credibility' and 'fiscal responsibility in the national interest'. In this speech, the shadow chancellor showed that Labour was above all concerned with its reputation:

> People know we are the party of jobs, living standards and fairness for working people.
>   But they also need to know that we will balance the books and make the sums add up and that we won't duck the difficult decisions we will face if they return us to government.

Working people have had to balance their own books.

And they are clear that the government needs to balance its books too. So Labour will balance the books in the next parliament.[66]

There was an important addition to this announcement that had the effect of reducing the number of Labour's policy options. Under Balls's plans public borrowing for day-to-day expenditure was again ruled out, though he promised that Labour's public spending cuts would be fairer because they would not affect the most vulnerable. That is, Labour's deficit reduction plans would rely more on tax rises than on cuts to key public services.

Similarly, Ed Miliband used a speech that dealt exclusively with the deficit to promise that Labour's 'tough and balanced approach will balance the books through an economy based on high wages and high skills, common sense spending reductions and fair choices on tax'.[67] He also said Labour would put in place a 'mansion tax', would abolish the status of 'non-doms', and would target tax avoidance by multinational companies. To sweeten the pill for disappointed party supporters, Balls promised to protect and invest in the NHS by taxing tobacco companies, and to raise the minimum wage.

But this was a confused message, as Miliband's famous deficit omission during his address to the 2014 Labour Party Annual Conference suggested. The right was still unconvinced by the party's commitment to fiscal probity, whereas the left was discouraged by the absence of progressive policies. To complicate Labour's message further, Miliband and Balls insisted that the Coalition's austerity programme had failed to reduce the public deficit, and that in addition, the Conservatives were committed to an agenda of reducing the size of the State to a 1930s level. However, they failed to explain why their kinder and fairer austerity plan would have a different effect.

Three weeks before the general election, Labour made a last-minute attempt to gain economic credibility by sealing the party's embrace of austerity. Its manifesto stated that Labour's first electoral pledge was to reduce the deficit every year. The language used by Miliband was also telling of the party's concerns. To emphasise Labour's commitment to deficit reduction, the leader announced a 'triple lock of responsibility', which committed the party to not making promises that would require additional borrowing, cutting the deficit every year, and finally delivering a budgetary surplus and falling debt levels by 2020.[68] In short, Labour's triple lock was mostly about trying to fight the party's reputation for economic profligacy and economic incompetence.

However, the triple lock allowed room for manoeuvre in terms of borrowing for capital investment. Indeed, during the electoral campaign, the party's campaign chief, Lucy Powell, admitted that Labour could 'borrow to invest'. Moreover, there were still substantial differences between Labour and Conservative deficit reduction plans. Analysis by the respected Institute for Fiscal Studies showed that Labour's plans implied 'only relatively small cuts to departments other than aid, NHS and education spending – on top of the cuts already in place for 2015–16'.[69]

But these differences were barely noticed by voters, which was problematic for Labour, in particular in Scotland. The SNP's anti-austerity approach was a major threat for Labour in Scotland as it could deprive the party of a majority in the Commons. To a lesser extent, the Green Party's anti-austerity message was also problematic, as the rise of the Greens threatened to dent Labour's majority in more than twenty seats in England. On the other hand, voters in England were unpersuaded by Labour's commitment to fiscal probity.

The plan for growth

Accepting that the deficit and public debt were the most important challenges facing Britain's finances implied that Labour's reformist agenda was watered down. Indeed, the 2015 electoral manifesto made brief references to the party's plans to re-balance the economy and to increase productivity. In other words, the embrace of austerity had the effect of rendering Labour's departure from New Labour and neoliberalism less clear-cut. It also left Labour with a defensive economic programme with few positive messages. To use Peter Hall's terminology, Labour's economic programme was not comprehensible. In promising to 'balance the books' and produce a budgetary surplus (of the current budget) within the 2015 Parliament, Labour was unable to explain how it would fund its ambitious plans to transform capitalism and deliver a 'high wage, high skill' economy. Labour's nebulous public spending and public borrowing commitments were noted by the Institute for Fiscal Studies.[70] If in the long term the high-wage economy could result in higher revenue collected from taxation, the process of creating it would initially cost millions in public investment. Moreover, the different tax rises that were announced were not sufficient to fund such an ambitious programme of economic reform. Indeed, most had been ear-marked to invest in the NHS, or to fund childcare and some modest active labour market policies targeting the young unemployed.

There were also doubts about the ability of Labour's public service reforms to deliver 'big reforms without big spending'. By the same token, it was not enough to state that Labour's reform plans would only come to fruition after 2020, when the current deficit would be under control. Most voters make their electoral decisions based on what political parties promise to do within the short timeframe of a Parliament. To ask voters to make such a long-term investment in the Labour Party was a sign of either great confidence or utter despair.

But austerity was not the only limitation to Miliband's plans. The shadow chancellor Ed Balls was slow to convert to the idea of regional development underpinned by a devolution of economic and fiscal power from the Treasury to English cities and towns. Indeed, these ideas had been briefly spelled out by Miliband in the early days of his leadership, but it was only in the spring of 2014 that he finally persuaded

Ed Balls to endorse them. Only then did the shadow chancellor start to make the case for the devolution of fiscal and economic powers to English cities[71] as had been proposed by Lord Adonis's Growth Review.[72]

Lord Adonis's proposals for regional growth (which adapted the Coalition's plans to devolve powers to 'combined' authorities) enabled the party to present itself as fiscally prudent and pro-business, and to set out a transformative economic agenda. These proposals to devolve fiscal and financial powers to English cities and towns were also presented as a cost-effective way to deliver economic growth to the different regions of England. According to Lord Adonis, savings would be achieved through the pooling of resources across different towns and through the elimination of duplicate services and 'waste' (that old favourite bogeyman). Similarly, Labour's proposals to develop a long-term corporate culture, to give the Government a role in setting industrial priorities and in supporting companies in key economic sectors, were also presented as a new approach to economic management that would not involve new public spending commitments.

However, not all of Labour's new industrial policies were cost-free. The party admitted as much whenever they signposted future commitments to investments in public infrastructure, or to the development of the 'green economy', or in the new home-building programme, or apprenticeships. But given the party's ambiguous stances on public borrowing at the time of the general election there were still unanswered questions about how Labour's plans would be funded.

These were questions that were being asked by many inside the party, but also outside. For example, Patrick Diamond from the Policy Network said that there was a compelling case for an 'active, social investment state' but that Labour did not have a 'concerted strategy for how to create one'.[73] In particular, Labour had not explained how it would pay for those policies. The tax increases that Labour had announced, such as the return of the 50p tax rate and closing loopholes on tax avoidance, 'were not sufficient to boost long-term tax revenues'.[74]

The right of the party was also unhappy with Miliband's agenda of economic reform but for different reasons. The New Labour wing claimed that Miliband's economic agenda, and in particular his 'predator versus responsible capitalism' and 'cost-of-living crisis' narratives, were perceived to be too anti-business and not sufficiently 'aspirational'. In one of his typical outbursts, Lord Mandelson told an interviewer that Miliband had 'confused the party's message on business' and had failed to explain how Labour would 'bring about economic growth'.[75]

The Labour leader proved to be immune to these criticisms. For him, the concessions on the deficit, the commitment to Britain's EU membership (demonstrated by the party's refusal to hold a referendum on EU membership in the foreseeable future), his commitment to an active industrial policy, and the promise to maintain 'the most competitive tax regime in the G-7' were sufficient demonstrations of Labour's pro-business credentials. That much was clear in the speech he delivered in the autumn of 2014 to the Confederation of British Industry, where he was supposed to reassure the business community,[76] but where instead he emphasised his commitment to tackle the 'zero-zero' economy – that is, the economy that relied on low pay and facilitated corporate tax avoidance.

But there were other holes in Labour's active industrial policy. The German model of economic development was often invoked by Miliband and by Chuka Umunna as one of their inspirations for Labour's proposals to develop an extensive programme of apprenticeships and active industrial policy. However, one of its key components was missing from the party's plans. The success of the German model is predicated on the role played by the trade unions in defining industrial policy together with business and the national Government. In this corporatist model of economic management, there is constant consultation among employers, trade unions, and the State, and often the result is an agreement on wage moderation or a commitment to a long-term economic target.

But in this area Labour was ambivalent. If the party proposed to have workers' representatives on the boards of companies, in particular on remuneration committees, it shied away from making trade unions a key actor in economic policy. This omission is noticeable given the role of trade unions in the success of the German model. In addition, the defenders of pre-distribution were quite explicit about the part played by trade unions in preventing a winner-take-all economy. Indeed, both Hacker and Pierson linked the decline of trade unions to the rise of inequality.

The reasons that can explain Labour's stance on the role of trade unions are political. The first is related to the party's public perception. Labour did not want to promote the idea that Ed Miliband would rehabilitate the days of 'beer and sandwiches' at Number 10. Moreover, the fact that the Miliband owed his leadership to the trade unions affected his reputation and informed his terse relationship with leading trade unionists. The last thing Labour desired was to be seen as the party that strengthened the position of trade unions (especially following the Falkirk scandal).

Second, the party's leadership thought that British trade unions were different from Germany's. Whilst in Germany trade unions were highly representative of the workforce, in Britain trade union membership had been in decline for decades. Moreover, and according to Peter Hain, British trade unions 'had not shown much enthusiasm' for the German model.[77] Finally, British trade unions were not considered as responsible as their German counterparts to deserve that role.[78] For that reason, Miliband's senior policy adviser Lord Wood contended that Labour did not plan to change trade unions' legislation in order to give them new rights.

Wood's perception seemed to be quite widespread in the party. The MP John Denham, who advised Miliband in the early stages of his leadership, spoke with fatalism about declining trade union membership. Indeed, the idea that the Labour Party, originally a party of workers, could promote greater trade union membership seemed anathema to many leading Labour figures. In Denham's view the problem lay with the trade unions themselves: 'we would like to see more people from the private sector in trade unions, but we have a trade union leadership that appears to be institutionally incapable of understanding what needs to be done to organise [workers]', he argued.[79] When asked if Labour could do anything to give the trade unions a bigger role in economic policy, Denham said: 'no, there is actually no problem with trade union legislation'.[80] Even Peter Hain, a former trade unionist who believed that trade unions should have a greater role in economic life, admitted that trade unions had problems in recruiting new members.[81] With such a strong resistance to the idea of empowering trade unions it is unclear how workers' representation on remuneration committees, as the party proposed, would result in a British version of the German model of economic development, or would promote the pre-distribution ideas on market reforms or the high-wage economy the Labour leader seemed so committed to developing.

Tackling banks and their excesses

Labour's plans to re-balance the economy included as well ideas to tackle the financial services industry, which was seen by Miliband as 'a poor servant of the economy'.[82] The party admitted that whilst in government New Labour had not done enough to regulate the banks. Thus, Labour's proposals to re-balance the British economy were designed to offer, as Miliband put it in a speech delivered in Birmingham in January 2014, a new reckoning with the financial services industry.[83] But as in other areas, the rhetoric of the party was far grander than the policy proposals. Indeed, Labour's incremental and timid banking reforms were not proportional to the party's angry anti-bankers rhetoric.

Labour signalled a desire to introduce tighter regulation to the banking industry with the purpose of reducing risk and increasing competition. In that spirit, Miliband endorsed the Vickers report on banking regulation, proposed the creation of new banks to increase competition, and supported new legislation to prevent banks from becoming too big. He also promised to reform the bonus system prevalent in the financial services industry,[84] to separate retail and investment banking activities, and committed the party to introducing new taxes on bankers' bonuses. Finally he argued that the banking industry would benefit from a more diverse financial ecosystem that would see the re-emergence of mutualist banks. Indeed, the party went as far as defending the mutualisation of recently bailed-out and partly nationalised banks.

But there was a gap between Miliband's rhetoric and the policy proposals that accompanied it. The reforms to the banking industry that Labour endorsed were modest in scope. Subsequent banking scandals showed that the Vickers proposals could only be seen as a starting point to the regulation of the financial services industry. Moreover, the gap between rhetoric and policies was particularly visible in Labour's approach to the EU's proposal to introduce a financial transactions tax. In the early days of his leadership, Miliband supported the proposal without conditions. At the 2011 Labour Party Annual Conference, Miliband said he would back the tax, even if it only went ahead in Europe. 'We are in favour of this. It is a hard thing to do but I think it is necessary, important and the right thing to do. You have got to do it globally for it to work, or at the very least in Europe', he said.[85] In other words, Miliband expressed a preference for a global financial transactions tax but accepted and supported its implementation in Europe as a starting point.

However, in less than a year Labour's position has changed. Labour was in principle supportive of the tax, but in practice only when it was adopted universally. This change of tact suggested that protecting the City of London was still paramount for Labour, as opposing this tax enabled the party to present a pro-business stance. In an article published in the *Evening Standard*, Ed Balls claimed that adopting the tax on financial transactions only in Europe risked damaging the City, which he claimed to be committed to supporting as 'one of the world's most successful financial centres'.[86] Stewart Wood made a similar argument. 'For us it's very important that a financial transactions tax does not lead to perverse incentives.'[87] In concrete terms, Labour feared that the introduction of the financial transactions tax could weaken Britain's tax base.[88]

Its stance regarding the tax on financial transactions (or Tobin tax) suggests that Labour was still ambivalent about the banking industry. If, on the one hand, the party promised a big reckoning with the financial services industry, on the other, Labour was not interested in dramatically changing its role in the British economy. In a telling statement, the shadow business and skills secretary Chuka Umunna said that 'when we talk about diversifying our economy, we are not talking about reducing the size of our financial services sector but growing the size of other sectors of the economy.'[89]

The gap between rhetoric and policy reflected a number of things. First, it showed that the party, and in particular the frontbench team, did not share the same analysis about what caused the global financial crisis. According to an insider, Ed Balls saw the crisis as an aberration, and not, like Miliband, as a crisis created by structural flaws in the make-up of global capitalism. Second, Labour's proposals were not consistent with the party's desire to bring a 'big reckoning' with the banking industry, which was promised by Miliband when he became leader of the Labour Party. At best, they represented a timid approach to banking regulation that suited the interests of the banking industry itself.

Concluding remarks

This chapter has showed that the Labour Party under Ed Miliband sought to develop a programme that addressed the structural economic problems laid bare by the global financial crisis and that offered an alternative to the austerity policies pursued by the Coalition Government. Put simply, Miliband's goal was to use the powers of the State to reform capitalism. To that effect, the party searched and debated new and old ideas that would deliver sustainable and balanced economic growth, create high-skill and well-paid jobs, and, of course, reduce the public deficit.

Some of these ideas reflected the intellectual 'zeitgeist' of the period, others were rehabilitated from the party's ideological keepsake box. New ideas such as pre-distribution, the 'entrepreneurial State', and the German economic model were discussed alongside mutualism, guild socialism, and Polanyian insights about the role of small communities in creating and reforming markets. Both new and old ideas were consistent with the Labour leader's stated goals, but also with the party's core values and traditions. Indeed, Miliband brought back to the Labour Party a social democratic critique of capitalism that had been absent from the party's rhetoric and policies during the New Labour era.

Some of the ideas discussed in this chapter were visible in his narrative but were never transformed into substantial policy proposals. It was the case with ideas on mutualism. The leadership of the party was rhetorically committed to them, but its approach to bank regulation and to the financial services industry meant that mutualism had a modest role in Labour's economic blueprint. It is true that Labour proposed the mutualisation of Northern Rock, under public control since 2007, and to create regional banks, however these ideas were not developed further.

In other instances, only parts of those ideas were adopted and adapted by the party. For example, Labour was ambivalent about the adoption/adaptation of the German model of economic development because of its problematic relation with the trade unions. Similarly, the pick-and-mix approach to the ideas around 'pre-distribution' and the entrepreneurial State reduced their potential to reform and transform capitalism.

In some instances, Miliband was unable to convince relevant actors to support his policies. Members of the shadow cabinet and several backbenchers were sceptical of his approach. Many wanted Labour to develop a more pro-business agenda whilst others resisted the proposals to reform the State. As a result of these disagreements and of his weak grip over the party, he compromised. But that compromise was achieved at the expense of clarity and radicalism.

In other instances, Miliband's ideas were diluted or neglected simply because they were neither persuasive nor comprehensible. Ideas such as pre-distribution or the entrepreneurial State generated hundreds of column inches in media commentary, but they were not easily translated into attractive and easily understood policy proposals. To use Peter A. Hall's criteria, they did not resonate with voters' experiences. Because they were difficult to comprehend they also failed to persuade.

But crucially these ideas failed to get a hearing because Labour had lost its economic credibility. The fact that the global financial crisis happened under a Labour Government was a severe constraint to the development of a transformative economic programme. The Coalition parties, with the support of the media, were successful in blaming Labour's alleged profligacy for the rise of the public deficit and public debt. It did not help that Labour's last chief secretary to the Treasury, Liam Byrne, left an allegedly ironic note to his successor where he admitted that 'there [was] no money'. This letter was constantly invoked and shown by the Conservatives, and had a role (especially during the electoral campaign) in persuading voters that Labour was careless with the public finances.

Labour did very little to dispel this perception. This proved to be fatal, because Labour had no credibility to promote an alternative to the public spending cuts of the Coalition Government. For a while Labour tried to challenge the prevailing public narrative about the deficit. Miliband and Balls even tried to articulate a Keynesian alternative to austerity, but those attempts were neither very persistent nor convincing. Indeed, Keynesian approaches to deficit reduction challenged voters' understanding of economics. By contrast, austerity ideas were attractively simple to understand as they resonated with voters' experiences of managing their own domestic economies.

But Miliband's alternative to austerity also failed to attract the support of relevant actors. The Labour leader was under pressure to develop a credible approach to the economy that implied the acceptance of austerity. The media too played an important role in pressuring Labour to endorse public spending cuts as the only credible recipe to reduce the public deficit. From the *Daily Mail* to the BBC, and including the *Guardian*, Labour was cornered into accepting a definition of economic credibility that implied the acceptance of some form of austerity measures.

But the endorsement of austerity – albeit a lighter version – did not end Miliband's woes. Labour's reluctant embrace of austerity was neither entirely comprehensible nor persuasive. The party's message on the deficit lacked intellectual coherence. It continued to attack the Coalition's public spending cuts and deficit reduction targets, though Labour had just adopted a similar approach. It was equally difficult to understand how public spending cuts would match Labour's ambitious plans to reform capitalism and launch the foundations of a more productive economy, which required a hefty investment by the State. Though Labour planned to borrow to invest, the endorsement of austerity led to the dilution of its transformative economic agenda.

Voters reacted in predictable fashion. Disillusioned progressive voters felt Labour did not offer a distinctive programme. In Scotland they abandoned Labour and voted overwhelmingly for the SNP. In England, they turned to the Green Party or simply stayed at home on polling day. By contrast, floating centrist voters were unconvinced by Labour's endorsement of austerity and by its ability to manage the economy. This being said, some of Miliband's ideas – such as the proposal to freeze energy prices, to tackle pay-day lenders and zero-hours contracts, to promote the living wage, to regulate the banking industry through new taxes on bonuses – were popular with the public. But it was precisely these ideas that some party insiders, media commentators, and business people attacked on the grounds that they lacked economic credibility.

In sum, the Labour Party under Ed Miliband was unable to develop an alternative to austerity policies that would effectively reform British capitalism. Labour's lack of economic credibility and the prevalent public discourse and obsession with the public deficit constituted considerable constraints to the development of a distinctive, coherent, transformative, and credible economic agenda.

Notes

1   Ed Miliband, 'The New Generation: Speech to the 2010 Labour Party Annual Conference', 28 September 2010, www.labour.org.uk/ed-miliband–a-new-generation,2010-09-28 (accessed 10 January 2012).

2   Colin Crouch, *The Strange Non-Death of Neoliberalism* (Cambridge: Polity Press, 2011), p. 179.

3   Crouch, *The Strange Non-Death of Neoliberalism*; Andrew Gamble, *The Spectre at the Feast: Capitalist Crisis and the Politics of Recession* (Houndmills: Palgrave Macmillan, 2009); Andrew Gamble, *Crisis without End? The Unravelling of Western Prosperity* (Houndmills: Palgrave Macmillan, 2014); Mark Blyth, *Austerity: The History of a Dangerous Idea* (Oxford: Oxford University Press, 2013).

4   Chris Rogers, '"Hang on a Minute, I've Got a Great Idea": From the Third Way to Mutual Advantage in the Political Economy of the British Labour Party', *British Journal of Politics and International Relations* 15 (2013): 53–69 (p. 59).

5   Gordon Brown, 'The Mansion House Speech', 20 June 2007, http://ukingermany.fco.gov.uk/en/news/?view=Speech$id=4616377 (accessed 10 October 2012).

6   Roger Liddle and Patrick Diamond, 'Towards a Progressive Capitalism', *Policy Network*, 2 July 2014, http://www.policy-network.net/pno_detail.aspx?ID=4696&title=Towards-a-progressive-capitalism (accessed 5 September 2014).

7   Polanyi is quite explicit on this point: 'While laissez-faire economy was the product of deliberate state action, subsequent restrictions on laissez-faire started in a spontaneous way. Laissez-faire was planned; planning was not.' Karl Polanyi, *The Great Transformation: The Political and Economic Origins of Our Time* (Boston, MA: Beacon Press, 2001), p. 147.

8   Maurice Glasman, 'My Blue Labour Vision Can Defeat the Coalition', *Observer*, 24 April 2011.

9   Glasman, 'My Blue Labour Vision'.

10 Alan Finlayson, 'Should the Left Go Blue? Making Sense of Maurice Glasman', 27 May 2011, http://www.opendemocracy.net/ourkingdom/alan-finlayson/should-left-go-blue-making-sense-of-maurice-glasman (accessed 3 August 2015).

11 Maurice Glasman, 'Labour as a Radical Tradition', in Maurice Glasman, Jonathan Rutherford, Marc Stears, and Stuart White (eds), *The Labour Tradition and the Politics of Paradox: The Oxford London Seminars 2010–11* (n.p.: Oxford London Seminars, 2011), pp. 14–34 (pp. 32–33).

12 Jon Cruddas and Jonathan Rutherford, *One Nation: Labour's Political Renewal* (London: One Nation Register, 2014), http://www.joncruddas.org.uk/sites/joncruddas.org.uk/files/OneNation%20by%20Jon.pdf, p. 12.

13 Neal Lawson, private Interview, 10 May 2013.

14 Peter Hain, *Back to the Future of Socialism* (Bristol: Policy Press, 2015), pp. 81–88.

15 Roger Liddle, 'Is Social Democracy in Need of a New Economic Model?', http://www.social-europe.eu/2010/12/is-social-democracy-in-need-of-a-new-economic-model/ (accessed 16 June 2013).

16 Alan Johnson, 'The Unions' No-Cuts Agenda Is Delusional', *Guardian*, 17 January 2012.

17 Jacob S. Hacker and Paul Pierson, *Winner-Take-All Politics: How Washington Made the Rich Richer – and Turned Its Back on the Middle Class* (New York: Simon and Schuster, 2010), p. 15.

18 Hacker and Pierson, *Winner-Take-All Politics*, pp. 34–40. See also Jacob S. Hacker, 'The Institutional Foundations of Middle-Class Democracy', Policy Network, 6 May 2011, http://www.policy-network.net/pno_detail.aspx?ID=3998&title=The+institutional+foundations+of+middle-class+democracy (accessed 7 September 2012), p. 33.

19 Jacob Hacker, 'The Free Market Fantasy', Policy Network, 23 April 2014, http://www.policy-network.net/pno_detail.aspx?ID=4628&title=The-Free-Market-Fantasy (accessed 28 August 2014).

20 Thomas Piketty, *Capital in the Twentieth-First Century* (London: Belknap Press, 2014), pp. 20–22.

21 Hacker, 'The Institutional Foundations', p. 35.

22 Maurice Glasman and Duncan Weldon, 'German Lessons for Miliband's Growth Agenda', *Financial Times*, 3 August 2011.

23 Stewart Wood, 'Business, Government, and Patterns of Labour Market Policy in Britain and the Federal Republic of Germany', in Peter A. Hall and David Soskice (eds), *Varieties of Capitalism: The Institutional Foundations of Comparative Advantage* (Oxford: Oxford University Press, 2013), pp. 247–274 (p. 248).

24 Stewart Wood, private interview, 17 January 2013.

25 Chuka Umunna, 'Introduction: How Britain Can Harness the Winds of Change', in Chuka Umunna (ed.), *Owning the Future: How Britain Can Make It in a Fast-Changing World* (London: Policy Network, 2014), pp. 1–9 (p. 7).

26 Mariana Mazzucato, *The Entrepreneurial State: Debunking Public vs. Private Sector Myths* (London: Anthem Press, 2013), p. 5.

27 Mazzucato, *The Entrepreneurial State*, p. 5.

28 Mariana Mazzucato, 'Small and Inclusive Growth', in Umunna, *Owning the Future*, pp. 63–72 (p. 70).

29 Ha-Joon Chang and Antonio Andreoni, 'Rebuilding the UK Industrial Base', in Umunna, *Owning the Future*, pp. 103–112 (pp. 108–11).

30 Alan Finlayson, 'From Blue to Green and Everything in Between: Ideational Change and Left Political Economy after New Labour', *British Journal of Politics and International Relations* 15 (2013): 70–88 (p. 79–80).

31 Anthony Painter, 'Co-operatism as a Means to a Bigger Society', in *What Mutualism Means for Labour: Political Economy and Public Services* (London: Policy Network, 2011), pp. 27–35 (p. 27).

32 Tristram Hunt, 'Reviving Our Sense of Mission: Designing a New Political Economy', in Robert Philpot (ed.), *The Purple Book: A Progressive Future for Labour* (London: Biteback Publishing, 2011), pp. 61–79 (p. 75).

33 Patrick Diamond, 'Mutualism and Social Democracy', in *What Mutualism Means for Labour: Political Economy and Public Services* (London: Policy Network, 2011), pp. 7–13 (p. 11).

34 When Ed Miliband proposed freezing energy prices his ideas were compared to the Venezuela of Hugo Chávez.

35 Ed Miliband, 'Interview with Ed Miliband: "We Need to Tax the Better-Off" ', *Independent*, 30 August 2010.

36 Ed Miliband, 'Why I Want to Lead the Labour Party', *Guardian*, 15 May 2010.

37 Ed Miliband, 'Ed Miliband Speech at Senate House', 13 November 2014, http://press.labour.org. uk/post/102524244299/ed-miliband-speech-at-senate-house (accessed 14 November 2014).

38 Douglas Alexander and Ed Miliband, 'We Will Defend the State', *Guardian*, 5 February 2010, http://www.theguardian.com/commentisfree/2010/feb/05/defend-state-osborne-nu dge-equality (accessed 17 August 2015).

39 Ed Miliband, 'Building a Responsible Capitalism', *Public Policy Research* 19:1 (2012): 17–25 (p. 17).

40 Miliband, 'Building a Responsible Capitalism', p. 18.

41 Ed Miliband, 'Ed Miliband's Speech to the Policy Network Inclusive Prosperity Conference', 3 July 2014, http://press.labour.org.uk/post/90646112699/ed-miliband-speech-to-the-policy-network-inclusive-propserity-conference (accessed 4 July 2014).

42 Miliband, 'Building a Responsible Capitalism', p 19.

43 Ed Miliband, 'Ed Miliband's Speech to Labour Party Conference', 27 September 2011, http://archive.labour.org.uk/ed-milibands-speech-to-labour-party-conference (accessed 3 April 2012).

44 Stewart Wood, 'The God that Failed', *New Statesman*, 29 September 2011.

45 Stewart Wood, 'Responsible Capitalism Is Labour's Agenda', *Guardian*, 9 January 2012, http:// www.theguardian.com/commentisfree/2012/jan/09/responsible-capitalism-labour-david-cameron (accessed 17 August 2015).

46 In the speech 'The Fabric of Our Country', Miliband outlined his economic programme. Ed Miliband, 'The Fabric of Our Country – Speech by Ed Miliband', 8 April 2015, http:// press.labour.org.uk/post/115841294434/the-fabric-of-our-country-speech-by-ed-miliband (accessed 12 August 2015).

47 Ed Balls, 'Striking the Right Balance for the British Economy', 3 June 2013, http://www.labour. org.uk/striking-the-right-balance-for the-british-economy.html (accessed 5 June 2013).

48 Miliband, 'The New Generation'.

49 Miliband, 'Speech to Labour Party Conference', 2011.

50 Ed Balls and Ed Miliband, 'Ed Miliband and Ed Balls Press Conference', 14 March 2011, http://www.labour.org.uk/ed-miliband-and-ed-balls-press-conference,2011-03-14 (accessed 20 January 2012).

51 Eunice Goes, 'The Left and the Global Financial Crisis: The Labour Party in Search of a New Economic Narrative', in João Cardoso Rosas and Ana Rita Ferreira (eds), *Left and Right: The Great Dichotomy Revisited* (Cambridge: Cambridge Scholars, 2013), pp. 183–200 (pp. 190–191).

52 Ed Balls, 'There Is an Alternative – Speech to Bloomberg', 27 August 2010, http://www.edballs. co.uk/blog/?p=907 (accessed 10 January 2012). See also Ed Balls, 'Now Let's Offer a Real

Choice – and Nail the Tory Lie on Cuts', *Guardian*, 26 September 2010, www.guardian.co.uk/commentisfree/2010/sep/26/offer-choice-nail-tory-cuts-lie (accessed 10 January 2012).

53 Anthony Painter and Hopi Sen, 'Labour Must Make Fiscal Honesty the Key to Responsible Capitalism', *Guardian*, 1 December 2011. See also Graham Cook, Adam Lent, Anthony Painter, and Hopi Sen, *In the Black Labour* (London: Policy Network, 2011), http://www.policy-network.net/publications/4101/-in-the-black-labour (accessed 3 August 2015).

54 Tony Blair, 'Labour Must Search for Answers and Not Merely Aspire to Be a Repository for People's Anger', *New Statesman*, 11 April 2013.

55 Balls, 'Striking the Right Balance'.

56 Ed Miliband, 'One Nation Plan for Social Security Reform', 6 June 2013, http://www.labour.org.uk/one-nation-social-security-reform-miliband-speech (accessed 21 June 2013).

57 Ed Miliband, 'The Discipline to Make a Difference', 22 June 2013, http://www.labour.org.uk/the-discipline-to-make-a-difference–ed-miliband (accessed 24 June 2013).

58 Peter Hain, private interview, 25 March 2015.

59 Patrick Diamond, 'Wanted: A Tax-and-Spend Policy that Makes Sense', *Guardian*, 27 March 2014.

60 Mark Serwotka, 'Miliband's Offer of Austerity in a Red Rosette Is Failing Voters', *New Statesman*, 24 June 2013, http://www.newstatesman.com/print/politics/2013/06/milibands-offer-austerity-red-rosette-failing-voters (accessed 24 June 2013).

61 Neal Lawson, 'Labour and the Tories – Spot the Difference', *Guardian*, 24 June 2013, http://www.guardian.co.uk/commentisfree/2013/jun/24/labour-tories-austerity-investing-grow-economy (accessed 24 June 2013).

62 John Rentoul, 'Recovery Means … Dumping Labour Policies', *Independent*, 23 June 2013, http://www.independent.co.uk/voices/comment/recovery-means-dumping-labour-policies-8669703.html (accessed 24 June 2013).

63 Adam Lent, Hopi Sen, and Anthony Painter, 'Moving Labour "into the Black" ', Policy Network, 19 June 2013, http://www.policy-network.net/pno_detail.aspx?ID=4422&title=Moving-Labour-%E2%80%98into-the-black- (accessed 16 August 2015).

64 Lent, Sen, and Painter, 'Moving Labour "into the Black" '.

65 It is important to note that by promising to deliver a budget surplus Ed Balls was talking about the 'current' budget. Ed Balls, 'Beyond the Third Way: A New Inclusive Prosperity for the 21st Century', 30 June 2014, http://www.edballs.co.uk/blog/?p=5244 (accessed 28 August 2014).

66 Ed Balls, 'Speech to the Labour Party Conference', 22 September 2014, http://press.labour.org.uk/post/98137818419/speech-by-ed-balls-mp-to-labour-party-annual (accessed 23 September 2014).

67 Ed Miliband, 'Speech by Ed Miliband MP on the Deficit', 11 December 2014, http://www.labour.org.uk/pages/news (accessed 11 December 2014).

68 Ed Miliband, 'Britain Can Better: The Manifesto Launch Speech', 13 April 2015, http://labourlist.org/2015/04/britain-can-be-better-the-full-text-of-milibands-manifesto-launch-speech/ (accessed 14 April 2015).

69 Rowena Crawford, Carl Emmerson, Soumaya Keynes, and Gemma Tetlow, *Post-Election Austerity: Parties' Plans Compared* (London: Institute for Fiscal Studies, 2015), p. 4.

70 Crawford, Emmerson, Keynes, et al. *Post-Election Austerity*, p. 18.

71 Ed Balls, 'Conservative Complacency Won't Help Working People', *Guardian*, 24 July 2014. In this article, Balls argued that a stronger and more balanced economy required the devolution of power and funding to city and county regions.

72 Final report of the Adonis Review, *Mending the Fractured Economy: Smarter State, Better Jobs* (London: Policy Network, 2014). Ed Balls hosted the Policy Network conference on industrial policy.

73 Diamond, 'Wanted'.

74 Diamond, 'Wanted'.

75 Georgia Graham, 'Ed Miliband Is Confused and Unconvincing, Lord Mandelson Says', *Daily Telegraph*, 19 June 2014, http://www.telegraph.co.uk/news/politics/ed-miliband/10911015/Ed-Miliband-is-confused-and-unconvincing-Lord-Mandelson-says.html (accessed 3 September 2014).

76 Ed Miliband, 'Ed Miliband's Speech to the CBI', 10 November 2015, http://press.labour.org.uk/post/102276146664/ed-milibands-speech-to-the-cbi (accessed 14 November 2014).

77 Hain, private interview, 25 March 2015.

78 Wood, private interview, 17 January 2013.

79 John Denham, private interview, 16 July 2013.

80 Denham, private interview, 16 July 2013.

81 Hain, private interview, 25 March 2015.

82 Ed Miliband, 'Ed Miliband's Economy Speech in Full', 17 January 2014, http://www.politics.co.uk/comment-analysis/2014/01/17/ed-miliband-s-economy-speech-in-full (accessed 4 August 2015).

83 Ed Balls, 'Speech to the Labour Party Conference'.

84 Ed Miliband, 'Speech to the CBI', 25 October 2010, http://www.labour.org.uk/leader-of-the-labour-party-ed-milibands-speech-to-the-cbi,2010-10-25) (accessed 10 January 2012).

85 Ed Miliband, 'Speech to Labour Party Conference', 2011.

86 Ed Balls, 'Don't Cripple the City – London Can Lead the Recovery', *Evening Standard*, 31 October 2011, http://www.standard.co.uk/news/dont-cripple-the-city-london-can-lead-the-recovery-6363131.html (accessed 16 August 2015).

87 Wood, private interview, 17 January 2013.

88 Wood, private interview, 17 January 2013.

89 Chuka Umunna, 'Future of Financial Services', 15 April 2013, http://www.labour.org.uk/future-of-financial-services–chuka-umunna.html (accessed 30 April 2013).

4

Labour and equality I

Minding the gap

Tackling inequality is the new centre ground of politics.

Ed Miliband[1]

Equality – or the lack of it – occupied a central role in Ed Miliband's thinking and approach to politics. Indeed, it was the reason why he ran for the leadership of the Labour Party. At least that is what he said in a speech to the Resolution Foundation in 2011: 'I believe we should be willing to talk about the inequality in our society. It is why I am in politics',[2] he said. This was a particularly striking comment to make given the record of New Labour in this area. Despite the introduction of several redistributive policies, New Labour did not seem overly concerned with rising social inequalities, provided that there was a reduction in absolute poverty. This thinking was behind Blair's infamous justification for his unwillingness to raise taxation on the highest-income earners. As he told a BBC *Newsnight* presenter, it was not his 'burning ambition … to make sure David Beckham earns less money'.[3]

Miliband's egalitarian agenda, then, marked a departure from New Labour in terms of thinking but also in terms of policy approach. In many respects, which will be explained in this chapter, his approach offered a corrective to New Labour, and marked a return to social democratic ideas and values. Miliband's egalitarian agenda suggests an understanding of social democracy that places equality as a core value that is juxtaposed to the values of liberty and democracy.

Miliband's focus on equality was not merely the result of a personal commitment to social democracy, but also reflected zeitgeist ideas and the particular political and economic context in which his thinking and policies were developed and formulated. The aftermath of the global financial crisis and following debt crisis brought concerns about the rise of social inequalities to the centre stage of political debate. This being said, the very loud talk about inequality did not result in a concerted political approach to tackle it.

This chapter explores Ed Miliband's approach to equality with a view to establishing whether he steered the Labour Party away from New Labour and in a social democratic direction. For that purpose, it analyses the context, different ideas, and political traditions that shaped the Labour leader's approach to equality. But that analysis would not be complete without an understanding of the political, institutional, economic, and ideological factors that constrained his policy response to the problem. Thus, the chapter examines as well how the interplay among the ideas and political and institutional factors influenced, first, the party's narrative on equality, and second, its policy proposals. It argues that under Ed Miliband the Labour Party departed from New Labour, renewed the party's commitment to greater equality, and searched for older Labour traditions and new ideas to find fresh strategies to deliver that goal. However, there was a clear gap between the rhetoric and the policies proposed. The party's narrative suggested a transformative approach to equality, whereas the policies proposed were rather minimalist in scope.

Context and the legacy of New Labour

Miliband's approach to equality stemmed from his analysis of the causes of the global financial crisis, and in particular from his criticism of what he called the 'stale mindset' that no longer delivered prosperity for the majority.[4] But before he could address the inadequacies and failings of the Coalition Government, Miliband had to recognise the legacy of New Labour in this area. The task was difficult because New Labour's legacy was complex. New Labour had been committed to wealth redistribution – through investment in public services and through the creation of the minimum wage and a complex system of tax credits – but its commitment to greater equality was ambiguous.

New Labour's approach had been reliant on an economic model geared up to generate high rates of economic growth, whose proceeds would then be redistributed to the poorest sections of society through tax credits, benefits, job creation schemes, investments in public services, and Sure Start children's centres. However, New Labour's economic model relied as well on supporting a lopsided economy, based on high levels of consumption and consumer debt, and crucially on low wages. In other words, New Labour's approach to equality could be disentangled neither from its endorsement of the Thatcherite legacy, nor from an uncritical approach to globalisation.

In terms of policy, this approach was translated in New Labour's acceptance of a low-waged economy (the low-paid would receive a subsidised top-up to their salaries in the shape of tax credits) and the championing of flexible labour markets. Indeed, Blair took pride in the fact that Britain had the most restrictive trade union legislation in the Organisation for Economic Co-operation and Development (OECD). Another aspect of New Labour's attitude to equality was its approach to work. The promotion of work, and of the work ethic, became almost an end in itself.

Thus, New Labour's thinking on equality was closer to a Christian democrat concern with poverty levels than to a social democratic focus on reducing inequalities. Indeed, New Labour was not too concerned with income inequality. Peter Mandelson's legendary comment on how Labour was now a party 'intensely relaxed about people getting filthy rich provided they pay their taxes' is a clear reflection of this thinking. Even Gordon Brown, who implemented a complex system of tax credits to help the low-paid, went to extreme lengths to explain how his approach to equality was fairly minimalist. Whenever he addressed the subject he made the point of explaining the meaning of equality. Brown always distinguished 'equality of income' (which he deplored) from 'equality of opportunity' (which he supported). It is noteworthy that social democrats or socialists (with perhaps the exception of George Bernard Shaw) never make that distinction. They talk simply about equality or greater equality.

Gordon Brown was also the architect of one measure that had a negative impact on low-income earners. His 'clever' bribe to Middle England – the reduction of the basic rate of income tax from 22 per cent to 20 per cent – was funded by the elimination of the 10 per cent income tax rate. As a result of this measure, the tax bills of low-income earners doubled from 2008. Several Labour backbenchers rebelled against such a measure, but Gordon Brown insisted on its fairness. Interestingly, Ed Miliband announced that a future Labour Government would correct Gordon Brown's mistake by reintroducing this income tax band.[5] Furthermore, New Labour's policies in this area reflected too a Fabian approach to public-services delivery, as it relied on the powers of the central State to deliver progressive outcomes.

In short, New Labour's record on reducing inequalities reflects the ambiguous aims of its agenda. Instead of equality, New Labour preferred to talk about 'fairness' and to tackle 'social exclusion'. Thus, despite its efforts in reducing poverty and in promoting work, as well as in improving the earnings of the lowest-paid workers, inequality rose during the New Labour era.[6]

Ideas: old and new

Ed Miliband's approach to equality critically acknowledged the legacy of New Labour, and affirmed the desire to follow a different path. Miliband admitted that the 'new inequality' that worried him so much 'was there under Labour'.[7] He went as far as recognising the complacency of New Labour in this area when he said that inequality still grew despite the anti-poverty policies implemented by the party.[8] In a direct reference to Mandelson's infamous statement, Miliband said: 'We were intensely relaxed about what happened at the top of our society. I say – no more.'[9] Using a softer but nonetheless unequivocal tone, Liam Byrne also recognised the shortcomings of New Labour in this area when he wrote:

At times we looked too comfortable, too cosy you might say, with the newly power-ful that this new globalisation created. We did not do enough to stand alongside the newly powerless. We were basically too optimistic about the financial markets' ability or ambition to regulate themselves well, and too optimistic that the undoubted gains from global growth would distribute themselves fairly.[10]

In terms of thinking, Ed Miliband's approach to equality marked a clear departure from New Labour, and reflects the zeitgeist in which his ideas gestated. When he became leader of the Labour Party in September 2010, rising inequalities were the dominating theme in policy discussions not only in Britain but also across Europe and in all those countries that had been adversely affected by the global financial crisis.

Several factors contributed to this ideational zeitgeist. First, the global financial crisis exposed the widening gap between rich and poor. In the United States and across the world, several Occupy protests, involving thousands of people, denounced the unfair power of the 1 per cent. Second, some unorthodox analysis (which soon became mainstream) on the causes of the financial crisis linked its origins to rising social inequalities. It was the case of Richard Wilkinson and Kate Pickett's *The Spirit Level*, a work that was translated in many European countries and that had a great impact in public debates about inequality in Britain.[11] More importantly, the book argued that inequality affects everyone in society (and not only the poor) in a wide range of areas (from education to health and crime).

If Wilkinson and Pickett's conclusions and methodology were disputed by some, the link between rising inequalities and the global financial crisis was an axiom that was accepted by many policy-makers. Several IMF and OECD studies either established the same correlation, or simply pointed to the fact that social inequal-ities were on the rise and they affected economic performance. This evidence was widely discussed in the international media by popular economists such as Paul Krugman, or via documentaries on the causes of the 2008 financial crash such as Charles H. Ferguson's *Inside Job*, or in books such as Michael Sandel's *What Money Can't Buy*.[12] Even Conservative commentators echoed these concerns and ideas in books such as Ferdinand Mount's *The New Few*.[13]

But it was within Labour circles that the arguments of *The Spirit Level* had greater resonance. Just before the 2010 general election, Douglas Alexander and Ed Miliband published an article in the *Guardian* where they made a direct reference to the book. 'Richard Wilkinson and Kate Pickett's *The Spirit Level* demonstrates graphically how living in a society where some prosper and most flounder is self-defeating for all.'[14] In his first speech as Labour leader, Miliband reflected Wilkinson and Pickett's main argument when he said: 'the gap between the rich and poor does matter. It doesn't just harm the poor, it harms us all.'[15] Similarly, in 2014 Thomas Piketty's best-seller *Capital in the Twenty-First Century*, which was much read and quoted in Labour cir-cles, brought back to the political central stage the idea that the dramatic rise in social inequalities is incompatible with democracy, and has a detrimental impact on economic growth and social stability.[16] Finally, the work of the Resolution Foundation on low pay, inequality patterns, and declining living standards also offered Labour substantial statistical evidence to back its new egalitarian agenda.

This debate also questioned the morality of wealth pursuit. One important contribution to it was made by the American political philosopher Michael J. Sandel, who addressed the Labour Party Annual Conference in 2012. In his address, Sandel spelled out a vision of the common good that did not require strict equality but that imposed limits on markets. Underpinning Sandel's argument was a critique of a particular economic model that over-emphasised the values of economic growth and consumerism. Similarly, Robert and Edward Skidelky attacked wealth pursuit and made the case for a good life, based on ideas about economic sufficiency.[17]

Hence, the intellectual zeitgeist of the time contributed to the centrality of this theme, but there were other ideas and traditions that shaped Miliband's approach. The myriad of ideational traditions ranged from new ideas such as 'pre-distribution' and 'relational equality' to the egalitarian concerns of ethical and guild socialists such as R. H. Tawney and G. D. H. Cole (a tradition much celebrated by Blue Labour thinkers and by Marc Stears), the cooperative ideas of mutualism, and the democratic ideas of the New Left, as well as the civic republican concern with relations of domination and power distribution.

All of them were intensely scrutinised and debated, but pre-distribution gained the status of 'big idea' within the Labour Party and media circles. There were several reasons for this. First, 'pre-distribution' sounded like a 'wonky' idea that seemed to confirm Miliband's reputation as a 'Hampstead socialist'. Second, it was a new, freshly minted idea that seemed to be tailored to the challenges of Britain's economic recession and debt crisis (though it was conceived with the United States in mind). Third, it was an idea that dovetailed with older Labour intellectual traditions and values, in particular with those that sought to address inequalities of power through democratic empowerment.

As we saw in the previous chapter, the starting point of Jacob Hacker's concept of pre-distribution was 'the realisation of vast wealth differentials between the very rich and the rest of the population in the United States'.[18] According to Hacker, the widening of the wealth gap was the result of a deliberate winner-take-all politics. In other words, governments had played a role in allowing for wage stagnation amongst the middle classes, for the infiltration of corporate interests within the democratic process, for the erosion of labour and social rights, and for the undermining of trade unions as genuine vehicles for workers' interests. To address this problem, Hacker proposed 'pre-distribution' as a strategy 'to stop inequality before it starts'.[19]

From this starting point he went on to argue that pre-distribution implies a different, more critical approach to capitalism. The purpose of pre-distribution was quite ambitious: 'to focus on market reforms that encourage a more equal distribution of economic power and rewards even before government collects taxes or pays out benefits'.[20]

Pre-distribution had also political advantages. It enabled progressive politicians to bypass voters' resentment with redistributive policies and welfare spending.[21] However, Hacker did not explain how the vision of pre-distribution could be translated into concrete policies, leaving an almost empty canvas on which centre-left politicians could add the colours and shapes they wanted. This being said, he argued that a pre-distribution agenda would be composed of three main elements. The first one was spending in public services, in particular in those areas that are 'more oriented towards providing opportunity'.[22] Education, childcare provision, and housing were the type of services Hacker had in mind. The second component was a strategy aimed at improving standards in the labour market through either a minimum wage or a living wage, flexible working patterns, and greater protection for workers. The third component revolved around what he defined as 'regulation at the top', which could include policies that re-energised the organisational capacities of the middle classes, namely through trade unions and cross-class civic organisations. These were, however, long-term strategies that could result in significant structural changes to what he defined as a 'middle-class democracy'.

Hacker's work on pre-distribution had the virtue of being simultaneously aspirational and vague on prescriptions. Certainly he made recommendations, but he did not develop detailed policy proposals. This lack of detail allowed for some creativity in the way 'pre-distribution' was interpreted by several Labour figures. Offering his own interpretation, Miliband argued that pre-distribution was about fighting the assumption that Britain could only grow if it relied on a low-wage economy.[23] Thus, for Miliband pre-distribution was about giving people 'higher skills, higher wages and an economy that works for working people'. He also linked pre-distribution to redistribution when he said that 'redistribution will always remain necessary'.[24]

Likewise, Stewart Wood viewed pre-distribution as a complement to redistribution but also as a tool 'to intervene earlier – to reform markets so that economic power and rewards are more evenly distributed, even before taxes and transfers kick in'.[25] In other words, Wood focused on the idea that markets were flawed, and that as a result the role of the State was to intervene in order to correct them. In policy terms, he associated pre-distribution with measures to curb excessive pay, vocational education that would lead to well-paid jobs, and the living wage.

The shadow education secretary Tristram Hunt, on the other hand, offered a different reading of pre-distribution. He linked it to Labour's traditions of mutualism.[26] Interestingly, Hunt talked of pre-distribution instead of redistribution.[27] He viewed pre-distribution as an alternative to the traditional political methodology of social democracy. As he put it, 'out go flashy new ways of spending money and in come smart, inexpensive interventions that have the power to reshape the existing rules of the market'.[28]

Whilst pre-distribution was attracting most of the media's attention, in the discreet seminar rooms of influential think-tanks such as the IPPR other ideas were being discussed, and shaping Miliband's approach to equality and social justice. One of these ideas – relational equality – had a civic republican lineage that came directly from Anglo-American political theory debates. This idea was developed by the political philosopher Elizabeth S. Anderson, and it matched Miliband's interest in the traditions of guild socialism and ethical socialism, as well as in ideas about the relational State (which will be analysed in the next chapter).

Anderson's conception of democratic equality is one that looks at individuals as members of communities and views 'equality as a social relationship'.[29] As such, it offers a thicker conception of equality because it looks beyond socio-economic inequalities, and focuses on preventing relations of domination that restrict individuals' ability to live the life of their choice. In contrast with Rawlsian egalitarians who emphasised the distributional implications of egalitarian strategies, Anderson's relational equality stressed the value of reciprocity: mutual respect as well as the social embeddedness of individuals. Anderson argued that 'democratic equality regards two people as equal when each accepts the obligation to justify their actions by principles acceptable to the other, and in which they take mutual consultation, reciprocation, and recognition for granted'.[30] This approach implied that 'democratic equality is sensitive to the need to integrate the demands of equal recognition with those of equal distribution'.[31]

This conception of equality had interesting implications for distributive politics. Anderson argued that 'democratic equality conceives of equality as a relationship among people rather than merely as a pattern in the distribution of divisible goods ... It lets see how injustices may be better remedied by changing social norms and the structure of public goods than by redistributing resources'.[32] As a result, this was a concept that accepted income inequalities as long as 'all citizens enjoy a decent set of freedoms, sufficient for functioning as an equal in society'.[33] Nonetheless, Anderson argued that the 'relational egalitarian agenda is much wider than distributive concerns alone',[34] especially because it is concerned with the effects of inequality on power relations. This is so because 'people are vulnerable to having to enter into relationships of subordination just to get by'.[35]

It was precisely this broader and thicker conception of equality that informed the IPPR's report, *The Condition of Britain: Strategies for Social Renewal*. The authors of the report argued that the centre left should broaden its commitment to equality 'beyond merely distributional concerns', and should aim for a more equal distribution of power, to give greater recognition to individual agency, promote stronger social relationships, and place (like Anderson) liberty at the same level of priority as equality.[36]

The idea of relational equality was particularly admired by Miliband's speech-writer, adviser, and friend, Marc Stears. Indeed, he wrote that Labour was shifting its focus from 'material redistribution' to be 'more focused on questions of belonging and identity'.[37] Like Anderson, Stears did not emphasise the role of distributive politics. In his view, distributive politics has a role in reducing social inequalities, but egalitarian politics should be mostly about the relationship between individuals and communities. The implication of this approach is that the State does not have a central role in promoting greater equality. Instead, local communities should take control of their own lives and work together to achieve their own goals, because the State can also be unresponsive.[38] In similar vein, Jon Cruddas emphasised the role of relationships – or fraternity – in promoting what he called the good life. He also claimed that the emphasis on nurturing relationships was embedded in Labour's history. 'Labour built its history organising working people to defend their family life, to struggle for fair wages and a decent home, and to create a better future for their children.'[39]

Thus, Labour's interest in relational equality served three purposes: it enabled a richer and multi-dimensional understanding of inequality, which considered the equal worth of individuals but also their duties towards their communities. In other words, it was congruent with a socialist tradition whereby greater equality was promoted through the values of solidarity, fellowship, and community. Second, it enabled Labour to articulate a different – more critical – approach to the State. Third, relational equality enabled Labour to move the discussion on equality from the focus on redistribution of wealth to the distribution of power. This concept accepted inequality provided that every individual had an equal right to some basic minimums that would enable him/her to participate in society. This being said, it is important to emphasise at this point that Labour's current critique of redistribution did not aim to dismiss it. Instead it sought to draw attention to its limits.

The ideas of pre-distribution and relational equality were not in direct competition with each other but they differed in emphasis in two important points. First, relational egalitarians were more accepting of inequalities. Second, relational egalitarians favoured a methodology that focused on democratic processes, grassroots activism, and promoting relations instead of State action, whereas pre-distributionists emphasised the role of market reforms, which rely on State intervention.

However, both concepts emphasised one key point that was made by several Labour politicians, and this point was that there was more to egalitarian politics than just redistributive strategies. In addition, both ideas constructed a critique of the managerial and unresponsive State espoused by New Labour, and argued for a greater role for non-State actors and democratic politics in reducing the wealth and power gap (this aspect of Labour's equality agenda will be addressed in the next chapter).

Furthermore, these two ideas complemented Labour's earlier traditions of pluralism, guild socialism, and ethical socialism. As Ben Jackson explained, these traditions of the Left 'wanted to foster a community characterised by "fellowship", in which citizens of equal standing treated one another with mutual respect, free from 'invidious comparisons of superior and inferior', and fairly shared the fruits of their collective labour'. The redistribution of economic resources, educational opportunities, and productive obligations was therefore the means to the achievement of a wider set of civic goals.[40] It is noteworthy how this conception of 'fellowship' resonates with Anderson's take on democratic equality and with current Labour politics. Indeed, Marc Stears stressed the contribution of the guild socialist movement in current Labour thinking about localism, citizen empowerment and democratic engagement, and the good life.[41]

Similarly, Jon Cruddas claimed to be interested 'in questions of industrial democracy, in questions of how people lived full and rewarding lives'.[42] Borrowing from the traditions of the Independent Labour Party, Cruddas argued that the meaning of socialism was more about 'a deeper sense of fulfilment' than only about 'subsistence'.[43] That sense of fulfilment was based on ideas about duties and obligations. Moreover, Cruddas emphasised these traditions with a view to establishing parallels between the managerialism of New Labour and the scientific approach of the Fabians. Finally, Tristram Hunt linked the ideas of pre-distribution to the ethical socialism of John Ruskin and R. H. Tawney and to the mutualist traditions of the party.[44]

The referencing of a diversity of Labour traditions shaped the party's approach to equality in terms of the aims, but also with regard to the means to promote greater equality. In terms of means, it is clear that redistribution of wealth continued to play a role, but there was a myriad of other policy instruments that could be deployed to achieve those egalitarian aims. In addition, this approach to equality necessitated a different response from the State, and relied on grassroots activism and active community life. In fact, in this conception, the process of fighting for greater equality was almost as important as obtaining it. Such a conception of equality assumed that individuals achieved greater personal fulfilment when involved in a collective or community endeavour.

Labour's borrowing from earlier Labour traditions has also had an impact on the aims of the party. Indeed, the references to Cole, Tawney, Ruskin, George Lansbury, and the mutualist tradition enabled Labour to move away from materialistic considerations to concentrate on questions about the uneven distribution of power, as well as on ideas to promote the good life. Thus, the pluralism in Labour's egalitarianism was one that sought to focus simultaneously on questions about the communal good life and on ideas about the empowerment of individuals through a life embedded in the community.

As a result of these debates and influences, Labour's egalitarian agenda sought to implement policies that could lead not only to a 'sufficient' but also to a fulfilling and good life. Work should be pursued but so would the conditions – such as a living wage and fair working conditions – to live that fulfilling life. This was an argument deployed by Jon Cruddas, Ed Miliband, and the shadow work and pensions secretary, Rachel Reeves, in many speeches. Whereas Cruddas tended to offer a more philosophical approach to the good life agenda, both Miliband and Reeves were explicit in their references to the life beyond work and inside the family unit. For instance, Reeves argued for the living wage on the grounds that it would also enable parents 'to spend more time with their family and children'.[45] A similar point was made by Ed Miliband in his speech to the 2013 Labour Party Annual Conference, where he spoke of those times in the 1980s when economic growth enabled people to 'spend time with kids, not working all the hours that god sends'.[46]

Constraints

Thus far we have seen how the Labour leader put equality at the centre of his agenda of change. Miliband's focus on equality reflected his own values, his own interpretation of the role of the Labour Party in British politics, and it also echoed zeitgeist ideas and political and academic debates about equality that took place in progressive circles. But the Labour leader had to calibrate his agenda to the political context and economic realities of Britain, and to translate some of those ideas into a language that could resonate with voters' concerns.

The need to reduce the public deficit imposed severe constraints on Labour's ability to make ambitious public spending commitments. Moreover, poll after poll confirmed that voters opposed higher welfare spending. Polling conducted by YouGov showed that the public was very concerned with the affordability of the benefits system, and around two-thirds of the public thought that 'welfare scroungers' constituted a 'significant minority'.[47] The *British Social Attitudes* (*BSA*) annual survey confirmed that trend. The 2013 report surveying thirty years of public attitudes noted that 'the hardening in public attitudes towards welfare spending, although far from uniform, shows little sign of abating'.[48] In addition, the *BSA* report noted that despite the recession and prolonged economic stagnation, 'only a very small proportion of the public – one in twenty – now support increased spending on social security benefits'.[49] These trends were again confirmed in the *BSA* 2014 report.[50]

Public resistance to higher public spending on welfare was an important obstacle to Labour's ambitious plans to reduce inequalities of income and of power. Some Labour backbenchers, mostly from the Blairite wing (but not exclusively) thought the party looked soft on welfare and public spending, and called on the party leader to address that perception.[51] For them, Labour could only gain credibility if it developed a 'tough' message on welfare centred on the ideas of rewarding work and discouraging welfare dependency. This concern explains Rachel Reeves's comments, made shortly before the start of the 2015 electoral campaign, about welfare claimants. In an interview with the *Guardian* she said that Labour was not the party 'of people on benefits'. She also claimed that Labour did not want to be seen as 'the party to represent those who are out of work'.[52]

These constraints had an impact on Labour's approach to equality and to welfare policy in general. Though many of Labour's flagship welfare policy ideas – such as the living wage and a greater emphasis on vocational education and apprentice-ships to tackle youth unemployment – had been presented in 2010, Miliband's vision remained undeveloped for the first three years of his leadership. It was only from the summer of 2013 that Labour's frontbench decided to spell out the party's approach to equality and social security spending.

In two speeches delivered in the summer of 2013 Ed Balls and Ed Miliband announced a three-year cap on structural social security spending. A year later they announced that once in government Labour would stop paying the winter fuel allowance to richer pensioners and would introduce a cap on child benefit.[53] The language of the 'spending cap' aimed to demonstrate that a government led by Ed Miliband would be a responsible manager of the economy but also that the party favoured a 'tough' approach to the social security budget.

Labour's plans were presented as a long-term strategy to reduce the social secur-ity budget, as they were predicated on having more tax-payers than benefit claimants and on a much larger housing stock (which would have an impact on how much the State would spend on housing benefits). However, Labour's plans implied consider-able public investments, which would have a short-term impact on the budget, and on the levels of public borrowing. For instance, the proposal to give local author-ities the ability to negotiate lower rents with landlords would produce, according to the party's estimates, immediate savings; however, the plan to invest in building new houses, and the introduction of vocational training and apprenticeships would involve greater public spending and public borrowing.

Regarding in-work benefits, Labour estimated that the gradual and modest increase of the minimum wage, the expansion of the living wage, and greater childcare provision would result, in the medium to long term, in lower welfare spending and higher tax revenues. But again, these were policies with a price tag attached. More free childcare provision in the early years, and after-school care, would be provided by the State (funded by a tax on bankers' bonuses), and the ini-tial stages of the promotion of the living wage would imply a State subsidy of the companies that would endorse it. However, Labour did not explain when and how some of its flagship policies would be implemented or funded.

In addition, the party was very careful in its use of language. Miliband's office created the rule that no frontbencher should use the word 'welfare' when discussing any issue that in the past would have been presented as a 'welfare policy'. Instead the emphasis was on sponsoring specific policy ideas such as the minimum wage, or on showing Labour's opposition to the so-called 'bedroom tax', or stressing Labour's cap on social security spending. These semantic manoeuvres suggested that Miliband's team was wary of public opinion and of negative headlines in the Conservative press.

However, the party was very open about its redistributive commitments. If Tony Blair and Gordon Brown challenged the idea that Labour was a tax-and-spend party, Miliband and his team (though some shadow cabinet ministers were not entirely comfortable with it) were explicit in their support for redistributive measures. Indeed, the Labour leader seemed to relish the rhetoric on wealth redistribution and justified the funding of several redistributive measures with higher taxes for those high-income earners, banks, bankers, and 'mansion' owners. From his first day as Labour leader Miliband showed his commitment to reinstating the top rate of income tax introduced by the Gordon Brown Government, which had been repealed by the chancellor George Osborne in the 2012 budget.[54] This approach to taxation was ferociously attacked by the right-wing media, and was mildly criticised by the right of the party, but it was popular with the public.

Greater equality

Notwithstanding these important constraints, it was clear that addressing rising inequalities and the unequal distribution of power were dominant themes on Miliband's agenda. His starting point was that there was a 'new inequality' that had damaging and lasting effects on society. Echoing the arguments of Piketty, and Wilkinson and Pickett, the Labour leader spoke often about the detrimental effects of this 'new inequality' on economic growth, on employment, and on public finances. He also argued that 'inequality makes social mobility far harder to achieve',[55] because it 'reinforces privilege and opportunity for the few'.[56] As he repeated incessantly during the 2015 electoral campaign, inequality was 'our generation's greatest challenge'.[57]

Miliband seemed immune to the criticisms that his egalitarian agenda could undermine the party's economic credibility. Indeed, even when his leadership was attacked because he was not sufficiently pro-business, Miliband claimed to be exercised by the fact that Britain was a country that 'increasingly doesn't work for the many', and attacked the 'most mistaken view of all, that the success of the country depends on just a few at the top'.[58]

These arguments were of an instrumental variety but Miliband's narrative on equality reflected as well a thicker concept, one that was concerned with more than just issues of distributive justice. His egalitarian agenda was based on the idea of equal worth (this aspect of Miliband's agenda is analysed in Chapter 5) and on considerations about the good society. In his first speech as Labour leader he said that the good society contains the 'things that business cannot provide', namely, 'strong families, time with your children, green spaces, community life, love and compassion', as well as 'community, belonging and solidarity'.[59] In this tract, Miliband presented a political vision that went beyond transactional relations and affirmed the value of a good life where valuable public goods were not necessarily exchanged in the market. In an indirect reference to guild socialism and to the concept of relational equality Miliband said that he wanted his children to live 'in a country where people look after each other, look out for each other, care for each other, where compassion and responsibility to one another are valued'.[60] This vision of the good life was fleshed out more fully in Miliband's 'One Nation' speech presented at the 2012 Annual Party Conference, where he argued that 'inequality matters':[61]

> At the heart of the idea of One Nation is a belief in us prospering together as a country. We will not tolerate a widening gap between the richest and poorest. The route to economic recovery will be through addressing the living standards crisis being suffered by millions of families, not through helping millionaires get richer still.[62]

Though his One Nation approach was clearly borrowed from the Conservative politician Benjamin Disraeli, it was also influenced by those earlier Labour traditions of ethical socialism and mutualism that stressed the value of fellowship. This 'good life' agenda was well received by the intellectuals within and around the party, and to a certain extent by the grassroots of the party; however, it ran the danger of sounding too abstract to the general public. Moreover, an important section of the shadow cabinet was weary of Miliband's high ideals and preferred instead to focus on tangible, pragmatic offers to voters, which people like Jon Cruddas considered to be a minimalist and 'economicist' (as he put it) agenda. As a result, references to the good life disappeared from Miliband speeches, though some aspects of it could be detected in the Policy Review document and in the 2015 electoral manifesto. Thus, the party concentrated on promoting issues that had no price-tag attached and that were popular with voters. This was the case in Miliband's attack on 'zero-hours' contracts, the proposal to freeze energy prices and modestly increase the minimum wage, the promise to repeal the 'bedroom tax', or to cut tuition fees.

Labour used three main narratives to promote its egalitarian agenda: (1) the narrative about the challenges facing the 'squeezed middle', the 'cost of living crisis' and the 'zero-zero economy'; (2) the narrative about the promotion of work; (3) the narrative about the contributory principle. These three narratives were then pegged to policies such as the rise of the minimum wage, the promotion of the living wage, vocational education (inspired by the German model), tackling oligopolies, and opposition to the Coalition's welfare reforms.

The cost-of-living crisis

The central plank of Labour's equality agenda focused on what had been identified as the 'cost-of-living crisis' and the 'zero-zero economy'. The first venture into this new ground was an article Miliband published in the *Sunday Telegraph* in 2010, where he declared himself to be 'on the side of the squeezed middle'.[63] By the 'squeezed middle' he meant the people who 'played by the rules, but did not feel that society rewarded responsibility', the people who 'found themselves working harder than ever' but who found it more difficult 'to get by'.[64] In a speech to the Resolution Foundation in 2011, Miliband linked the phenomenon of the 'squeezed middle' to the 'new inequality' and to the Coalition's austerity policies: 'the 21st century inequality, the fairness div-ide in our economy, threatens to be about a division between the richest at the top who have been doing well, and the majority – lower and middle-income – who have been struggling to keep up: working harder for longer for less'.[65]

But by the summer of 2013 macroeconomic figures were signalling faint economic growth, and the Coalition tried to make the most of the situation by emphasising the end of the recession. This created difficulties for Labour's economic policies and message. Though the spending cuts introduced by the Coalition had failed to elim-inate the deficit and had slowed down the recovery, Labour had lost the economic argument. In fact, Labour was still blamed for having caused the deficit crisis. This meant that Labour had to change tack and emphasis. And that is precisely what Miliband did at the 2013 Labour Party Annual Conference.

Instead of focusing on the Coalition's austerity approach, Labour shifted the emphasis to the crisis of living standards. The message was simple: the economy was faintly growing, but the proceeds of that growth were not equally shared. The 'squeezed middle' could not feel the benefits of economic growth because their wages had stagnated and the cost of living had increased. As he put it to voters, 'You were the first into the recession but you are the last one out'.[66] In his speech to the 2013 Labour Party Annual Conference, Miliband presented this idea as an attack on 'trickle-down economics'. 'They used to say a rising tide lifts all boats, now the ris-ing tide just seems to lift the yachts',[67] he said. According to the Labour leader the British economy favoured a race to the bottom in terms of wage policies, labour rights, and working conditions with many workers having to end up 'working for their poverty'.[68] This line of argument was endlessly repeated during the 2015 elect-oral campaign.

To remedy this situation, Miliband and other Labour frontbenchers proposed a panoply of big and small policy ideas, such as the living wage, vocational education and apprenticeships, free childcare provision, and home building, but the one that grabbed the headlines was the proposal to freeze energy bills for twenty months from the moment Labour formed a government and then to regulate the energy market to prevent the over-charging of consumers.

The idea to use the State to regulate the market was then extended to other areas. Miliband also promised to address the problem of the predatory practices of pay-day lenders, which affected mostly the low-paid. The Labour leader identi-fied this problem – what he called the 'Wonga' economy, in a direct reference to the famous pay-day lender – as a symptom of a bigger one. This bigger problem was 'the cost-of-living crisis' that he associated with low-skilled jobs, wage stagnation for low-to-middle-income earners, and what he called the predatory behaviour of utility providers.[69] He also linked this problem to the failures of markets. Indeed, the 2015 party manifesto explicitly presented this idea as a 'mending markets' proposal.[70] The party then extended the idea to the water supply industry and to the letting market. Seeking to attract young voters, Labour's sixth electoral pledge was a 'new deal for those who rent their homes' that would create three-year tenancies and where private rents could not rise above inflation.[71]

Miliband's proposal to freeze energy prices was received with derision by the Conservative Party and by some media commentators who accused the Labour leader of endorsing the Marxist politics of this father. However, with this promise he succeeded in setting the political agenda. Opinion polls showed that Miliband's proposal was popular with voters.[72] Even the former Conservative prime minister John Major admitted he was in favour of imposing a levy on the 'excessive profits' of the energy companies so that people were not forced 'to choose between food or fuel'.[73]

In his last speech to the Labour conference before the general election he returned to the theme of the 'squeezed middle', but this time the focus was on the problems of 'precariousness and insecurity' in the labour market. In that spirit he promised to tackle low pay by increasing the minimum wage, tackling 'zero-hours' contracts, and dealing with the 'growing army of the self-employed'.[74] Moreover, the party decided to make the campaign against the under-occupancy penalty, colloquially known as the 'bedroom tax', a flagship policy. At the 2014 Annual Party Conference, the shadow secretary for work and pensions, Rachel Reeves, opened her speech with the promise to repeal the 'bedroom tax': 'the very first thing I will do if I am Secretary of State for Work and Pensions next May is repeal it. It's unfair, it's unworkable, and it's on its way out – across the whole of the United Kingdom. Scrapped, binned, axed, abolished, put out of its misery, consigned to the history books.'[75] The Labour leader was equally committed to abolishing the bedroom tax and also to addressing the deep inequalities in Britain's labour market, which were characterised by low pay, zero-hours contracts, and a shortage of affordable housing. In a bid to target disillusioned Liberal Democrat voters, Labour promised as well to reduce the annual cost of tuition fees to £6,000.[76] Last but not least, Miliband reinforced his commitment to equality by promising to protect and invest in the NHS.

Promoting work

Ed Miliband followed the well-established Labour tradition – which had strong Fabian, ethical socialist, and also New Labour roots – of promoting work and the work ethic. In the spirit of that tradition, the Labour leader showed how he disapproved of those who chose not to work and to live on benefits, and asserted his commitment to promoting the work ethic. 'Labour – the party of work – the clue is in the name', he said in his 2013 seminal speech on social security.[77] And though New Labour developed several welfare-to-work policies aimed at addressing welfare dependency and long-term unemployment, Miliband conceded that New Labour 'did too little to ensure responsibility at the bottom' and was seen 'as the party of those ripping off our society'.[78]

But Labour's defence of the work ethic was mostly a response to the prevailing media narrative about welfare dependency and in particular to the Conservatives' rhetoric about 'skivers' and 'strivers'. This divisive rhetoric framed the political debate on welfare spending, and forced Labour to recalibrate its message. In any major speech about welfare policy, Miliband and other Labour frontbenchers talked with disapproval about those who lived on benefits.[79]

However, there was a qualitative difference between Miliband's approach to welfare dependency and that followed by New Labour or by the Coalition. Whereas New Labour had accepted the New Right ideas and assumptions about the 'dependency culture', the Labour leader stressed that welfare reform was not 'about stereotyping everybody out of work, it's about transforming their lives'.[80] In other words, he viewed this problem not as the result of a 'skiver' mentality but as the outcome of failed economic policies. Similarly, Stewart Wood disapproved of the Coalition's 'skivers versus strivers' narrative on economic grounds: 'the Government wants to portray people out of work as somehow at fault for unemployment ... This is wrong. It's not that it's wrong morally. It's wrong economically.'[81]

As Labour rejected the Coalition's negative rhetoric on welfare, the emphasis was placed on promoting work through vocational training and apprenticeships for the young, and on helping mothers to return to the labour market by offering twenty-five hours of free childcare. The argument that Labour was making was that unemployment, and in particular youth unemployment, was a consequence of an unskilled workforce. This argument was forcefully made by Lord Adonis. Quoting data from the OECD, Adonis argued that the lack of skills was the key factor in explaining Britain's high rate of youth unemployment.[82] This analysis backed Labour's promise of a 'real jobs guarantee' to the young unemployed. The initiative would be funded by a tax on bankers' bonuses that would be used to provide training to those under twenty-five who would sign up to the scheme. With a nod to the *Daily Mail* reader (and also to Sydney and Beatrice Webb), Labour presented this proposal as a 'Compulsory Jobs Guarantee' and stressed that 'saying no is not an option'.[83]

In parallel with this initiative, Labour promised a new emphasis on vocational education with the proposal to create a Technical Baccalaureate and the promotion of apprenticeships.[84] Miliband admitted that this was a long-term project as it required a change of attitudes towards apprenticeships and vocational education, but announced the party's commitment to it nonetheless. In a direct reference to the German model, Miliband said: 'In Germany, middle-class parents boast about their kids doing great apprenticeships. But in Britain, too often people think that if they don't go to university, they are written off by society.'[85] To change this culture Labour proposed the introduction of a target aimed at doubling the number of school leavers who enrolled on apprenticeships.

Miliband linked the problem of high welfare spending to what he identified as the 'the low pay emergency', and the high costs associated with social housing. To address the problem of in-work poverty, the Labour leader proposed several policies, namely the reform of zero-hours contracts to prevent the exploitative practices that Miliband associated with the Victorian era,[86] the rise of the minimum wage, and the promotion of the living wage. This latter proposal occupied a central place in his equality agenda. Indeed, in his first speech as Labour leader, he said the 'foundation of the economy in the future must be a living wage'; however, the party's promises in this direction were rather modest.[87]

The campaign for the living wage was initially presented as part of Labour's good life agenda and it reflected Miliband's strong interest in the issue. He made the living wage a commitment in the 2010 party manifesto and it was the dominant theme of his leadership campaign. In addition, Miliband's speeches on welfare were peppered with comments about how the quality of life of ordinary workers was affected by having to work so many hours in order to make a living. 'It is not good for our country for people to be working 60 or 70 hours a week, doing two or three jobs, not having time to see their kids.'[88] Miliband and Balls also stressed how insecurity about work had a damaging effect on social cohesion.

But the party's emphasis, especially during the 2015 electoral campaign, was on the pragmatic aspects of the policy. For instance, Rachel Reeves argued that the Government could save more than £6 billion 'in reduced spending on benefits and tax credits and increased income from taxation and national insurance if all employees were paid at least a living wage.'[89] Likewise, Miliband argued that the low-wage economy was too costly because low-paid jobs were subsidised by the tax-payer in the form of tax credits and benefits. As he put it in an article published in the *Evening Standard*, 'low-wages aren't just bad for families; they short-change the taxpayer too'.[90] Thus, in his speech to the last Annual Party Conference before the general election, Miliband declared that 'the first national goal' of a Labour Government was to 'halve the number of people in low pay by 2025'.[91] This commitment occupied a central place in Labour's manifesto. One of the main lines of the manifesto was that 'Britain's route to prosperity and higher living standards' was through 'more secure and better paid jobs'.[92]

But if Miliband was strong on the moral and practical benefits of the living wage – and some of the rhetoric was fairly radical – his approach to the policy was far more cautious. Instead of proposing legislation to introduce the living wage – a demand made by some on the left – Miliband favoured a gradual and consultative approach.[93] This meant that Labour would *encourage* the adoption of the living wage, by offering companies that implemented it a twelve-month tax rebate, but it would not make it statutory. In addition, in the period just before the general election, Miliband talked less of the living wage and emphasised more the party's commitment to a modest raise in the minimum wage to £8.00 per hour by 2020.

This approach was criticised by some influential activists. For instance, Mark Ferguson from LabourList criticised Labour's plans for 'not being bold enough'. In his view, the party should 'raise the minimum wage to the living wage' because the living wage is 'widely accepted to be the lowest amount that someone can actually live on'.[94] In the televised debates, even the prime minister, David Cameron, used the modesty of Labour's proposals on the minimum wage to claim that 'hard-working people' would be better off under a Conservative Government. But the frontbench team feared negative headlines in the right-wing press and believed that a stronger commitment would contribute to the party's reputation as anti-business.

To off-set the rather modest proposals on the living wage and on the minimum wage the party focused instead on policies that were easier to deliver and that had resonance with voters. The attack on 'zero-hours' contracts was a case in point, and from the autumn of 2014 it became the centre of Miliband's cost-of-living agenda. In what became known as the 'fight-back' speech delivered in November 2014, he talked about the 'zero-zero' economy, which was defined by the increase on 'zero-hours' contracts and by the 'zero-tax' for those at the top.[95] More importantly, the Labour leader linked these ideas to his more ambitious egalitarian agenda. As he argued, the 'zero-zero' economy was a symptom of 'a deeply unequal, deeply unfair, deeply unjust country'.[96] Labour was short on detail on how it would put an end to the practice of zero-hours contracts; however, Miliband seemed to relish the opportunity to name-and-shame employers that relied on this type of practice. During the electoral campaign Labour focused its campaign on denouncing what Miliband described as 'the epidemic of zero-hours' and promised to 'ban' the practice.[97] But here again, there was a gap between the rhetoric and proposed policies. In truth, under Labour proposals, workers who had been hired on zero-hours contracts for more than twelve weeks would gain the legal right to obtain a 'regular contract'.

Contributory principle

The third main theme in Labour's welfare agenda was the re-assertion of the contributory principle. This theme gained prominence in 2013 and was promoted in the IPPR's report *The Condition of Britain* as 'the second pillar on which to build a strong society', but there had been references to it in earlier speeches by the Labour leader.[98] For instance, at the 2011 Labour Party Annual Conference Ed Miliband argued for the introduction of the contributory principle on the grounds of promoting responsibility: 'Do we treat the person who contributes to their community the same as the person who doesn't? My answer is no. Our first duty should be to help the person who shows responsibility.'[99] Around that time, Liam Byrne (who was then Labour's spokesman on work and pensions) made the case for the contributory principle in an article published in *The Purple Book*. In this article, he said that citizens' place in the queue for benefits was affected by whether they 'are doing the right thing, getting a job, paying taxes, being a good tenant and neighbour and so on'.[100] But it was only in June 2013 that the Labour leader developed the idea of the contributory principle and fleshed out some of the policies that would be associated with it.[101] For Miliband the recognition of the contributory principle via the social security system implied offering more affordable childcare to working families, recognising contributions to the social security system.[102]

But introducing a contributory element to Britain's complex system of in-work and out-of-work benefits was far from straightforward, as it implied the dilution of the universality principle. In addition, if it was easy to understand the shift in focus from unemployment benefits to help with childcare costs and vocational training, it was harder to justify benefit rises or cuts depending on how much individuals had contributed. Similarly, Labour's proposals to withdraw the winter fuel allowance from wealthier pensioners, or child benefit from wealthier parents, were not related at all to the contributory principle (as richer pensioners and parents are paying larger contributions to the social security system). Rachel Reeves admitted as much in her first interview as shadow work and pensions secretary: 'It's not easy. If you increase what you give to some people then presumably you have to reduce it for others. We are not in an environment where there is more money around. It is a difficult thing to achieve.'[103]

Nonetheless, in Labour's manifesto there was a commitment to promoting the contributory principle. The party promised to 'introduce a higher rate of Job Seekers [*sic*] Allowance for those who have contributed over years'.[104] But as this vague promise demonstrates, the party's ideas were undeveloped. Labour neither explained how it would fund this policy, nor offered any detail about the value of that higher rate of Job Seeker's Allowance or how many years of contributions were necessary to be entitled to it.

Concluding remarks

Under the leadership of Ed Miliband, the Labour Party clearly moved its approach to equality away from New Labour and into social democratic territory. That movement was evident in the party's rhetoric and also in its policy proposals. In contrast with New Labour, Ed Miliband claimed that inequality mattered and that the party was committed to reducing it. Moreover, he seemed eager to correct the mistakes of New Labour: namely to challenge the low-wage economic paradigm that New Labour had supported; to restore the 10p tax rate; and to complete the welfare reforms of New Labour, by addressing the problem of in-work poverty through higher wages rather than State-funded tax credits.

Miliband's focus on equality reflected the intellectual zeitgeist in which many of his ideas gestated. As explained at the beginning of this chapter, the rise of inequality across the world and in particular in Europe and in North America was (and still is) intensely debated and discussed by public intellectuals, politicians, academics, journalists, and international institutions. After decades of neglect, ideas and concerns about equality reached the top of the political agenda. Like other social democratic parties, the Labour Party identified this new political concern with rising social inequalities as the new centre ground of politics.

The Labour Party, supported by a large epistemic community of academics, think-tank researchers, party activists, and public intellectuals, sought to develop a political agenda that addressed this problem in a way that was consistent with its ideological traditions. The process of developing that agenda was long and intense, and thrived on the conversations, exchanges, and dialogues among these different actors. Obviously, those debates considered the economic, political, and electoral circumstances that the party had to address in order to win the 2015 elections, but they did not shy away from ambitious goals.

From the different ideas and possibilities that were debated in Labour circles there were two ideas that stood out. They were Jacob Hacker's ideas on pre-distribution, and Elizabeth Anderson's concept of relational equality, which was later adopted by the think-tank IPPR and transformed into a series of policy proposals. Both pre-distribution and relational equality had the merit of addressing specific and current policy puzzles whilst at the same time they could be associated with the older Labour traditions of guild socialism, mutualism, and ethical socialism. Indeed, both pre-distribution and relational equality sought to address the unpopularity of redistributive ideas by shifting attention to policies that would tackle inequality before redistributive measures would be considered necessary. This being said, the Labour Party under Ed Miliband was very explicit about its support for redistributive measures (though some frontbenchers were concerned by it). In fact, Miliband never sounded apologetic when he defended the reintroduction of the 50p tax rate, or the introduction of a mansion tax, or the tax on bankers' bonuses, or measures to tackle tax evasion by multinational corporations.

Miliband was also rhetorically committed to a more ambitious egalitarian agenda, upon which the ideas of pre-distribution and relational equality depended. Indeed, these two ideas were predicated on a more ambitious egalitarian agenda that focused on protecting individuals from domination and promoting a conception of equal worth that relied on building relationships. This agenda would link the promotion of equality to the strengthening of democratic culture and institutions, and to individual empowerment. It is noteworthy that this thicker conception of equality had a long lineage in the Labour Party, in particular in the traditions of guild socialism.

These ideas found a place in Miliband's narrative. This outcome was not necessarily an accident, given that Marc Stears was Miliband's speech-writer and adviser, and Jon Cruddas led the party's policy renewal process, and both of them drafted Labour's 2015 electoral manifesto. In speech after speech, Miliband revealed that the main purpose of his project for Britain was to address the problems of the inequalities of wealth and of power. He was also clear about his intellectual and ideological sources.

References to the guild socialists, to Wilkinson and Pickett, to Sandel, to the idea of pre-distribution, and to the importance of relationships found their way into Miliband's speeches. These references were indicative of his ambitions in this area. For instance, the rejection of the bedroom tax can be associated with the ideas of relational equality that emphasise respecting human dignity and equal treatment and respect. Similarly, the method Labour chose to promote the living wage owed a lot to the old Labour traditions of ethical socialism and mutualism, but also to Elizabeth Anderson's concept of 'relational equality' (though it also reflected the party's concern with being perceived as anti-business). Rather than proposing legislation on the living wage to make it statutory, Labour proposed a consultative process of decision-making that aimed to be business-friendly but also empowering, as it relied on grassroots campaigns.

But the transformation of these ambitions into concrete policy proposals was not easy. Miliband and his team operated in a constrained environment. There was little space in the media and in public debates to promote such ambitious ideas. The pursuit of greater equality was seen as a utopian, and even dangerous, project, especially considering Britain's public deficit. Given that Labour was constrained by its own commitment to 'balance the books' the party focused on highlighting its cost-free proposals. Hence, Miliband, Reeves, and Balls re-doubled the attacks on zero-hours contracts, promised to repeal the popularly named 'bedroom tax', and presented their modest proposal of a minimum wage increase as a policy that would transform Britain's low-wage economy. But in reality these policies would only address what Miliband considered to be a narrow approach to equality.

In addition, public attitudes to welfare policies had hardened considerably. Finally the Labour Party was divided between those, like Miliband, who defended an ambitious transformative agenda, and those, normally coming from the right of the party, who feared that an egalitarian agenda would compromise the party's efforts to be seen as economically credible and pro-business. But in the end, as Jon Cruddas conceded, the 'economicist argument' prevailed over the 'good life argument'.[105] Instead of talking about the good life, Labour's 2015 electoral campaign focused on retail offers on issues such as the bedroom tax, zero-hours contracts, and the minimum wage.

Any party leader would have had to consider these ideational, political, and institutional constraints, but for Miliband it was particularly difficult. Isolated in the party, with a serious image problem, and bounded by his cautious personality, the Labour leader had no choice but to compromise on his goals. As a result, the party failed some of Peter A. Hall's criteria to ascertain the success of ideas. On the whole, Labour's egalitarian agenda was intellectually and ideologically coherent; however, some of the party's policy proposals were rather minimalist in scope. It was the case of the party's approach to the minimum wage and to the living wage. Labour's proposals in this area represented an incremental improvement to the living conditions of low-paid workers, but were very far from challenging inequalities of power.

Moreover, some aspects of Miliband's agenda failed the persuasion and comprehensibility tests. Ideas such as pre-distribution or relational equality had no resonance with the lives of ordinary voters. More importantly, the party's proposals for redistributive policies challenged popularly held assumptions (promoted by the media) about the role of the State in tackling inequality. This being said, proposals such as repealing the bedroom tax, reforming 'zero-hours contracts', raising the minimum wage, tackling the cost-of-living crisis, and taxing bankers were popular with voters. But crucially – and this leads us to Hall's third criterion – these ideas were dismissed by the right of the party and by important sections of the media on the grounds that they were anti-business. Indeed, Miliband struggled to find 'relevant' supporters for his transformative programme.

As a result of these constraints, Miliband's ambitious egalitarian agenda was less than the sum of its parts. There was a clear commitment to reducing inequality through redistributive and pre-distributive measures, and the myriad of small policies Labour proposed would have a cumulative effect in the lives of low-paid workers, but the larger agenda that focused on promoting the 'good life' was abandoned.

Notes

1 Ed Miliband, 'The Hugo Young Lecture', LabourList, 10 February 2014, http://labourlist. org/2014/02/ed-milibands/hugo-young-lecture-full-text/ (accessed 15 April 2014).

2 Ed Miliband, 'The Cost of Living Crisis in Britain: Speech to the Resolution Foundation', 28 February 2011, http://www.labour.org.uk/the-cost-of-living-crisis-facing-britain-ed-miliband (accessed 20 March 2011).

3 Jeremy Paxman, transcript of BBC *Newsnight* interview with Tony Blair, 2001, http://news. bbc.co.uk/1/hi/events/newsnight/1372220.stm (accessed 18 August 2015).

4 Ed Miliband, '2014 Labour Conference Speech', 23 September 2014, http://www.labour.org. uk/blog/entry/2014-labour-conference-speech (accessed 25 September 2014).

5 Ed Miliband said: 'We would put right a mistake made by Gordon Brown and the last Labour government'; Ed Miliband, 'Rebuilding Britain with a One Nation Economy', 14 February 2013, https://www.labour.org.uk/rebuilding-britain-with-a-one-nation-economy-ed-miliband (accessed 7 May 2013).

6 John Hills, 'Labour's Record on Cash Transfers, Poverty, Inequality and the Lifecycle 1997–2010', CASE Working Paper 5 (July 2013), p. 37.

7 Ed Miliband, 'Speech to Progress Annual Conference', 21 May 2011, http://www.labour.org. uk/ed-milibands-speech-to-progress-annual-conference (accessed 14 May 2013).

8 Ed Miliband, 'Speech to London Citizens', 10 January 2013, http://www.labour.org.uk/ labour-will-deliver-fairness (accessed 15 January 2013).

9 Ed Miliband, 'Responsibility in 21st Century Britain', 13 June 2011, http://www.labour.org.uk/ ed-miliband-speech-responsibility-2011-06-13 (accessed 25 November 2013).

10 Liam Byrne, 'Eliminating "Power Failures": A New Agenda for Tackling Inequality', in Robert Philpot (ed.), *The Purple Book: A Progressive Future for Labour* (London: Biteback Publishing, 2011), pp. 129–143 (p.131).

11 Richard Wilkinson and Kate Pickett, *The Spirit Level: Why More Equal Societies Almost Always Do Better* (London: Allen Lane, 2009). In a later work Wilkinson and Pickett advocated a series of policies (including greater democracy in the workplace) with a view to promoting greater equality. They also called on the progressive forces to develop an inspiring concept of the good

life 'which is not only environmentally sustainable, but in which the real quality of life is better for the vast majority'. Richard Wilkinson and Kate Pickett, *A Convenient Truth: A Better Society for Us and the Planet* (London: Fabian Society/Friedrich Ebert Stiftung, 2014), p. xvii.

12 Michael J. Sandel, *What Money Can't Buy: The Moral Limits of Markets* (London: Penguin, 2013).

13 Ferdinand Mount, *The New Few; or, A Very British Oligarchy* (London: Simon and Schuster, 2012).

14 Douglas Alexander and Ed Miliband, 'We Will Defend the State', *Guardian*, 5 February 2010, http://www.theguardian.com/commentisfree/2010/feb/05/defend-state-osborne-nudge-equality (accessed 17 August 2015).

15 Ed Miliband, 'The New Generation: Speech to the 2010 Labour Party Annual Conference', 28 September 2010, www2.labour.org.uk/ed-miliband---a-new-generation,2010-09-28 (accessed 10 January 2012).

16 Thomas Piketty, *Capital in the Twentieth-First Century* (London: Belknap Press, 2014).

17 Robert Skidelsky and Edward Skidelsky, *How Much Is Enough? The Love of Money, and the Case for the Good Life* (London: Allen Lane, 2012).

18 Jacob S. Hacker, 'The Institutional Foundations of Middle-Class Democracy', Policy Network, 6 May 2011, http://www.policy-network.net/pno_detail.aspx?ID=3998&title=The+institutio nal+foundations+of+middle-class+democracy (accessed 7 September 2012).

19 George Eaton, 'Jacob Hacker: Ed Miliband's Wonkish Pin-Up', *New Statesman*, 11 July 2013.

20 Hacker, 'The Institutional Foundations'.

21 Hacker, 'The Institutional Foundations'.

22 Jacob Hacker, Ben Jackson, and Martin O'Neill, 'The Politics of Predistribution: Jacob Hacker Interviewed by Ben Jackson and Martin O'Neill', *Renewal* 21:2–3 (28 August 2013): 54–64 (p. 56).

23 Ed Miliband, 'Speech to Policy Network – Labour's New Agenda', 6 September 2012, http://www.labour.org.uk/labours-new-agenda (accessed 22 August 2013).

24 Miliband, 'Speech to Policy Network'.

25 Stewart Wood, 'Responsible Capitalism Is Labour's Agenda', *Guardian*, 9 January 2012, http://www.theguardian.com/commentisfree/2012/jan/09/responsible-capitalism-labour-da vid-cameron (accessed 17 August 2015).

26 Tristram Hunt, 'Reviving Our Sense of Mission: Designing a New Political Economy', in Robert Philpot (ed.), *The Purple Book: A Progressive Future for Labour* (London: Biteback Publishing, 2011), pp. 61–79 (pp. 67–72).

27 Hunt, 'Reviving our Sense of Mission', p. 65.

28 Tristram Hunt, 'One Nation Labour', in Owen Smith and Rachel Reeves (eds), *One Nation: Power, Hope, Community* (London: One Nation Register, 2013), pp. 145–159 (p. 156).

29 Elizabeth S. Anderson, 'What Is the Point of Equality?', *Ethics* 109 (January 1999): 287–337 (p. 313).

30 Anderson, 'What Is the Point of Equality?', p. 313.

31 Anderson, 'What Is the Point of Equality?', p. 314.

32 Anderson, 'What Is the Point of Equality?', p. 336.

33 Anderson, 'What Is the Point of Equality?', p. 326.

34 Nick Pearce, 'Elizabeth Anderson: Juncture Interview', *Juncture* 19:3 (2012): 188–193 (p. 188).

35 Pearce, 'Elizabeth Anderson', p. 189.

36 Kayte Lawton, Graeme Cooke, and Nick Pearce, *The Condition of Britain: Strategies for Social Renewal* (London: IPPR, 2014), pp. 14–16.

37 Marc Stears, 'In the Battle to Reshape Labour, a New Force is Emerging', *Liberal Conspiracy*, 13 February 2011, http://www.liberalconspiracy.org/2011/02/13/in-the-battle-to-reshape-labour-a-new-force-is-emerging (accessed 17 June 2013).

38 'People feel disempowered by the State and by the market. It is equally frustrating when you're on the telephone trying to get through to a call centre and there are layers of bureaucracy and they say it's a private provider. It is disempowering and people feel loss of control. And in the same way they feel the same about the interaction with the State services. In some State services people felt that they did not have enough control over the dynamic of that process. There's a democratic deficit in the State and in the market in recent years and one of the things that we've been thinking about is how to address both of those problems.' Marc Stears, private interview, 18 June 2013.

39 Jon Cruddas, 'Speech on Love and Work', 29 January 2015, http://www.joncruddas.org.uk/sites/joncruddas.org.uk/files/FINAL%20Love%20and%20Work%2028.1.15.pdf (accessed 2 February 2015). See also Jon Cruddas and Jonathan Rutherford, *One Nation: Labour's Political Renewal* (London: One Nation Register, 2014), http://www.joncruddas.org.uk/sites/jon-cruddas.org.uk/files/OneNation%20by%20Jon.pdf (accessed 3 August 2015), p. 35.

40 Ben Jackson, *Equality and the British Left: A Study in Progressive Political Thought, 1900–64* (Manchester: Manchester University Press, 2007), p. 27.

41 According to Marc Stears, the guild socialist movement 'was about finding new mechanisms of democratic participation for working people so that they could shape the industries in which they worked, their own towns and cities, and then eventually influence national politics through the Labour Party'. Stears argues that this is a 'historical theme' within the Labour Party. 'With the end of the New Labour years those issues reasserted themselves unsurprisingly after a long period in government', he argued. Private interview, 18 June 2013.

42 Jon Cruddas, private interview, 2 September 2013.

43 Cruddas, private interview, 2 September 2013.

44 Hunt, 'One Nation Labour', pp. 150–151.

45 Rachel Reeves, 'The Labour Agenda for Tackling Low Pay', 4 September 2013, http://www.rachelreeves.mp.co.uk/the_labour_agenda_for_tackling_low_pay (accessed 4 May 2014).

46 Ed Miliband, 'Ed Miliband MP's Speech to the Labour Party Annual Conference 2013', 24 September 2013, http://press.labour.org.uk/post/62160282657/ed-miliband-mps-speech-to-labour-party-annual (accessed 25 September 2013).

47 Peter Kellner, 'A Quiet Revolution', *Prospect* 192 (March 2012): 30–34.

48 Nick Pearce and Eleanor Taylor, 'Government Spending and Welfare', in Alison Park, Caroline Bryson, Elizabeth Clery, John Curtice, and Miranda Phillips (eds), *British Social Attitudes 30* (London: NatCen Social Research, 2013), pp. 33–61 (p. 35).

49 Pearce and Taylor, 'Government Spending and Welfare', p. 38.

50 Peter Taylor-Gooby and Eleanor Taylor, 'Benefits and Welfare', *British Social Attitudes 32*, http://www.bsa.natcen.ac.uk/media/38977/bsa32_welfare.pdf (accessed 5 May 2015).

51 Joe Murphy, 'Labour MPs Tell Ed Miliband to Toughen Up on Welfare', *Evening Standard*, 8 April 2013.

52 Rachel Reeves quoted in Amelia Gentleman, 'Labour Vows to Reduce Reliance on Food Banks if It Comes to Power', *Guardian*, 17 March 2015.

53 Ed Balls, 'Speech to Labour Party Conference', 22 September 2014, http://press.labour.org. uk/post/98137818419/speech-by-ed-balls-mp-to-labour-party-annual (accessed 25 September 2014).

54 Ed Miliband, 'Rebuilding Scotland, Rebuilding Britain', 19 April 2013, http://www.labour. org.uk/ed-miliband-scottish-conference (accessed 7 May 2013). See also Ed Miliband, 'One Nation Labour: Britain Can Prevent a Lost Decade', 23 March 2013, http://www.labour.org. uk/one-nation-labour-britain-can-prevent-a-lost-decade (accessed 7 May 2013); Ed Balls, 'My Speech to the Fabian Society', 24 January 2014, http://www.edballs.co.uk/blog/?p=4747 (accessed 4 February 2014).

55 Ed Miliband, 'Speech on Social Mobility to the Sutton Trust', 21 May 2012, http://www. labour.org.uk/ed-milibands-speech-on-social-mobility-sutton-trust,2012-05-21 (accessed 21 July 2012).

56 Ed Miliband, 'Ed Miliband's Speech to Labour Party Conference', 27 September 2011, http:// archive.labour.org.uk/ed-milibands-speech-labour-party-conference (accessed 3 April 2015).

57 Ed Miliband, 'Ed Miliband's Speech to the Fabian Conference', 17 January 2015, http://press. labour.org.uk/post/108338079199/ed-milibands-speech-to-fabian-conference (accessed 2 February 2015).

58 Ed Miliband, 'Ed Miliband Speech at Senate House', 13 November 2014, http://press.labour.org. uk/post/102524244299/ed-miliband-speech-at-senate-house (accessed 14 November 2014).

59 Miliband, 'The New Generation'.

60 Miliband, 'Responsibility in 21st Century Britain'.

61 Ed Miliband, 'Speech to Labour Party Annual Conference 2012', 2 October 2012, http://www. labour.org.uk/ed-miliband-speech-conf-2012 (accessed 4 October 2012).

62 Ed Miliband, 'Preface', in Smith and Reeves, *One Nation*, pp. 7–9 (p. 7).

63 Ed Miliband, 'My Vision to Rebuild Trust', *Sunday Telegraph*, 25 September 2010.

64 Ed Miliband, 'Full Transcript: Ed Miliband, Speech to the Fabians', 15 January 2011, http:// www.newstatesman.com/the-staggers/2011/01/labour-government-politics (accessed 22 March 2012).

65 Miliband, 'The Cost of Living Crisis in Britain'. He also used this narrative to attack the austerity policies of the Coalition when he said that Cameron's 'failed plan' of austerity had made 'silent victims' out of the 'squeezed middle'. Ed Miliband, 'Speech to the IPPR', 24 November 2011, http://www.labour.org.uk/economic-gamble-has-failed,2011-11-24 (accessed 30 November 2011).

66 Miliband, 'Speech to the Labour Party Annual Conference 2013'.

67 Miliband, 'Speech to the Labour Party Annual Conference 2013'.

68 Ed Miliband, 'Ed Miliband's "Cost of Living Crisis" Speech – Full Text', LabourList, 5 November 2013, http://labourlist.org/2013/11/ed-milibands-cost-of-living-crisis-speech-full-text (accessed 5 November 2013).

69 Miliband, ' "Cost of Living Crisis" Speech'.

70 *Britain Can Be Better: The Labour Party Manifesto 2015* (London: Labour Party, 2015), p. 25.

71 Ed Miliband, 'Speech in Stockton-on-Tees', 27 April 2015, http://press.labour.org.uk/post/117508448409/ed-milibands-speech-in-stockton-on-tees (accessed 1 May 2015).

72 Will Dahlgreen, 'Voters: Energy Prices Are Number One Threat', YouGov, 25 September 2013, http://yougov.co.uk/news/2013/09/25/energy-prices-economic-threat/ (accessed 3 August 2015).

73 Owen Bennett, ' "Windfall Tax on Energy Companies to Stop Heating or Eating Choice" Argues Sir John Major', *Express*, 22 October 2013, http://www.express.co.uk/news/uk/438504/Windfall-tax-on-energy-companies-to-stop-heating-or-eating-choice-argues-Sir-John-Major (accessed 18 August 2015).

74 Miliband, '2014 Labour Conference Speech', 23 September 2014.

75 Rachel Reeves, 'Speech to Labour Party Annual Conference', 22 September 2014, http://press.labour.org.uk/post/98144482264/speech-by-rachel-reeves-mp-to-labours-annual (accessed 29 September 2014).

76 Ed Miliband, 'Britain Can Be Better – The Full Text of Miliband's Manifesto Launch Speech', 13 April 2015, http://labourlist.org/2015/04/britain-can-be-better-the-full-text-of-milibands-manifesto-launch-speech/ (accessed 14 April 2015).

77 Ed Miliband, 'One Nation Plan for Social Security Reform', 6 June 2013, http://www.labour.org.uk/one-nation-social-security-reform-miliband-speech (accessed 11 June 2013).

78 Miliband, 'Responsibility in 21st Century Britain'.

79 In her first media interview following her appointment as work and pensions spokeswoman, Rachel Reeves emphasised the party's tough message on benefits: 'If you can work you should be working, and under our compulsory jobs guarantee if you refuse that job you forgo your benefits'; Toby Helm, 'Labour Will Be Tougher than Tories on Benefits, Promises New Welfare Chief', *Observer*, 13 October 2013.

80 Miliband, 'The New Generation'.

81 Stewart Wood, private interview, 17 January 2013.

82 Andrew Adonis, 'Youth Unemployment: It's Not the Age that Matters but Lack of Skills', *Guardian*, 1 July 2013.

83 Ed Miliband, 'Speech to Labour's Youth Conference', 16 March 2013, http://www.labour.org.uk/ed-milibands-speech-to-labours-youth-conference,2012-03-16 (accessed 2 December 2013).

84 Miliband, '2014 Labour Conference Speech'.

85 Miliband, 'Speech on Social Mobility'.

86 'All of the risks in the economy which we used to believe should be fairly shared between employers and working people [*sic*]. Now placed on the individual worker alone [*sic*]. That's why the worst of these practices owe more to the Victorian era than they do to the kind of workplace we should have in the 21st century'. Ed Miliband, 'Speech to the TUC', 10 September 2013, http://www.labour.org.uk/speech-by-ed-miliband-to-the-tuc (accessed 2 December 2013).

87 Miliband, 'The New Generation'.

88 Miliband, 'Miliband's "Cost of Living Crisis" Speech'.

89 Rachel Reeves, 'Meeting the Fiscal Challenge', in John Denham (ed.), *The Shape of Things to Come: Labour's New Thinking* (London: Fabian Society, 2012), p. 6.

90 Ed Miliband, 'The Living Wage Benefits All, Not Just the Low-Paid', *Evening Standard*, 4 November 2013.

91 Miliband, '2014 Labour Conference Speech'.

92 *Britain Can Be Better*, p. 23.

93 Miliband, '2014 Labour Conference Speech'.

94 Mark Ferguson, 'Cut to the Chase, Ed – and Raise the Minimum Wage to the Living Wage', LabourList, 4 November 2013, http://labourlist.org/2013/11/cut-to-the-chase-ed-and-raise-the-minimum-wage-to-the-living-wage/ (accessed 20 November 2013).

95 Miliband, 'Speech at Senate House'.

96 Ibid.

97 Ed Miliband, 'Speech in Huddersfield', 1 April 2015, http://press.labour.org.uk/post/115200074924/ed-miliband-remarks-zero-hours-contracts (accessed 17 August 2015).

98 Lawton, Cooke, and Pearce, *The Condition of Britain*, p. 53.

99 Ed Miliband, 'Ed Miliband's Speech to Labour Party Conference', 27 September 2011, http://www.labour.org.uk/ed-milibands-speech-to-labour-party-conference (accessed 22 February 2012).

100 Byrne, 'Eliminating "Power Failures"', p. 140.

101 Miliband, 'One Nation Plan'.

102 Ibid.

103 Helm, 'Labour Will Be Tougher'.

104 *Britain Can Be Better*, p. 48.

105 Jon Cruddas, private interview, 4 March 2015.

5

Labour and equality II

Power to the people

I care about inequality of income and opportunity. But I care about something else as well. Inequality of power. Everyone – not just those at the top – should have the chance to shape their own lives.

Ed Miliband[1]

Ed Miliband's egalitarian agenda went beyond considerations about distributive justice. Whilst he believed that redistribution of wealth was an important tool to reduce inequalities he also thought it was not enough. The Labour leader was equally exercised by what he defined as 'inequalities of power', and those could not be addressed by merely tinkering with the tax system or by creating the conditions for a high-wage economy. To address inequalities of power a more ambitious agenda was required. This more ambitious agenda was based on a thicker, though also more ambivalent, concept of equality.

This agenda was a key component of Milibandism, however it received scarce attention in the first years of his leadership. Certainly, he made a few references to it in some speeches, but it was always in a piecemeal and discreet fashion. It was only in 2014 that this agenda began to be fleshed out. By then, the sceptics within the party reluctantly accepted some of its policy implications. Moreover, the political dynamic unleashed by the campaign for the referendum on Scottish independence created space for this agenda.

As we saw in the previous chapter, Miliband's egalitarian and emancipatory agenda was characterised by a commitment to wealth redistribution and pre-distributive measures, but given that he did not think these measures were sufficient to deliver real equality of opportunity, his approach entailed as well a commitment to citizens' empowerment, democratic renewal, and a programme of power devolution from the State to citizens. The party's democratic renewal agenda was thus composed of four main strands: (1) devolution of power to local authorities; (2) a reform of public services based on ideas about relational equality and the relational State; (3) the promotion of movement politics and; (4) political reforms aimed at increasing the transparency, democratic accountability, and accessibility of representative institutions.

In order to understand fully Miliband's 'power to the people' agenda, this chapter starts by mapping the different cognitive and normative ideas and intellectual traditions that were discussed at the policy level and that influenced the party's agenda. Second, it outlines how these ideas permeated Miliband's narrative, how they were communicated to the public, and how they were transformed into policy proposals. Along the way, the chapter discusses the context whereby these ideas evolved, and identifies the political and institutional constraints Miliband and his team encountered that help to explain the party's policy proposals. The remaining sections of the chapter focus on analysing how these ideas influenced the party's policy proposals for a 'power to the people' agenda.

Context

Ed Miliband's programme of democratic renewal only became apparent after he delivered the 2014 Hugo Young Annual Lecture. In speeches delivered during the leadership campaign and afterwards he certainly addressed many aspects of this agenda; however, he did it in a haphazard manner. The reason for this neglect was the absence of a congenial setting for the promotion of these ideas. The party was mostly focused on developing a credible economic programme, and given Labour's difficulties in developing it there was little appetite within the party for political reforms. Moreover, the party was divided, and as a result the relevant factions had to be persuaded about the necessity of such an agenda. Finally, Miliband himself was for a long time undecided. If intuitively he agreed with some of its assumptions, he did not feel the same enthusiasm for it as the chair of the party's Policy Review, Jon Cruddas, or his speech-writer, adviser, and friend, Marc Stears.

For these reasons, it can be argued that there were no immediate political triggers for the development of this agenda. Indeed, many in the party believed that there were 'no votes' to be won with the 'power to the people' agenda, though it was abundantly clear, at least since the MPs' expenses scandal of 2009, that there was a widening chasm between the political elites and voters, and that there was growing popular discontent with Westminster politics. The Occupy movements of 2009–10, the student protests in 2010, and the different grassroots campaigns against austerity showed as well that there was an appetite, especially amongst the young, for more transparent, horizontal, and participatory forms of politics. But it was only in the spring of 2014 that Miliband secured the support of key Labour frontbenchers for the main planks of the 'people's power' agenda, and in particular to develop and promote his ideas about devolution of power from Westminster to English cities and towns. It was only then that he abandoned his earlier reluctance to embrace it.

By then, and partly thanks to the Scottish independence referendum campaign, this agenda gained a momentum of its own.

Ideas: old and new

The 2014 Hugo Young Lecture offered Miliband an opportunity to outline his approach to the State and articulate his vision on political and democratic reforms. His focus on unaccountable power, the unresponsive State, movement politics, and the crisis in politics reflected debates that took place within Blue Labour circles and the think-tank IPPR, and to a smaller extent within the Progress party group. These different debating circles did not work in isolation. Indeed, there was substantial dialogue and overlap between them. In addition, Marc Stears and Jon Cruddas – key figures in Miliband's team – provided points of contact between these two epistemic communities, as well with other party traditions. For instance, Marc Stears contributed to the debates surrounding Blue Labour, and to those about relational equality and the relational State at the IPPR, whereas Jon Cruddas was closer to the Blue Labour circles, but he nonetheless claimed to be inspired by the Brazilian political theorist Roberto Mangabeira Unger, who visited Britain at the invitation of the IPPR. Along the way, other ideas, such as Paul Hirst's associational democracy, Roberto Unger's concept of deep freedom, E. P. Thompson's celebration of ordinary workers' contribution to progressive causes, and Elizabeth S. Anderson's concept of relational equality (discussed in the previous chapter) contributed to these discussions. Some of the debates culminated in concrete policy proposals whilst others just provided an intellectual and political backdrop that helped to agenda-set certain themes and policy ideas.

The Blue Labour grouping which was so influential in the first years of Miliband's leadership certainly falls into the latter category. As discussed in previous chapters, the Blue Labour debates offered a cogent analytical framework to many of the policy puzzles Labour had to tackle, such as the global financial crisis or immigration. And though the Blue Labour project was at some point disowned by some Labour figures it continued to provide 'mood-music' to the Miliband project.

Blue Labour emerged as a reaction against the social democratic accommodation of neoliberalism, but it was equally concerned with the centralising and unresponsive traditions of New Labour's statecraft, and sought to revive Labour's older traditions of mutualism, pluralism, and guild socialism.[2] Out of this critique Blue Labour developed a political vision based around ideas of organic models of democracy, but also around ideas about belonging and reciprocity. The focus of Blue Labour was then on nurturing a democratic culture and praxis. Maurice Glasman, the central figure of Blue Labour, argued that its purpose was to remind 'the party that only democratic association can resist the power of capital and that the distinctive practices of the Labour movement are built upon reciprocity, mutuality and solidarity'.[3] In a clear reference to the tradition of guild socialism and also to Thompson's account of how progressive causes relied on the dissenting and campaigning activities of the English working class, Glasman contended that Labour politics was 'rooted in the democratic resistance to the commodification of human beings'.[4] Glasman claimed that Labour had to 'build a politics of the common good by returning citizenship to all our cities, re-establishing guildhalls, and restoring institutions of vocational self-regulation within them'.[5] Similarly, Jonathan Rutherford argued that 'relationships must be at the heart of Labour's revival'.[6] The most concrete policy idea that Blue Labour proposed was the promotion of movement politics as it was practised by grassroots associations, such as Citizens UK with their campaign for the living wage.

Whilst Blue Labour linked this focus on democracy to the historical roots of the party – and in particular to its culture of dissent and democratic radicalism – it distanced itself from the post-1945 Labour Party. This emphasis on building 'relational power' could also be seen, as Stuart White argued, as an attempt to renew 'the left as a pluralistic, coalitional force'.[7] However, by emphasising 'relational power' Blue Labour attacked the Labour Party's traditional statecraft, which was deemed authoritarian, unresponsive, and ineffective. Blue Labour's references to the State, and even to the Labour legacy of 1945, were, at best, dismissive. Most were highly critical of the 'bureaucratic beast' Labour had created.

But despite the attack on Labour's traditional statecraft, Blue Labour failed to offer a credible account of the State. It limited itself to critiquing Labour's traditional statecraft but did not offer a vision of what the role of the State would amount to in their idealised Labour Government. Blue Labour thinkers seemed to believe that organic community life would take over the responsibilities of the State. Underpinning Blue Labour's critical take on the State was a somewhat romantic belief that workers' rights, free health care, and education could all be protected and managed by the sheer efforts of local communities and citizens' engagement (and almost as Thompson had described in *The Making of the English Working Class*).[8]

By contrast, the debate about the relational State, promoted by the IPPR in several pamphlets and in the 2014 book *The Condition of Britain: Strategies for Social Renewal*, was at the same time more layered and more concrete, in terms of policy discussions and proposals. It was also more technocratic, and as such, its audience was composed mostly of policy-makers and academics. Nonetheless, it was extremely influential. Its starting point was a desire to seek 'a society in which people relate to each other as free and equal citizens, and in which unjust social hierarchies of power, esteem and standing are progressively overcome'.[9]

The enactment of this vision implied a new approach to the State and to public services delivery that contrasted with New Labour. Indeed, the starting point of the 'relational State' agenda was a critique of New Public Management (NPM), which had been embraced by New Labour.[10] For the advocates of the relational State, NPM delivered worse public services and resulted in higher costs for the tax-payer. Geoff Mulgan, who worked in Downing Street during the Blair years, and who was now one of the strongest advocates of the relational State, admitted as much. 'Even if the targets were met they often "missed the point", not connecting to the things the public actually value', he argued.[11]

In general terms, ideas about the relational State emphasised the need to develop relations and downplayed the transactional aspects of public services delivery that were associated with the 'choice' agenda espoused by New Labour. Thus, and as the columnist and keen observer of 'Milibandism' Rafael Behr explained, ' "relational" thinking put the emphasis on building institutions, integrating services, pooling resources and deploying professionals at a local level across different areas and in collaboration with charities and volunteers'.[12] The purpose was then to empower public service users, by giving them access to information and a voice, by changing the focus to prevention and by insisting on shared responsibility with providers of public services. The relational State also promised to demonstrate fiscal responsibility by producing savings in public spending. As Graeme Cooke and Rick Muir argued, the relational State would drive costs down because 'local, flexible decision-making will be more capable of adapting to particular circumstances, avoiding waste and driving innovation, while opening up the space to make logical spending switches, such as towards low-cost preventative measures in healthcare'.[13] From these general premises the relational State could then follow different paths. In Labour circles the debate polarised around two main conceptions. Whilst one, espoused by Geoff Mulgan, still relied on State power to deliver egalitarian aims, the other, articulated by Marc Stears, was far more critical of the State, less concerned with its potential unequal outcomes, and more interested in promoting individual autonomy.

Mulgan saw the relational State as an answer to the problems of trust, legitimacy, and public value that affected the quality of the State's relationships with the public.[14] He viewed relationships as a goal to be promoted alongside others such as better public health, a stronger economy, less crime, and so on. Consequently, Mulgan's approach argued for a State that was more responsive to citizens' personal needs and that governed with the people, but that would still play a central role in policy-making. Perhaps reflecting his experiences as a policy-maker, he argued that there were limits to the relational State. For instance, he argued that the relational State could not be developed in defence policy. He also said that there was still room for a State that does things to and for the people, because 'nearly as bad as a government that never listens is a government that is addicted to conversation'.[15]

By contrast, Stears was sceptical about the relational State and argued instead for a State that supported relationships. For him, the relational State was not sufficiently empowering because its approach was still too top-down, uniform, and standardised, and it still treated citizens as 'passive players'.[16] In its place, Stears called for a State that enabled citizens to relate more effectively to each other and that treated those relationships as an end in itself: 'There are also ways in which the state can play an active part in shaping the conditions in which a more relational culture can flourish, by doing what it can to help provide the places, time, organisation and power that people need – and then stepping away'.[17]

For Stears the nurturing of relationships offered as well 'the right response to the power of capitalism'. As he explained: 'It is what Labour used to call "combination" that potentially makes the difference, with people coming together to identify shared concerns and building a movement of solidarity through which they seek to face down the gravest of all evils that rampant capitalism places on them.'[18] He also saw relationships as part of the process of achieving other goals. 'It reminds us that we cannot have equality, social justice and human rights simply provided for us by someone else. Those crucial goals require us, the citizens, to be part of the process by which they are created', he argued.[19] Taking this argument to its full conclusion, he accepted the contingency of those democratic relationships. In other words, as Cooke and Muir argued, the destination of politics could not be prescribed by a central authority but should be 'constantly' contested through an active relational life'.[20]

The implication of this was that for Stears the central role of a centre-left Government was to foster a democratic culture.[21] In particular, he argued that Labour needed to recognise that the immediate task was 'to help release the relational capacity of its own party members, supporters, and the broader citizenry'.[22] Interestingly, Stears suggested that the political leader who wished to promote relations should adopt a different political language. Instead of speaking in universal and abstract terms about their values and aims, political leaders 'need to find a language that is rich in respect – or even better, love – for the actual relational strengths of the British people, be they grounded in traditions, stories, or places'.[23] This meant that the political narratives developed by politicians should make 'concrete references to real people, places and actions'.[24]

The debate between Mulgan and Stears highlighted the different possibilities of the relational State but it also identified the tension among the concepts of equality, liberty, and localism.[25] This tension pointed to the different positions within Labour circles concerning the ends and means of social democracy, and how the values of equality, liberty, and democracy should be articulated and prioritised. However, these tensions should not be overemphasised. Indeed, the subsequent debate focused on the overlapping areas between these two approaches. In particular, it concentrated on the shortcomings of the over-centralised and unresponsive State, and it argued for the development of a public sector reform agenda that devolved power from the centre to local communities and to citizens.[26] This would be done in two ways: public services providers would gain greater control over budgets, and citizens would be given the choice to purchase the public services they desired.

These concrete proposals to devolve power to communities and citizens have a strong genealogy. Most recently they are directly related to Paul Hirst's associational democracy ideas, with which they share their premises. In Hirst's formulation, associational democracy starts as a criticism of market values and of State centralism, and defends the position that the 'organization of social affairs should as far as possible be transferred from the state to voluntary and democratically self-governing associations'.[27] In other words, political authority should be decentralised, whereas the social functions of the State should be devolved to voluntary associations. Likewise, the 'deep freedom' concept of Roberto Unger – a much admired author in some Labour circles, especially by Jon Cruddas[28] – overlaps with the relational State's agenda for the devolution of power. His ideas were also present in Stears and Cruddas's promotion of a greater and deeper democratic culture. In Unger's definition, deep freedom meant 'freedom grasped and realised through change of our institutions and practices – not just through a one-time change but through a practice that can generate future, ongoing changes in the institutional order of society'.[29] In concrete terms, a politics of deep freedom would promote constitutional and political reforms that would exploit the potential of further decentralisation of power, and would incorporate features of direct and horizontal forms of democracy in representative institutions.

The debate about the shortcomings of the State incorporated as well insights from older Labour traditions such as guild socialism, English pluralism, mutualism, and what Jon Cruddas liked to call the romantic traditions of the Independent Labour Party (ILP) and of the New Left. For instance, the advocates of Blue Labour often quoted R. H. Tawney, G. D. H. Cole, Karl Polanyi, and the New Left tradition (in particular Raymond Williams and E. P. Thompson). Similarly, associational democracy finds some of its roots in the English pluralism of John Neville Figgis and Harold J. Laski, and in guild socialism. In addition, two key figures in Team Miliband – Marc Stears and Jon Cruddas – referenced this lineage but placed special emphasis on different authors and movements. Whereas Stears paid particular attention to guild socialists such as Cole, Cruddas referenced the tradition of the ILP (and in particular the legacy of George Lansbury) and that of Tawney.

These disparate intellectual traditions had some common ground – in particular their criticism of Fabian statecraft, which they considered too centralising, top-down, and stifling of democratic institutions. They also supported an agenda of radical decentralisation of the economy and of the political system, participatory democracy, and horizontal decision-making processes. But as Patrick Diamond rightly observed, historically these traditions had little resonance within the labour movement.[30] David Marquand concurred, but with one subtle qualification. He argued that 'Guild Socialist theories matter less than the mood and tone of the movement.'[31] In its time, says Marquand, 'Guild Socialism was a cry of revolt – against capitalism, of course – but also against bureaucracy, subordination and unaccountable power.'[32]

It is precisely a cry of revolt that current Labour references to guild socialism invoke. This modern cry of revolt has two main targets linked to the New Labour years, namely the crisis of market capitalism and the unresponsive State. Marc Stears justified the rationale of reviving these traditions exactly in those terms. 'There is a democratic deficit in the state and in the market in recent years and one of the things that we've been thinking about is how to address both', he claimed.[33] Guild socialism has also enabled some figures within the current Labour Party to promote an agenda of democratic renewal.

Interestingly, the current use of the tradition of guild socialism also reflected its inherent tensions, in particular the tensions between equality and freedom. In his study of Labour's concept of equality, Ben Jackson argued that Cole's critique of Fabianism meant that his proposals for a radically democratic guild socialism 'side-stepped distributive questions and focused instead on inequalities in power as the principal theoretical division between his pluralism and what he saw as Fabian statism'.[34] This very same tension is present in Stears, Cruddas, and Unger's prioritisation of freedom over equality. Stears framed this criticism in terms of a dichotomy between those, like the Fabians and New Labour, who promoted equality through the centralised and standardising State and at the expense of democracy, and the tradition of guild socialism, which argued that it was not the role of the State to tell people how they should live their lives. This did not mean that Stears dismissed equality but simply that he placed a greater emphasis on the value of individual autonomy and democracy (as a means to empowering individuals to lead the lives they want) and on emancipation rather than on socio-economic outcomes. Echoing Elizabeth Anderson's concept of 'relational equality' (discussed in the previous chapter), he defined his approach as 'active equality', which he described as a 'form of equality that is more comfortable with decentralisation and democratisation, even contingency and chance'.[35] That implied that truly democratic politics was 'an open-ended politics, and therefore a truly democratic pursuit of equality had to be an open-ended pursuit as well'.[36] Thus, for Stears, there was no trade-off between equality and democracy – but it required the selection of a different conception of equality. For him, treating people as equals meant 'allowing them the opportunity to enjoy an "active equality"' and 'welcoming them as part of the process itself'.[37]

The legacy of the ILP was another older Labour tradition quoted by figures close to Ed Miliband that was related to the agenda of democratic renewal. The traditions of the ILP enabled Labour to promote organic styles of democracy and community politics but also to fight the bureaucratic State. Jon Cruddas's engagement with this tradition was more about capturing a mood and an attitude than about endorsing a specific policy toolbox. For Cruddas, 'the great pioneers of Labour – Lansbury, Attlee – all came out of a specific tradition that was anti-centralist, utopian'.[38] This working-class, romantic form of the Labour tradition, as he put it, interested him because it represented 'what socialism was about'. This tradition was interested in 'questions of industrial democracy, and in how people lived full and rewarding lives rather than simply skimming a bit of money off the top ... questions about a deeper sense of fulfillment rather than just subsistence'.[39] This sentiment was reflected in many of Cruddas's writings and speeches.[40]

Mutualism was also quoted by Labour backbenchers and thinkers as a tradition that offered solutions to the economic crisis and to rising inequalities. Regarding public services, Labour figures such as Patrick Diamond and Tristram Hunt were advocates of 'social mutualism'. This form of mutualism involved an 'approach to the organisation and delivery of public services, where both employees and those using public services could acquire greater control over their management and operation',[41] but it also implied 'an ethos of shared responsibility which encourages autonomy and self-reliance'.[42] According to Tristram Hunt, the mutualist and cooperative approach could give citizens 'a real voice in deciding how those services should be run'.[43]

These debates across different groupings in the Labour Party, which incorporated new and old ideas, found some resonance in Miliband's narrative. Many of the themes (such as power distribution) and policy ideas (for instance, the relational State) were referenced in his speeches, provided justifications for specific courses of action, and on some occasions informed new policy approaches. Above all, they signalled a willingness by the party's leadership to address the shortcomings of the market economy and of the unresponsive State not only via active economic redistribution but also through citizen empowerment, power devolution, democratic renewal, and State reform. The tensions underlying these debates were also reproduced by the Labour elite. Indeed, if there was a genuine attempt to devolve powers to citizens there was also a strong attachment to the idea of an active and powerful State.

Miliband's vision

The living wage campaign became symbolic of the values and themes Ed Miliband wanted to prioritise. In particular, it signalled his concern with rising social inequalities and with the plight of the low-paid, and it reflected his vision of Labour as a party of workers, but it also pointed to his interests in deeper forms of democracy and in particular in movement politics. For example, in a speech delivered during the leadership campaign, Miliband referred to the living wage campaign as an example of the kind of political change he wanted to bring about to the Labour Party. 'It is this kind of movement we need: bringing Labour Party members, trade unionists, but also those interested in the environment, young people – all people who share our values', he said.[44]

In his first speech as Labour leader, Ed Miliband devoted some time to outlining his ideas on political reform, and he identified the main themes that later on were developed and transformed into policy proposals. He also spoke about broken politics and identified a number of ways whereby citizens' trust in politics could be restored. For instance, he argued for public services reform, because 'unless reformed, unless accountable, unless responsive, government can impede the good society'.[45] A few months later, in a speech to the Fabian Society, he lamented that in the New Labour era the party 'lost sight of people as individuals, and of the importance of communities', and claimed he wanted to correct that. In particular he said he would like to revive the party's 'alternative strand', which 'saw Labour as a grass-roots, democratic movement to enable people to lead the most fulfilling lives'.[46]

He talked as well about the need to promote a new democratic culture by devolving power to local authorities, the Scottish Parliament, and the Welsh and Northern Irish assemblies.[47] He supported the reform of the House of Commons, electoral reform, the democratisation of the House of Lords and its transformation into a Senate of the Nations and Regions,[48] and the codification of the constitution, and he called for the creation of a democratic constitutional convention. This agenda appealed to several figures in the party, namely to those backbenchers and peers who were closer to Blue Labour, and to those who were keen to revive the localist traditions of guild socialism and mutualism. Figures such as Lord Adonis, John Denham, Liz Kendall, Steve Reed, Hilary Benn, Jon Cruddas, Stella Creasy, Lisa Nandy, and Rowenna Davis were enthusiastic in their endorsement of this agenda.

But there was also strong opposition to it. As a result, this aspect of Miliband's vision was often overlooked because, though he was interested in it, he was reluctant to push it through. Deeper democracy and the reform of public services were not issues that commanded widespread support within the party, in particular within the shadow cabinet. Many thought this was an issue that did not interest the electorate, which was far more worried with falling living standards and immigration, whilst others were more concerned with Labour's reputation as anti-business.

In short, there were serious disagreements about the desirability of this agenda. The left disliked Miliband's critique of Labour's traditional statecraft and saw this agenda as stealth Blairism and back-door privatisation.[49] However, the resistance coming from the shadow cabinet was of a different nature. According to Jon Cruddas, some members of the shadow cabinet 'were fiercely against the notion of devolution of power' and believed in the efficacy of the Westminster model of government.[50] Cruddas explained the party's resistance to these ideas on the grounds that they were somehow 'alien' to Labour: 'Issues of democracy are alien to the party in many respects because partly we're so Westminster focused, partly because of the command and control machine that Blair built which was very effective for quite a long time at winning elections; but there was a cost to that in terms of the essential nature of it, the texture of the political party, its vibrancy.'[51] Cruddas framed this debate in terms of disagreement between radical reformers and those who applied a 'safety first' approach to Labour's electoral strategy.[52] He claimed that there was a generation of Labour backbenchers who used to be policy advisers and who were intellectually anchored to New Labour's 'revisionism', but for whom it was difficult to 'change lanes intellectually in that process'.[53]

The greatest resistance came from the shadow chancellor, Ed Balls.[54] Reflecting his experience in the Treasury and his closeness to Gordon Brown, Balls was seen as a natural centraliser. In particular, he seemed to support the view that the Treasury should be the controlling department in the machinery of government. But Balls was not the only Labour figure who had reservations about this agenda. Miliband was also undecided. Though he agreed with the diagnosis he was ambivalent about the prescription. Like Balls, his experience in government led him to believe in the ability of the levers of the State to deliver progressive outcomes. Indeed, it was this resistance that led a group of representatives of a 'progressive community' (which included organisations such as Compass, Policy Network, the Fabian Society, LabourList, and Progress, amongst many others) to publish a letter in the *Guardian* urging Labour to endorse the power devolution agenda developed by Cruddas.[55]

As a result of party opposition and of his own ambivalence, Miliband devoted few speeches to this theme, and when he did, his comments tended to be fairly general and brief. Hence, it was difficult to identify an overall and coherent vision on political reform and democratic renewal. It was only from the spring of 2014 that this commitment to power devolution and to the reform of public services became important items on Miliband's agenda of political change. These were also the most developed ideas of the party's 'power to the people' agenda.

The chair of the Policy Review, Jon Cruddas, is credited for having convinced Miliband to endorse this agenda. But the same can be said about Marc Stears who (as it was shown earlier) was a strong advocate of deepening democracy and of movement politics, and whose language and ideas peppered Miliband's narrative and justifications for policy proposals. It is noteworthy that in the 2014 Hugo Young Annual Lecture, Miliband quoted the exact same Walt Whitman poem – 'The Prairie Grass Dividing' – that Stears used to explain his conception of equal worth.[56] Their influence is also visible in Labour's 2015 electoral manifesto. Indeed, Labour's manifesto starts by lamenting the fact that 'Too much power is unaccountable, concentrated in the market and the state, at the expense of individuals and their communities', and by stating that Labour's 'governing mission is to break out of the traditional top-down, "Westminster knows best approach", and devolve power and decision-making to people and their local communities'.[57]

The main focus of Miliband's 'power to the people' agenda was Labour's approach to the State. He was critical of New Labour's top-down approach and was equally exercised by what he called the 'crisis of legitimacy' facing Britain's political system, which manifested itself in falling turnouts; declining party memberships; public anger over the MPs' expenses scandal; and the rise of populist parties such as UKIP, which relied on an anti-Westminster platform. To address these problems he promised to reform political institutions. However, he also argued that reform had to come from the grassroots. According to him, 'the only way we can rebuild the case for politics is from the ground up. The campaign for the local library, the local zebra crossing, the improvement of a school, must be our campaign.'[58]

This analysis resulted, then, in a four-pronged programme. The most important component was the plan to devolve power from central government to local authorities. Second, Labour proposed public sector reforms based on the ideas of relations, responsibility, transparency, and reciprocity. But there were other components that complemented this agenda, though not in a coherent manner. The third was the promotion of movement politics within the party and across the country. The fourth was about political and constitutional reforms designed to deliver greater transparency and accountability, and to strengthen representative institutions.

Power devolution

The most ambitious and developed policy proposals put forward by Labour were the plans to devolve fiscal powers to English local authorities in the areas of transport, housing, skills, planning, health and social care, employment, and economic development, drafted by Lord Adonis. The rationale for such a proposal was, in the words of Cruddas and Nandy, to allow communities to 'have a say in how money is spent in their area, define their own problems, and find their own solutions and work together to set the agenda'.[59] But Labour was not a trailblazer in this area of public policy. Indeed, Lord Adonis acknowledged that Michael Heseltine's 2013 proposals for regional growth influenced his review. In addition, the parties of the Coalition developed and implemented similar proposals.

Under Labour proposals, the Treasury would give further funds to local authorities and to Local Enterprise Partnerships to invest and manage their own programmes of regional development. Labour plans would give local councils new powers on welfare policy, apprenticeships, and housing. The rationale for such a change was that 'devolving power from Whitehall to our towns and cities is essential to generate the new jobs we need', and also to rebuild the middle class.[60] Labour's plans for power devolution were also justified on cost-effectiveness grounds. Labour argued that devolution would reduce duplication and waste in the delivery of public services and therefore would result in greater Government savings, though how much the Government would be able to save was far from clear.

But Miliband's plans for devolution of power reflected his own ambivalence towards 'people power', as well as the compromises he had to strike with Labour figures like Balls, who opposed the marginalisation of the Treasury. As a result, Labour's plans amounted to a power give-away to local authorities that would be tightly controlled by Whitehall. Under Labour's plans, local authorities would only win a 'devolution deal' if their plans for job creation met Whitehall-set targets. In addition, Labour did not propose to give new fiscal powers to local authorities. For the more radical power decentralisers in the party these proposals amounted to very little. A group of north-eastern Labour MPs attacked the proposals on the grounds that they 'lack[ed] vision and ambition'.[61]

But if these proposals did little to address the imbalances in economic development across the English regions, they did even less to address the problems created by the asymmetric devolution settlements affecting Scotland, Wales, and Northern Ireland. In the wake of the referendum on Scottish independence in September 2014, it soon became apparent that these proposals did not go far enough. The political forces unleashed by the campaign for the referendum on Scottish independence forced the main Westminster parties to concentrate on policy areas that thus far they had considered unimportant because it was assumed that there were no votes in them. But suddenly, furthering the devolution settlement in Scotland and Wales and addressing the West Lothian Question were brought to the top of the political agenda, and Labour found itself on the defensive.

Instead of leading the debate, Labour was responding to it. To convince Scottish voters to remain within the union, Labour proposed new powers for the Scottish Parliament. In particular, the party proposed new powers on employment policy, social care, housing, infrastructure, and land use. But Labour's proposals for fiscal devolution did not go as far as those of the Conservative Party and the Liberal Democrats. Indeed, both the Conservatives and the Liberal Democrats proposed full fiscal powers, whereas Labour only proposed the partial devolution of income tax to the Holyrood Parliament.

Labour's promises to give more powers to the Scottish Parliament only highlighted the imbalances of the devolution settlement. Consequently, the debate spilled over to other constitutional matters: in particular to the English Question and to the potential devolution to English regions, cities and towns. Here, Labour was on the defensive again. Whilst the Conservative Party quickly reclaimed the initiative by proposing English-votes-for-English-laws as a solution to the old West Lothian Question, Labour had nothing to offer apart from opposition to the Conservative plans, though the 2015 electoral manifesto promised 'to consider how English MPs can have a greater role in the scrutiny of legislation that only affects England' and in particular the proposal of developing a 'committee stage made up of English-only MPs'.[62] Miliband's proposal to hold a democratic constitutional convention[63] to deliberate on a wide range of constitutional matters, including plans for further English devolution, seemed sensible enough; however, it also contributed to the perception that the party had little to say on those matters.

The relational State

In parallel with proposals for greater power devolution across the United Kingdom, Labour developed plans to reform public services. Reflecting the tone of the debate between Blue Labour circles and the advocates of the 'relational State' and mutualism, Miliband's plans to reform public services stemmed from a critique of the State, which he believed to be too centralised, managerial, and unresponsive. In a direct reference to Richard Sennett's book *Respect*, he characterised the current culture in public services delivery as a 'compassion that wounds'.[64] This critique of the State would not be misplaced in Blairite circles, but in contrast with New Labour, Miliband did not view the market as the solution to better public services. For him the market logic was 'flawed' because often the proposed 'choice' was illusory and wholly inadequate to apply to the delivery of public services. Consequently, his plans for public sector reform aimed to bring a new culture centred on the values of voice, equality, accountability, and reciprocity.

According to Miliband, this new culture would not be an 'old-style, top-down central control, with users as passive recipients of services', nor defined by a 'market-based individualism', but about putting 'more power in the hands of patients, parents and all the users of services'.[65] In other words, public services, and in particular health care, social care, and education, would be tailored around people's needs. A key component of this empowering agenda was the proposal to grant individuals greater access to information and ownership of personal data, and devolution of power to local communities.

Miliband's proposals outlined in the 2015 manifesto were influenced by the ideas promoted by the IPPR and by the innovative cooperative model of public service delivery used in Labour-led councils such as Lambeth, Oldham, Sunderland, Newcastle, Plymouth, Rochdale, and several others. Indeed, Lambeth Council has promoted deeper civic engagement in a range of activities – from public gardening to youth church groups – and has used the cooperative model in the delivery of youth services. Similarly, the council of Rochdale introduced the principles of mutualism to its housing services. Different experiments in deliberative polling and participatory budgeting were also identified as models to follow. For instance, Jon Cruddas talked about a deliberative poll in a town in Essex and participatory budgeting in Durham[66] as examples of a new approach to policy-making that involved people in decisions.[67] But perhaps aware that the language of the 'relational State' was more suited to think-tank seminars than to the door-step, the Labour leader defined this agenda as 'people-powered public services'.

In terms of policies, the ideas about the relational State were visible in the proposals to adopt personal budgets in the areas of health care, education, mental health, and social care. Andy Burnham's proposals to integrate health and social care were another example of this approach to public service delivery. As Miliband put it, the purpose of these reforms was 'to drive power down' because citizens 'want more control over their lives'.[68]

Miliband's ideas represent an interesting synthesis of the relational State debate. If the rationale and rhetorical style (in particular Miliband's tendency to quote real people in his speeches) reflect the influence of Marc Stears, the policy solutions are closer to Mulgan's approach to the relational State. This should not come as a surprise. Stears himself acknowledged that when he explained Miliband's experience in government. According to him, the Labour leader 'appreciated the intricacies of the tax-benefit system and always evinced a faith that the cause of social equality could at least partially be progressed through effective administration'.[69] This faith in the State implied that 'the instinctive democratic capacities of his youth did not find a natural outlet in such a role'.[70]

Alongside ideological and theoretical considerations and aspirations, the relational State also aimed to provide an answer to the fiscal challenges of the State in a post-recession scenario. According to its advocates, the devolution of power would put an end – in the Jon Cruddas sentence that all Labour figures repeated – to 'the salami slicing of public spending' and to the overlapping and duplication of services. This pooling of resources, alongside a strategy focused on prevention, would result in savings to the public purse.[71] Equally, Liz Kendall and Steve Reed (who pioneered the cooperative model in the Lambeth Council) argued that more public spending in public services did not always translate into better public services. By contrast, savings could be achieved if the focus were on prevention and also on a model of public service delivery built around 'a new relationship of cooperation between service providers and service users'.[72]

These proposals were innovative and seemed to challenge the authoritarian and homogeneous ethos of public service delivery; however, it was not entirely clear how they would challenge NPM. Private companies –and many for-profit companies – were involved in the delivery of public services, in particular in the areas of education, health care and social care, and expected to make profits. More importantly, market approaches to public services delivery are not necessarily compatible with relational services that are based on ideas of cooperation (the current crisis in the delivery of social care is a very good example of the tension between the two models).

The party's rhetoric on this issue was robustly anti-privatisation of public services. In its electoral manifesto, Labour promised to 'end the wasteful and poorly performing Free Schools programme', but its most ambitious proposals concerned the NHS. For instance, when Andy Burnham presented his proposals for the integration of health and social care he warned against what he called 'the Tory market experiment in the NHS'. He argued that if market forces were allowed 'to continue to take hold, they will eventually break the NHS apart'.[73] Similarly, Ed Miliband pledged that under a Labour Government the NHS would be managed around the values of 'care, compassion and co-operation', and 'Not competition, fragmentation and privatisation'.[74]

Moreover, Labour proposed two new rules of engagement for the private-sector providers of public services. The first was a rule about procurement according to which private-sector providers would be required to comply with 'a public good' criterion.[75] The second was announced by Miliband in the party's electoral campaign launch and was about introducing a cap on the profits that private health companies could make on delivering health care.[76] Finally, Labour's electoral manifesto made a commitment to repeal the Health and Social Care Act, introduced by the Coalition Government, and to ensure that the NHS would be protected from the Transatlantic Trade and Investment Partnership Treaty (TTIP).

However, Labour's radical plans to reform public services only seemed to apply to health and social care and to free schools. Regarding other areas of public services Labour's plans were undeveloped. Indeed, Miliband refrained from defending the nationalisation of the railways (though Labour's proposals on public procurement left that option open), and was silent on the continued use of Public Private

Partnerships in public services delivery and on the programme of Academies for secondary schools.

Movement politics

The proposals to devolve power and to reform public services around ideas about the relational State and localism were part of a larger programme of democratic renewal that included as well plans to empower citizens and to promote 'movement politics'. During Labour's leadership campaign David Miliband was the champion of 'movement politics'. His 'Movement for Change', developed by Citizens UK, galvanised young supporters and seemed to offer a new model of party organisation based on relational principles but also on the methodologies of the American legendary community organiser Saul Alinsky. Moreover, Barack Obama's success in mobilising youth support, and raising funds through grassroots organisations during the 2008 presidential campaign, showed what could be done in terms of youth mobilisation. In a Fabian Society pamphlet, Will Straw and Nick Anstead called on Labour to learn from Obama's electoral campaign techniques, namely grassroots mobilisation, volunteer management, blogging, fundraising, and use of data. They also argued that the party needed to change its hierarchical culture, to become more tolerant of dissent, and to give organisers the tools to self-organise.[77]

The dynamics of the Occupy movement and the success of the unorthodox, and irreverent methods of the campaign groups UK Uncut and Focus E15 showed that there was an appetite for a type of politics that was less hierarchical and formal and more relational and democratic. Finally, the popularity of the student protest movement, and of campaigns about housing or against the TTIP, also suggested that the politicisation of the younger generations did not follow the traditional party-political route with its left–right alignments. All these factors combined led to a renewed interest in promoting citizen engagement, and in horizontal forms of democracy.

Once elected leader, Ed Miliband tried to bring the culture and methods of Movement for Change to the Labour Party as a way to reverse the trend of declining party membership. He believed that such an approach would attract new members and supporters to the party. Many Labour activists felt that one way of injecting energy and new blood into the party was to support community-based initiatives on issues such as the living wage campaign promoted by Citizens UK. Thus, organisations of this nature were recruited to teach Labour the tools of movement politics. In this area of policy, the influence of Blue Labour was crucial. Maurice Glasman was passionate about community empowerment and was determined to obtain the support of the Labour Party for his ideas. In 2009, Glasman persuaded Ed Miliband to include a commitment to the living wage in Labour's 2010 electoral manifesto.[78]

After the party's leadership election Glasman introduced Miliband to Arnie Graf, the American campaigner who had mentored the young Barack Obama's activist career in Chicago and who was a follower of the campaigning techniques of Saul

Alinsky.[79] Initially, Miliband was very enthusiastic about Graf's involvement in Labour's campaign. He felt that Graf's methods would force Labour to do politics differently by mobilising new supporters.[80] Following this meeting Miliband invited Arnie Graf to conduct a root-and-branch review of the party and to promote 'movement politics' in a way that would improve Labour's chances at the ballot box.

Graf accepted the challenge and was very open about his desire to create a platform for a more open, more relational, and more transparent party. But he encountered formidable obstacles that made his work very difficult. He counted on the support of the Labour leader, Jon Cruddas, Ian McNicol, and Tom Watson, but there was great resistance to his ideas within the party. The main obstacle was Labour's culture, which, according to some activists and supporters, suffered from a democratic deficit. For instance, Jon Cruddas admitted to the party's hierarchical culture, which dictated that in the Labour Party 'the clever people did the policy and the foot-soldiers did the campaigning'.[81] In similar vein, Neal Lawson from Compass argued that the Labour was still a party where members had no say in policy-making and that was closed to outsiders.[82] Lawson's assessment seems to be supported by the evidence. In fact, Labour struggled with a membership of only 190,000 people, who were only called to contribute during electoral campaigns but who were rarely (if ever) consulted on policy. Indeed, Graf reached similar conclusions in his first review of the party. He said that Labour was a party 'that had a bureaucratic culture rather than a relational one'.[83]

To change Labour's culture, Graf proposed new campaign methods that relied on grassroots initiatives and local campaigns on concrete issues, such as pay-day lenders and the living wage. However, several Labour frontbenchers, backbenchers, and activists were sceptical of his innovative methods and considered some of his themes too anti-business. Some Labour figures felt his ideas were not at all suited to a political party. Others did not approve of the cultural change Graf was advocating.[84] For example, Kevin Meagher, writing for Labour Uncut, aptly expressed the resistance felt in some Labour circles towards movement politics: 'There is a level of collective discipline – even bureaucracy – that is needed to manage a political party which is culturally quite different to the freedom in community organisations to decide locally what you want to achieve and how you go about getting it.'[85] Douglas Alexander, who was appointed in late 2013 to organise Labour's electoral campaign, was equally unimpressed by Graf's methods and financial cost to the party, and succeeded in side-lining him.

But if Graf was side-lined by Alexander it is nonetheless clear that he left his imprint on Labour politics. First, he changed the way Miliband campaigned. Instead of relying on traditional campaign methods such as cold-calling and knocking on doors, he started to favour direct contact with voters, such as 'meet-the-people' sessions in town squares.[86] Graf's influence was also felt across the party. Labour's secretary-general, Ian McNicol, promoted these campaign techniques in the different local constituency parties, and those MPs and first-time candidates who were supportive of this agenda were quick to endorse them too. In fact, the 2015 electoral campaign relied on these techniques. A few months before the start of the official campaign, Miliband said that Labour would win the election 'by having millions of conversations'.[87] He went as far as promising to hold four million conversations by polling day, a promise that the party actually delivered.

Finally, Graf's influence was visible in the Collins Review on party reform which was approved in early 2014. In his review of the party, Graf proposed open primaries for the party, as well as the creation of a community membership, which would allow voluntary associations to join as collectives, and the creation of a supporters' network.[88] The changes to the Labour Party proposed by the Collins Review included open primaries to nominate the Labour candidate to the post of London Mayor, as well as the opening of the party to new members and supporters.

On the other hand, Graf's ideas and the Collins Review did not alter the fundamentals of Labour's organisational structures. The changes brought by Miliband did little to open the process of policy-making to the rest of the party. Certainly, the National Policy Forum and the National Executive Committee are consulted and vote on the party's policies. But the process of setting out priorities and developing policy is mostly concentrated in the hands of the leadership. The 2015 electoral manifesto was no exception to this rule. The manifesto is based on the Policy Review led by Jon Cruddas and also by Angela Eagle (who was key to ensuring that party members were actually behind the leader); however, it was drafted by Miliband's office. Jon Cruddas, Marc Stears, and Jonathan Rutherford drafted the manifesto, and then the shadow cabinet amended it and approved it. In short, if Labour seemed eager to attract new supporters and to champion local campaigns, it had done little to ensure that these voices actually influenced the party's policy decisions.

Reforming representative institutions

The least coherent and developed aspect of Labour's proposals for a 'power to the people' agenda were those meant to reform representative institutions. Miliband and Labour figures such as Angela Eagle and Sadiq Khan tried to address what they defined as a 'flatlining democracy',[89] characterised by growing apathy and anti-Westminster feeling; however, Labour's policy proposals to deal with these problems were thin on the ground. Proposals for electoral reform, House of Lords reform, and the codification of the constitution were often discussed, especially in the wake of the referendum on Scottish independence, but they lacked visibility and were short on detail. Above all, Miliband's ideas in this area lacked coherence and they did not have an overarching narrative that united the disparate ideas for reform. Instead, the Labour leader made several proposals – many of them vague – that sought to improve the accountability and transparency of representative institutions, but that were far from offering a definite answer to the policy puzzles they aimed to address.

The most salient idea was the proposal to reform the rules on political party funding. This was a theme Miliband addressed when he became Labour leader and to which he often returned. 'We cannot solve our problems as a country unless we change what is wrong with our politics. And we cannot change what is wrong with our politics unless we change the way it is funded', he said.[90] The goal of taking 'big money out of politics' informed his proposals to cap donations to political parties at £5,000 and to introduce a new cap on campaign spending. However, he had little to say about the State funding of political parties.

Regarding House of Lords reform Miliband proposed the replacement of the House of Lords by a fully elected Senate for the Nations and Regions which would represent the regions of the United Kingdom. Indeed, Miliband's proposals for House of Lords reform sought to kill three birds with one stone, namely completing once and for all the reform of the second chamber of Parliament, solving the West Lothian Question, and also addressing calls for greater recognition of England as a political entity. Similarly, Miliband expressed support for electoral reform; however, following the rejection of the alternative-vote electoral system at the 2011 referendum, he did not flesh out any concrete proposals for the future. The 2015 electoral manifesto did not even consider electoral reform. This was a disappointment to Labour figures who considered electoral reform a crucial component of a democracy-and-citizenship agenda, but the reality was that the party was bitterly divided on the issue.[91]

Instead of electoral reform Miliband promised to lower the voting age to sixteen; to strengthen the powers of scrutiny of select committees; and to change the culture of the House of Commons, in particular the rituals and procedures surrounding Prime Minister's Questions. But none of these proposals was defended with zeal or with a sense that they would serve a greater purpose.

Concluding remarks

At a first glance, Miliband's 'people power' agenda looks like an after-thought. After all, it was only in 2014 that the Labour leader unveiled a fairly articulate agenda that sought to promote a democratic culture empowering citizens and renewing representative institutions. Hitherto, most of his energy had been devoted to developing a credible approach to the economy and to keeping the party united. But in reality, Miliband's team had been working on his 'people power' agenda since the early days of his leadership, and slowly the theme of democratic renewal and power redistribution became an important component of Miliband's agenda. Indeed, it was so important that John McTernan called it the 'third leg of Milibandism'.[92]

Proposals such as the devolution of power to English cities, public services reform around ideas on the relational State, and 'movement politics' had the clear imprint of Marc Stears and Jon Cruddas, but also of Blue Labour and the IPPR. Miliband's 'people power' agenda reflected some wider debates taking place within some Labour circles that sought to revive the traditions and values of mutualism, of guild socialism, and of the New Left, as well as to incorporate new ideas about power redistribution, localism, relational equality, and horizontal forms democracy.

By reviving these traditions, Labour was able to do a number of things. First, it enabled the party to demonstrate loyalty to its ideological roots, in particular to those that gave priority to the values of democracy and pluralism. Second, it enabled Labour to articulate an emancipatory concept of equality that relied on the promotion of organic forms of democracy. Third, it allowed Miliband to develop a critique of New Labour's approach to the State, in particular of its managerial and unresponsive features, and uncritical endorsement of market values.

By embracing this agenda, and in particular the ideas around movement politics, Miliband was also opening the door to collaborations with other political forces, such as grassroots campaigns, charities, and potentially other political parties. But the embrace of pluralism was also an exercise in political realism. With a more volatile electorate, declining party membership, and greater cynicism about politics, the Labour Party was acutely aware (especially following the 2014 local and European Parliament elections) that the days of winning comfortable majorities were gone, perhaps for a very long time. In order to be in government, Labour had to contemplate the possibility of opening dialogues and forming alliances with the Liberal Democrats, the SNP, Plaid Cymru, and potentially the Greens.

The transformation of these ideas into concrete policy proposals was relatively straightforward; however, they were not the easiest or most engaging ideas to promote. If the debates in Labour's policy circles were cogent and marked with a sense of urgency, it was difficult to translate them into a persuasive and comprehensible narrative and policy proposals. It did not help that this was not a policy area that normally galvanises public opinion. There was also a clear gap between the rhetoric about a 'people power' agenda and the modesty of some of its proposals.

As we saw, even Miliband's most ambitious proposals for the devolution of power from Whitehall to English cities and other devolved bodies did not represent the revolution in the devolution of power that he had suggested. In addition, Labour's proposals did not represent a qualitative difference, in terms of decentralisation of power, from those that were put forward by the Coalition Government. Indeed, in an attempt to outbid Labour, the Conservative-led Coalition has proposed the idea of elected Mayors and (without any sense of irony) imposed one in the area of Greater Manchester.

The timidity of Labour's proposals was a reflection of party splits concerning this agenda. As one insider put it, the 'economicist view' within the party, which privileged a minimalist electoral manifesto built around the cost-of-living crisis agenda, had prevailed.[93] But the party's timidity in this area also reflected Miliband's own ambivalence. The Labour leader was sympathetic to this agenda; however, he was too weary of internal opposition to it. He was also hesitant about it. If ideologically he agreed with a 'power to the people' agenda, his experience in government pushed him in a different direction. As Stears admitted, Miliband believed in the ability of State power to change people's lives. Thus, it was only in 2014 that Jon Cruddas was able to persuade the Labour leader to make this agenda a central plank of his programme of government. And he only endorsed it after securing the support of earlier sceptics such as Ed Balls. As a result of Miliband's hesitation and the party's scepticism, Labour's people-power agenda lacked a unifying narrative, and some of its proposals were undeveloped. In addition, this agenda was given very little prominence in Labour's electoral campaign. To use Peter A. Hall's criteria to assess the power of ideas, Labour's ideas were somewhat comprehensible, but some were too abstract or too remote from people's experiences to be fully persuasive.

There were other problems. Labour's ideas to renew democratic institutions were undeveloped. In Labour's policy circles, ideas about democratic culture were discussed in broad and abstract terms. Even after the referendum on Scottish independence, which had been preceded by exciting grassroots debates about constitutional reform, the Labour Party was not able to present an agenda of democratic and institutional renewal. At best, Labour presented a shopping list of ideas, such as lowering the voting age to sixteen, reforming party funding rules, and creating a fully elected Senate. Even in the area of public services reform, which was presented as Miliband's big idea, the proposals for devolving power to local authorities were not fully developed. It was unclear which powers local authorities would gain from central government, and, more importantly, how the 'relational State' would relate to the 'market-driven' areas of the public sector.

On the whole, then, Miliband's 'power to the people' agenda was more symbolic than transformative, given that it followed the gradualist pattern of change ingrained in Whitehall (and in the Labour Party) tradition(s). But the main problem for Labour was that in the wake of the referendum on Scottish independence in September 2014 – which reawakened older constitutional problems such as the English Question – and of the Coalition's power devolution agenda, Labour's proposals looked too timid and defensive.

Notes

1 Ed Miliband, 'The Hugo Young Lecture', LabourList, 10 February 2014, http://labourlist. org/2014/02/ed-milibands/hugo-young-lecture-full-text/ (accessed 15 April 2014).

2 Graeme Coooke, 'New and Blue', in Maurice Glasman, Jonathan Rutherford, Marc Stears, and Stuart White (eds), *The Labour Tradition and the Politics of Paradox* (n.p.: Oxford London Seminars, 2011), pp. 133–139 (p. 133).

3 Maurice Glasman, 'My Blue Labour Vision Can Defeat the Coalition', *Observer*, 24 April 2011.

4 Glasman, 'My Blue Labour Vision'.

5 Maurice Glasman, 'Labour as a Radical Tradition', in Glasman, Rutherford, Stears, and White, *The Labour Tradition*, pp. 14–34 (p. 32).

6 Jonathan Rutherford, 'Three Styles of Modern Leadership', in Glasman, Rutherford, Stears, and White, *The Labour Tradition*, pp. 72–74 (p. 72).

7 Stuart White, 'Blue Labour: A Republican Critique', 8 June 2011, https://www.opendemocracy.net/ourkingdom/stuart-white/blue-labour-republican-critique (accessed 6 August 2015).

8 E. P. Thompson, *The Making of the English Working Class* (London: Penguin, 2013).

9 Kayte Lawton, Graeme Cooke, and Nick Pearce, *The Condition of Britain: Strategies for Social Renewal* (London: IPPR, 2014), p. 11.

10 Graeme Cooke and Rick Muir, 'The Possibilities and Politics of the Relational State', in Graeme Cooke and Rick Muir (eds), *The Relational State: How Recognising the Importance of Human Relationships Could Revolutionise the Role of the State* (London: IPPR, 2012), pp. 3–19 (p. 8).

11 Geoff Mulgan, 'Government with the People: The Outlines of a Relational State', in Cooke and Muir, *The Relational State*, pp. 20–34 (p. 22).

12 Rafael Behr, 'Milibandism's Next Chapter: Reforming the State', *New Statesman*, 7 February 2014.

13 Cooke and Muir, 'The Possibilities and Politics of the Relational State', p. 13.

14 Mulgan, 'Government with the People', p. 22.

15 Mulgan, 'Government with the People', p. 23.

16 Marc Stears, 'The Case for a State that Supports Relationships, Not a Relational State', in Cooke and Muir, *The Relational State*, pp. 35–44 (p. 36).

17 Stears, 'The Case for a State that Supports Relationships', p. 44.

18 Marc Stears, 'Democracy, Leadership and Organising', in Glasman, Rutherford, Stears, and White, *The Labour Tradition*, pp. 57–71 (p. 63).

19 Marc Stears, 'Active Equality: A Democratic Agenda for the British Left', in James Purnell and Graeme Cooke (eds), *We Mean Power: Ideas for the Future of the Left* (London: Demos, 2010), pp. 151–163 (pp. 160–161).

20 Cooke and Muir, 'The Possibilities and Politics of the Relational State', pp. 8–9.

21 Marc Stears, 'In the Battle to Reshape Labour, a New Force Is Emerging', *Liberal Conspiracy*, 13 February 2011, http://www.liberalconspiracy.org/2011/02/13/in-the-battle-to-reshape-labour-a-new-force-is-emerging (accessed 17 June 2013).

22 Stears, 'Democracy, Leadership and Organising', p. 64.

23 Stears, 'Democracy, Leadership and Organising', p. 66.

24 Stears, 'Democracy, Leadership and Organising', p. 67.

25 Cooke and Muir, 'The Possibilities and Politics of the Relational State', p. 9.

26 Cooke and Muir, 'The Possibilities and Politics of the Relational State', p. 12.

27 Paul Hirst, *From Statism to Pluralism* (London: Routledge, 1997), p. 32.

28 Jon Cruddas quotes his conception of 'deep freedom'. And the IPPR invited Unger to talk at an event.

29 Roberto Unger, 'Deep Freedom: Why the Left Should Abandon Equality', *Juncture* 20:4 (Spring 2014): 93–100 (p. 98).

30 Patrick Diamond, *Governing Britain: Power, Politics and the Prime Minister* (London: I.B. Tauris, 2014), p. 69.

31 David Marquand, *Britain since 1918: The Strange Career of British Democracy* (London: Weidenfeld and Nicolson, 2008), p. 71.

32 Marquand, *Britain since 1918*, p. 71.

33 Marc Stears, private interview, 18 June 2013.

34 Ben Jackson, *Equality and the British Left: A Study in Progressive Political Thought, 1900–64* (Manchester: Manchester University Press, 2007), p. 63.

35 Stears, 'Active Equality', p. 159.

36 Stears, 'Active Equality', p. 160.

37 Stears, 'Active Equality', pp. 160–161.

38 Jon Cruddas, private interview, 2 September 2013.

39 Cruddas, private interview, 2 September 2013.

40 Jon Cruddas and Andrea Nahles, *Building the Good Society: The Project of the Democratic Left* (London: Compass, 2009), p. 11.

41 Patrick Diamond, 'Mutualism and Social Democracy', in *What Mutualism Means for Labour: Political Economy and Public Services* (London: Policy Network, 2011), pp. 7–13 (p. 7).

42 Diamond, 'Mutualism and Social Democracy', p. 12.

43 Tristram Hunt, 'Big Society, Big Danger', in *What Mutualism Means for Labour*, pp. 15–25 (p. 22).

44 Ed Miliband, 'A Mandate for Change', 30 August 2010, http://www.labourincoventry.org.uk/index.php?option=com_content&view=article&id (accessed 24 January 2014).

45 Ed Miliband, 'The New Generation: Speech to the 2010 Labour Party Annual Conference', 28 September 2010, www2.labour.org.uk/ed-miliband---a-new-generation,2010-09-28 (accessed 10 January 2012).

46 Ed Miliband, 'Full Transcript: Ed Miliband, Speech to the Fabians', 15 January 2011, http://www.newstatesman.com/blogs/the-staggers/2011/01/labour-government-politics (accessed 12 March 2012).

47 Ed Miliband, 'Devolution Is for Everyone: A No Vote Will Change All of Britain', *Guardian*, 14 September 2014, http://www.theguardian.com/commentisfree/2014/sep/14/scotland-has-shown-change-whole-country (accessed 4 August 2015).

48 Miliband, 'The New Generation'.

49 Rafael Behr, 'Miliband's Sheet Is Still Blank on Public Service Reform', *New Statesman*, 18 December 2013, http://wwwnewstatesman.com/print/politics/2013/12/milibands-sheet-still-blank-public-service-reform (accessed 20 December 2013).

50 Cruddas, private interview, 2 September 2013.

51 Cruddas, private interview, 2 September 2013.

52 Cruddas, private interview, 2 September 2013.

53 Cruddas, private interview, 2 September 2013.

54 Mary Riddell, 'Will Ed Balls Back the Miliband Power Give Away?', *Telegraph* blog, 10 February 2014, http://blogs.telegraph.co.uk/news/maryriddell/100258930/will-ed-balls-back-the-miliband-power-giveway/ (accessed 6 August 2015). See also J. C., 'Labour's Economic Plans: Departmental Determinism', *Economist*, 1 January 2014, http://www.economist.com/blogs/blighty/2014/01/labours-economic-plans (accessed 23 August 2015).

55 Neal Lawson, Patrick Diamond, Anna Coote, Andrew Harrop, David Clark, Mark Ferguson, *et al.*, 'Labour Must Adopt New Principles', *Guardian*, 24 March 2014.

56 This poem was quoted by Marc Stears in one of his contributions to the London/Oxford Seminars; Marc Stears, 'The Radical Potential of Conservatism', in Glasman, Rutherford, Stears, and White, *The Labour Tradition*, pp. 119–121 (pp. 120–121).

57 *Britain Can Be Better: The Labour Party Manifesto 2015* (London: Labour Party, 2015), p. 62.

58 Miliband, 'Speech to the Fabians'.

59 Jon Cruddas and Lisa Nandy, 'Only Labour Can Build the Big Society', *New Statesman*, 9 May 2014.

60 Ed Miliband, 'Ed Miliband's Speech on Tackling the Cost-of-Living Crisis', 8 April 2014, http://press.labour.org.uk/post/82080311502/ed-milibands-speech-on-tackling-the (accessed 8 April 2014).

61 'Labour MPs Revolt over Miliband's Economic Policy', *Northern Echo*, 17 June 2014, http://www.thenorthernecho.co.uk/news/local/northdurham/11281657.Labour_MPs_revolt_over_Miliband_s_economic_policy/ (accessed 23 August 2015).

62 *Britain Can Be Better*, p. 64.

63 Ed Miliband, '2014 Labour Conference Speech', 23 September 2014, http://www.labour.org.uk/blog/entry/2014-labour-conference-speech (accessed 25 September 2014).

64 Miliband, 'The Hugo Young Lecture'.

65 Miliband, 'The Hugo Young Lecture'.

66 Jon Cruddas, 'Power and One Nation, Speech to the NLGN Annual Conference', 12 February 2014, http://www.joncruddas.org.uk/node/595 (accessed 28 August 2014).

67 Jon Cruddas, 'Power and Belonging', Acevo Conference, 7 May 2014 http://www.joncruddas.org.uk/jon-cruddas-mp-power-and-belonging (accessed 28 August 2014).

68 Miliband, 'The Hugo Young Lecture'.

69 Stears, 'The Personal Politics of Ed Miliband', p. 128.

70 Stears, 'The Personal Politics of Ed Miliband', p. 128.

71 As Jon Cruddas put it, 'we will invest to prevent social problems rather than wasting money on reactive high cost services'. Cruddas, 'Power and Belonging'.

72 Liz Kendall and Steve Reed, 'People-Powered Public Services', in John Woodcock and Liz Kendall (eds), *Laying the Foundations for a Labour Century* (London: Policy Network, 2014), pp. 29–34 (p. 31).

73 Andy Burnham, 'Labour's 10-Year Plan for Health and Care', 27 January 2015, http://www.andyburnham.blogspot.co.uk/2015/02/andy-burnham-speech-on-labour's-10-year-plan-for-health-and-care (accessed 20 February 2015).

74 Ed Miliband, 'Ed Miliband Speech on the NHS', 27 January 2015, http://press.labour.org.uk/post/109289243889/ed-miliband-speech-on-the-nhs (accessed 2 February 2015).

75 Jon Cruddas, private interview, 4 March 2015.

76 Ed Miliband, 'Speech Launching Labour's General Election Campaign', 27 March 2015, http://press.labour.org.uk/post/114747701274/ed-miliband-speech-launching-labours-general-election-campaign (accessed 27 March 2015).

77 Will Straw and Nick Anstead, 'Introduction', in Will Straw and Nick Anstead, *The Change We Need* (London: Fabian Society, 2009), pp. 1–5 (pp. 3–4).

78 Rowenna Davis, *Tangled Up in Blue: Blue Labour and the Struggle for Labour's Soul* (London: Ruskin Publishing, 2011), pp. 95–97.

79 Rowenna Davis, 'Arnie Graf: The Man Ed Miliband Asked to Rebuild Labour', *Guardian*, 21 November 2012, http://www.theguardian.com/politics/2012/nov/21/arnie-graf-labour-party-miliband?cat=politics&type=article (accessed 3 August 2015).

80 Mark Ferguson, 'Ed Miliband Interview, Part Two: On Selections, Community Organising and the Future of the Labour Party', LabourList, 1 April 2013, http://labourlist.org/2013/04/ed-miliband-interview-part-two-on-selections-community-organising-and-the-future-of-the-labour-party/ (accessed 3 August 2015).

81 Cruddas, private interview, 2 September 2013.

82 Neal Lawson, private interview, 10 May 2013.

83 Arnie Graf quoted by Davis, 'Arnie Graf'.

84 Davis, 'Arnie Graf'.

85 Kevin Meagher, 'Sorry Arnie, Labour's a Political Party, Not a Community Group', LabourList, 23 April 2013, http://labourlist.org/2013/04/sorry-arnie-labours-a-political-party-not-a-community-group/ (accessed 4 August 2015).

86 Mary Riddell, 'Power to the People', 1 August 2013, *Fabian Review*, http://www.fabians.org.uk/power-to-the-people/ (accessed 6 August 2015).

87 Ed Miliband, 'Ed Miliband Speech in Salford', 5 January 2015, http://press.labour.org.uk/post/107208138389/ed-miliband-speech-in-salford (accessed 1 May 2015).

88 Davis, 'Arnie Graf'.

89 Angela Eagle, 'Why We Need a People's Politics Inquiry', LabourList, 24 April 2013, http://labourlist.org/2013/04/why-we-need-a-peoples-politics-enquiry/ (accessed 27 March 2015).

90 Ed Miliband, 'Taking Big Money out of Politics', 15 April 2012, http://www.labour.org.uk/taking-big-money-out-of-politics,2012-04-05 (accessed 23 May 2012).

91 Jon Cruddas argued that electoral reform should have been part of Labour's manifesto: 'It seems to me that if we are serious about democracy and citizenship and reimagining the State, about giving power back to the people, we should make sure that the way the people vote matters.' Cruddas, private interview, 4 March 2015.

92 John McTernan, 'Ed Miliband's Big, Bold Plan', *The Scotsman*, 13 February 2014.

93 Cruddas, private interview, 4 March 2015.

6

Labour and the politics of belonging

One Nation

Our story, as a party and as a country, is not what we achieved separately but what we achieved together. The story of the Scotsman, the Englishman, and the Welshman is not just the start of a good joke. It is the history of social justice in this country. It was a Scotsman, Keir Hardie, who founded the Labour party a hundred and twelve years ago. An Englishman, Clement Attlee, who led the most successful Labour Government in history. And a Welshman, Nye Bevan, who pioneered that Government's greatest legacy, our National Health Service. These are the achievements of our nations working together.

Ed Miliband[1]

Ed Miliband's One Nation narrative was more than a rhetorical device used to string together the different and apparently disjointed strands of his programme of political change. It also addressed issues related to the politics of belonging – such as the growing popular opposition to immigration and the rise in salience of an English national identity, as well as the ascendancy of UKIP as a party that could destabilise the party system – which Labour could not afford to ignore.

As the meteoric rise of UKIP suggests, these disparate but interrelated factors posed considerable electoral challenges to Labour. Many in the party – and in particular within the Miliband circle – recognised that a considerable number of working-class voters had abandoned Labour and were now voting UKIP. To prevent this from happening the party had to recognise the shortcomings of New Labour's uncritical embrace of globalisation and concomitant support for immigration, and to develop a narrative built around a politics of identity, belonging, and proud patriotism.

However, and like in other policy areas, the party was divided. If some Labour figures, in particular around Blue Labour, wanted to address the 'politics of belonging' head-on, others were deeply sceptical of such a strategy. Historically, Labour avoided patriotic politics as it did not want to be perceived as a parochial, xenophobic, or imperialist party. Moreover, playing the patriotic card was not risk-free. The party relied increasingly on the support of ethnic minorities, of women and of young professionals who felt at ease in an ethnically diverse Britain. Labour could lose the support of these progressive voters to the Greens or the SNP whilst targeting those disillusioned and left-behind Labour voters who were either supporting UKIP or not voting at all. Miliband's One Nation narrative sought to address these concerns but in a manner that reflected the party's traditions of radical patriotism and internationalism.

This chapter explores the different dimensions of Labour's politics of identity and belonging. It starts by contextualising its change of approach. Next, it maps the different normative and cognitive ideas as well as the debates that were taking place in the party at the policy level, and which influenced Miliband's thinking on the matter. The chapter then explains in broad terms Miliband's narrative on the politics of identity and belonging. In order to do so, it reflects how Labour's internal debates in this area – the political context as well as the different ideas discussed in Labour circles – shaped the Labour leader's narrative. The chapter shows how Miliband's narrative on the politics of belonging was transformed into policy proposals in three main strands: (1) immigration, (2) managing diversity, and (3) the English Question. Along the way, it also identifies the main political and institutional constraints Miliband confronted when developing his politics of belonging, and concludes with an assessment of Labour's politics of belonging.

Context

Long before UKIP started to create waves in British politics there was a small group of Labour politicians who had expressed concern with the loss of working-class voters and with the emergence of immigration as an important popular concern. During the 2005 electoral campaign, the Labour MP Margaret Hodge flagged up the salience of immigration as an important issue for her constituents, but at the time the threat Labour feared was the BNP and not UKIP. As the electoral threat posed by the BNP did not materialise in a parliamentary seat in those elections the issue of immigration was henceforth neglected.

But the large influx of Eastern European citizens into Britain following the enlargement of the EU in 2004, as well as the rise of Islamophobia that followed the 2005 London terrorist attacks, brought back this issue to the political centre stage. However, New Labour's reaction to this set of issues was, in the apt words of Robert Ford and Matthew Goodwin, 'a mix of frenetic activity and benign neglect'.[2] There were new rules on asylum aimed at restricting the number of refugees entering Britain and new immigration rules that restricted the entrance into

Britain of spouses and unqualified migrants; however, the big wave of Eastern European migrants who arrived after 2005 meant that these measures were mostly invisible.

Labour's neglect of immigration as a legitimate concern had a direct impact on the popularity of the party. Since 1997, and in particular since 2005, the party had lost five million voters; many of them (though not all) were the 'left behind' Labour voters who could be tempted to vote UKIP. Labour's disconnection from voters' concerns was further demonstrated by the infamous 'bigotgate' involving the former prime minister Gordon Brown with a Labour supporter he encountered during the 2010 electoral campaign. Gordon Brown's gaffe (he forgot he had a BBC microphone attached to his lapel when he said the voter was a 'bigot') showed that working-class voters in deprived areas of England perceived immigration in a radically different manner from the party's elite. Instead of seeing it as an economic opportunity, these voters saw it as threat to their employment prospects and to the social cohesion of their own communities.

Immigration continued to be a salient issue following the 2010 general election. According to research by Lauren McLaren, a significant proportion of the British public felt that immigration was a threat to British cultural connections. Moreover, these voters were not very confident about the ability of the main parties to control it.[3] By 2013 the British Social Attitudes Survey noted that 77 per cent of the population wanted to see immigration reduced.[4] Following UKIP's spectacular results at the 2014 European Parliament elections (where they obtained 27.9 per cent of the vote) it was clear that immigration had become one of the most salient issues on the political agenda.

In the meantime, UKIP started to make waves in national politics largely thanks to the salience of immigration as a top concern for voters. If by 2009 UKIP was already an electoral force to be reckoned with in certain parts of England, it was seen as mainly a threat to the Conservative Party. But by 2012 it became clear that the party was succeeding in targeting former Old Labour voters in traditional Labour heartlands in the north-east of England. Research conducted by Ford and Goodwin showed that 42 per cent of UKIP voters 'work in blue-collar jobs or do not work at all'.[5] These voters tended to be white, male, and working-class, with few qualifications and over fifty years old,[6] and according to Goodwin and Ford, tended to be politically conflicted as 'their "heads" are Labour, but their "hearts" are often with the social values of the Conservatives'.[7] More worryingly, Ford and Goodwin predicted that 'the more UKIP grows, the more it will hurt Labour'.[8] Their projection proved to be correct. In the autumn of 2014, Labour secured the safe seat of Heywood and Middleton at a by-election, but by only 617 votes. UKIP was the second largest party in this constituency. This trend was confirmed in the 2015 general election. UKIP made huge inroads into Labour's heartlands, becoming the second party in constituencies such as Stoke-on-Trent Central and even in Ed Miliband's Doncaster North constituency.

But if UKIP was identified as a threat to Labour, the party did not know how to respond to it. Though Miliband recognised this problem in his first speech as Labour leader, many in the party were still in denial about its existence. Moreover, and as the incident involving the MP Emily Thornberry during the by-election campaign in Rochester and Strood (provoked by the posting of a photo on Twitter of a house with English flags and a white van) showed, the party was extremely nervous about its approach to immigration and its strategy to neutralise UKIP's threat. If Miliband overreacted by dismissing Thornberry from the frontbench, she clearly underestimated popular sensibilities on immigration.

In parallel with concerns about immigration, two other related factors influenced Labour's re-assessment of its politics of belonging. The rise in salience of English national identity, as well as debates about what it means to be British in a highly diverse society, also informed the party's new approach to the politics of belonging. Last but not least, the English Question regained a new salience in the wake of the referendum on Scottish independence.

Ideas: old and new

Miliband's politics of belonging was influenced by Blue Labour, particularly in how this theme was framed in his narrative. But Blue Labour did not monopolise the party's debate in this area. Indeed, this was a highly contested ground and naturally there were ideational challenges to Blue Labour coming from the think-tanks and also from the politicians who were closer to New Labour. Another important influence on Miliband's politics of identity was that of the political philosopher Tim Soutphommasane, who proposed a liberal-inspired patriotism that would suit a multicultural society like Britain. There were marked tensions between the different strands of political thought. Blue Labour's patriotism had illiberal undertones, whereas the patriotism of Soutphommasane was strongly anchored in the liberal tradition and cherished some of the cosmopolitan values reviled by Blue Labour thinkers. Of the two main sets of ideas, Blue Labour was the most influential in terms of setting the tone and the political agenda. However, in terms of shaping the policy agenda the influence of Blue Labour was weaker.

Blue Labour draws inspiration from old English traditions of dissent and radical patriotism, as well as from the democratic cry of revolt of the early New Left. When Maurice Glasman argued that the traditions that influenced the formation of the Labour Party included as disparate events and legacies as the Norman Conquest and the non-established churches, he was placing Blue Labour as an inheritor of the tradition of English radical patriotism.

Likewise, Jonathan Rutherford called on Labour to 'rediscover England's radical traditions that are rooted in the long political struggle against dispossession,'[9] and that sought 'to conserve the integrity of the individual placed in conflict with the class structure of property rights and power'.[10] Jon Cruddas was equally explicit in his embrace of radical patriotism. 'For Labour to be part of the solution it must rediscover a rich English tradition of volatile, inspirational cultures of non-conformity, rebelliousness and creativity', he argued.[11] He also claimed that there was a direct link between this tradition of radical patriotism and the labour movement. As he put it, 'The Levellers Charters was ours', Labour was '[s]tanding with the crowd at Peterloo', and '[s]tanding with the Irishman Bronterre O'Brien and William Cuffay'.[12]

As these references show, Blue Labour also drew inspiration from the New Left, in particular from the early New Left associated with E. P. Thompson and Raymond Williams that rejected the abstract theorising of Continental philosophers and emphasised the role of feelings and emotions. Moreover, and like the New Left, Blue Labour thinkers rejected universal values – which they considered too abstract – and championed the traditions of working people located in specific times and places. This being said, Blue Labour thinkers like Glasman and Rutherford occasionally fell into abstract theorising. Indeed, their use of the word 'conservative' was more provocative than precise. For instance, Rutherford argued that 'Labour's future is conservative'.[13] But his conservatism was quite singular because it borrowed from the traditions of English ethical socialism but it also claimed 'the best of its Tory antecedents' (though he did not specify what those were).[14]

Similarly, Jon Cruddas admitted to being 'on the romantic and conservative side of socialism',[15] and he emphasised the place of conservative values such as the 'love of home, of place and of the local' in Labour traditions.[16] However, his references – John Ruskin, William Morris, the ILP, George Lansbury, and E. P. Thompson – were strongly anchored in Labour's history and traditions.[17] Thus, for Cruddas conservatism had more to do with localism and parochialism than with Burke's small platoons, patriarchal values and resistance to change. He defined his conception of conservatism as a form of resistance against globalised capitalism and its 'destructive effects' on families and communities.[18] His conservatism was also a rhetorical device to distance himself from what he called 'progressive cosmopolitanism'. Indeed, he argued that Labour's 'progressive cosmopolitanism tends toward an inability to comprehend the deep desire for the familiar and the parochial and the ordinary'.[19]

The Labour candidate and Blue Labour sympathiser Rowenna Davis admitted that 'conservative' was not a word that the Labour Party liked because it was seen as 'a roadblock against women, diversity, liberty and internationalism'.[20] But despite these reservations she endorsed it nonetheless. She called for a way of being conservative that was true to Labour: 'If what we mean by "conservative" is a politics that wants to safeguard the values and institutions that this country can be proud of, then this is perfectly possible. Family, neighbourliness, hard work and place are part of it. Dedication, honesty and compassion speak to it.'[21] She did not explain however why the values of the family, hard work, and neighbourliness were exclusively conservative.

As Davis predicted, Blue Labour's conservatism was attacked by Labour fig-ures.[22] For example, Hazel Blears voiced her disagreement with 'radical conser-vatism' in very strong terms. 'The labour movement has always been rooted in improvement and change – demanding the right to vote, marching and organising for better working conditions, creating the NHS to deal with poor health ... None of this was about conservation, it was about radical change to improve the lives of ordinary people', she said.[23] Philip Collins – Blair's former speech-writer, *Times* columnist, and participant in the famous Oxford London Seminars – was equally sharp in his criticism. He wondered how it was 'possible to be both conservative and radical'.[24]

Blue Labour also courted controversy by sounding nostalgic about the demise of patriarchy, and critical of the rise of feminism. When explaining the two main rival traditions of the party, Maurice Glasman gave them gender attributes:

> In Philosophical terms we have an Aristotelian Dad and a Platonic Mum, a Common Good Dad and a Progressive Mum, a traditional Dad and a Radical Mum ... The problem in the marriage was clear from the start. The Mum had all the advantages of class – resources, eloquence, confidence and science – and none of the experience of hardship ... The Dad had no power at work, and no power at home either.[25]

Glasman seemed to suggest that there was a natural order in society, and that in that natural order men were rulers. Similarly, Jonathan Rutherford made an expli-cit appraisal of patriarchal values. According to him, Labour had been a 'deeply patriarchal movement' but was now suffering from the effects of the disruption of patriarchy.[26] Though he admitted that the disruption of patriarchy had given greater independence to women, it had also strained their lives.[27] However, the great vic-tims of the disruption of patriarchy were men, who were no longer the main fam-ily breadwinners. For Rutherford, 'The loss of patrimony, the rise of single-parent households, and women's challenge to men's traditional roles have led to recurring moral panics about a crisis in masculinity, family and fatherhood.'[28]

Needless to say, this take on the 'disruption of patriarchy' antagonised femi-nists in the Labour Party. The backbencher Helen Goodman wrote a long pamph-let where she refuted almost line-by-line Blue Labour ideas on gender. She noted that 'Glasman characterises as female all the aspects of New Labour he dislikes, whereas all the characteristics he applauds he draws as male.'[29] She argued as well that Blue Labour seemed to blame working women, and in particular educated working women, for the anomie and atomism of contemporary society. Hazel Blears made similar criticisms. 'Appealing simply to male-dominated sectors of society would be electorally flawed, and I am concerned that the overt masculinity of radical conservatism would place us as diametrically opposed to modern femin-ism, and alienate many of the women who have been key to our electoral success', she argued.[30]

Another central theme in Blue Labour's thinking was the recognition of a distinct English national identity. The starting point of Blue Labour's take on Englishness was an analysis of Labour's poor electoral results in English constituencies, in particular amongst working-class voters. Blue Labour thinkers argued that Labour was too remote from the lives and concerns of English voters.[31] For Rutherford, Labour's fundamental problem was the championing of multiculturalism and a general mistrust of the popular symbols and iconography of Englishness. As Rutherford explained, the controversies over EU immigration and Islam were about a 'politics of belonging, fired up by economic insecurity' and by 'a reaction to the dispossession of men from the sources of their authority and entitlement, to the loss of people's capacities to determine their own ends, and to the loss of an identifiable national culture'.[32] Jon Cruddas echoed this thinking when he argued that Labour had recoiled from 'the visceral politics of loss and belonging' because 'it fears people's bigotry and xenophobia and has been contemptuous of those nostalgic for a past that they imagine was better'.[33] Cruddas contended that Labour had to recognise that the poorest communities were those who suffered the most with the migration flows, not only in terms of competition for work and public services, but also in terms of 'sheer changes in the national culture'.[34]

Both Cruddas and Rutherford argued that Labour could not afford to ignore English voters, and claimed that the way to regain their vote was to change the party's approach to immigration, to the EU (in particular with regard to the principle of free circulation of workers), and to the management of diversity. They also contended that this approach should be based on ideas of reciprocity and on a 'national intercultural dialogue that moves beyond the debates around assimilation and multiculturalism'.[35]

But this was a very sensitive policy area for the party, and Blue Labour advocates did not develop a unified position. Whereas figures such as Cruddas and Rutherford attempted a subtle position that recognised popular concerns with immigration but stressed its benefits as well, Maurice Glasman courted controversy when he called for all immigration to be 'frozen' and proposed that Labour should adapt their policies to the concerns of the far-right English Defence League.[36] His rather drastic proposals were immediately dismissed by Labour figures and led to the unravelling of the Blue Labour project.

The controversy about immigration showed that Blue Labour was more a forum for debate of challenging ideas than a purposeful and coherent political movement. Indeed, there were other inconsistencies in its thinking. For instance, Blue Labour's embrace of conservatism as well as the nostalgic narrative on patriarchy and Englishness were seen as a departure from the radical patriotism of E. P. Thompson. If Thompson was a traditionalist, the traditions he cherished were not conservative. In fact, as Michael Kenny pointed out, Thompson disliked the Conservative adulation of British political institutions and believed that the left's reclaiming of patriotism 'implied a willingness by radicals to tackle the inequalities of power, wealth and status which were fortified by conservative accounts of the nation'.[37] Thus, as Kenny argued, Thompson, who was now revered by Blue Labour, would have been 'concerned' if Labour 'signalled too great an accommodation with political forms of conservatism'.[38]

Moreover, Thompson's patriotism was not parochial. As Kenny explained, Thompson believed that 'the language and ethos of nationhood needed to be understood as deeply embroiled within political struggles, and not as alternatives to the strategic dilemmas and conflicts that politics involves'.[39] As such, it was a patriotism built around conflict and not around some consensus or nostalgia for a pastoral past. Moreover, his notion of Englishness was anything but Little Englander, as it 'was connected to the idea of developing forms of solidarity and co-operation with allies and movements beyond England'.[40]

In similar vein, Stuart White argued that both One Nation and Blue Labour could not be seen as a follow-up or a modernisation of Thompson's radical patriotism because they placed too much emphasis on a pastoral reading of the past and on the idea of harmony. As White rightly pointed out, Thompson's notion that democracy thrives on disagreements and debates was in stark contrast with Blue Labour's insistence on unity and nostalgia for a past that perhaps never existed. Thus, White argued that 'while One Nation Labour shares the national-historical approach, it seems ambivalent about the democratic and libertarian values that Thompson draws out of his historical narratives'.[41]

This conception of patriotism, which resulted from conflict and dissension, was articulated by Cruddas, and even by Ed Miliband in his One Nation speech, but it was somewhat absent from the narrative of Maurice Glasman and Jonathan Rutherford, who tended to emphasise conservative and patriarchal values as well as a nostalgic view of the past.

Blue Labour had a visible influence on Miliband's thinking and on his language about the politics of belonging but it was not the only influence that shaped his approach. By the hand of Jon Cruddas, the Labour leader was introduced to the ideas of the political philosopher Tim Soutphommasane on liberal patriotism. There were many areas of overlap between Blue Labour and Soutphommasane's liberal patriotism, in particular in their approach to immigration and in the emphasis on crafting and nurturing a national culture; however, there were also significant differences between them. Whilst Blue Labour emerged as a critique of liberalism and multiculturalism, Soutphommasane's liberal patriotism was strongly anchored in liberal values and argued for a greater recognition of ethnic and cultural diversity. In addition, it was also predicated on the idea that national cultures are not set in aspic, but change as a result of contact and dialogue with different groups and cultures that share the same public space.

Soutphommasane's ideas resonated with Miliband's personal background but also with his values and instincts as a Labour politician. Moreover, Soutphommasane's liberal patriotism was appealing because it was built around the concept of a dialogical/democratic relationship between the State and citizens, which was a theme that was dear to the Milibandite project (and analysed in the previous chapter). The Labour leader was also acutely aware that Labour could not only rely on the votes of 'left behind' Englishmen to the exclusion of other voters that composed Labour's electoral basis. Finally, he could not dismiss the internationalist traditions of the party to defend a pastoral vision of Britain.

Soutphommasane's approach, then, offered a contrast to the sometimes ethnically white and male-based patriotism of Blue Labour. If based on the abstract reasoning despised by Blue Labour thinkers, his liberal patriotism offered a subtle response to the problem of managing moral conflicts in diverse societies. As such, his liberal patriotism reflected more than two decades of debates between neutral liberals and multiculturalists, and absorbed insights from deliberative democracy advocates such as Seyla Benhabib, John Dryzek, David Miller, and others.

Its central contention was that 'the constellation of liberal political ideals – individual rights protected by the rule of law, a government administering impartial laws, a deliberative democracy, a welfare state that redistributes resources to those in want and need' – could only be achieved if there was 'a shared national identity among citizens motivating reciprocity and cooperation'.[42] In other words, this approach recognised that diverse societies present a challenge to patriotism because there 'appears to be something of a trade-off between solidarity and diversity'.[43] Furthermore it recognised that diversity had the potential to undermine ideals of redistributive justice.

Soutphommasane argued that multicultural states could address such conflict by using two mechanisms: first, the articulation of a civic or a liberal patriotism based on values and common history but crucially not on ethnic factors; second, the promotion of a deliberative culture whereby values and norms are negotiated and agreed daily amongst citizens.[44] As 'the shared characteristics that underpin a national culture are common institutions and shared values and norms – not ethnicity, lifestyle or biological descent', there was therefore room for 'many private cultures, including ethnic minority ones, to flourish within the borders of the nation'.[45]

In practice this meant that policies would be decided following processes of public deliberation open to all citizens.[46] National values would be agreed at as a result of a process of dialogue among different groups in society that would occasionally accommodate some demands for cultural or religious recognition by minority groups. However, this democratic dialogue would take place within a legally defined liberal framework that would prioritise democracy and the value of equality of worth, as well as a regime of civil liberties.[47]

This approach touched upon two important and salient policy areas: immigration and the integration of minorities. Regarding immigration, Soutphommasane argued that liberal patriotism ruled out an open-borders policy. Like Blue Labour thinkers, he argued that it was reasonable 'for a state to impose limits on immigration' and to pursue an admissions policy that used cultural criteria to decide whom to let into the country.[48] These restrictions would be informed by the admission that immigration can challenge the capacity of a state to exercise legal sovereignty.[49]

Regarding the integration of minorities, Soutphommasane called for a process of acculturation whereby the State would encourage migrant populations to accept key aspects of the national culture, and to learn the language, history, and civic culture of the country. But this process of acculturation implied as well a degree of reciprocity from the State. If minority communities made the effort to learn the language and to accept the values of the dominant culture, the State should in turn be able to include minority perspectives in public institutions, practices, and values.[50] However, this process of accommodation had limits. Soutphommasane argued that the recognition of identities should not extend to establishing distinct minority public institutions alongside existing ones. In other words, minority cultural identities should be subordinate to the dominant culture.[51]

Reflecting the influence of Soutphommasane's ideas, the think-tank IPPR offered a positive appraisal of the effects of migration in Britain and proposed a managed approach to immigration (interestingly the shadow home secretary Yvette Cooper used that precise term). In the pamphlet *Fair Deal*, the IPPR recognised that popular resistance to immigration was related to the pressure that population growth placed on public services in specific areas. To address this problem, the think-tank made a series of proposals aimed at helping local authorities to tackle those pressures.[52] In addition, the IPPR proposed measures that would restrict migrants' access to welfare benefits on the basis of their contribution to the social security system.[53] But, the IPPR also espoused an approach to integration that emphasised 'togetherness, solidarity and shared values' with a view to building 'stronger local communities'. The implication of this approach was that immigrants who had been welcomed in Britain were expected to play 'a full part in British society' and should speak English.[54] But like Soutphommasane, the IPPR emphasised that integration was 'always a two-way street'.[55]

Miliband's narrative: One Nation politics

Miliband's One Nation narrative became the obvious vehicle for Labour's particular brand of patriotism. This narrative not only reflected the themes and ideas discussed earlier but it also addressed new popular concerns and the sense of insecurity felt by 'left behind' voters. Moreover, it sought to unify the nation by appealing to a civic nationalism that recognised diversity but that asserted national (and liberal) common values. His vision tried as well to respond to new electoral challenges and to synthesise the different and occasionally opposing views within in the party.

Miliband's One Nation narrative led scholars like Mark Wickham-Jones to highlight the similarities with New Labour, in particular its emphasis on the ideas of community.[56] But whilst it is noteworthy that both Blair and Miliband sought to wrap the Labour Party in patriotic clothes it is also clear that their conceptions of patriotism were very different. Whereas Blair's narrative about the 'young country' was optimistic, and projected the image of a dynamic, entrepreneurial, cosmopolitan country that was mostly concerned with the winners of globalisation, Miliband's patriotism was more cautious and pessimistic. Its landscape was not Blair's 'Cool Britannia' but suburban England and Britain's 'squeezed middle'. To a certain extent, Miliband's One Nation offers a corrective to New Labour's neoliberal excesses and speaks mostly to those whose lives have been disrupted by globalisation in terms of job security, falling living standards, and anxieties about national identity. Indeed, he invoked that idea when he argued that Labour should be the defender 'of things that people value and which are threatened – sometimes by markets, sometimes by government'.[57]

However, his cautious and somewhat pessimistic approach was not an endorsement of Blue Labour thinking. If Miliband made references to the importance of protecting communities from commodification, he rejected Blue Labour's embrace of conservatism. As he argued in his first speech as Labour leader, 'we stand for these things not because we are social conservatives but because we believe in community, belonging and solidarity'.[58]

Miliband used as well his personal story as a son of Jewish migrants from Poland and Belgium who had escaped the Nazi occupation and settled in London, to weave a conception of patriotism, which he defined as 'progressive patriotism',[59] and which had the merit of sounding both genuine and loyal to Labour's ideological roots and history. Indeed, his conception of patriotism was not based on blood and ethnicity, but instead recognised overlapping identities bound together by a commitment to a notion of civic patriotism. As he put it: 'To me, Britain is a country where it is always possible to have more than one identity'.[60]

But if Miliband's conception of progressive patriotism was predicated on the possibility of overlapping identities, he still acknowledged an emerging English national identity. In a rare speech about England, he admitted that Labour had 'been too nervous to talk on English pride and English character'.[61] Given the rising salience of English national identity over the past decade he encouraged the party and the country to 'embrace a positive, outward looking version of English identity'.[62]

Presenting himself as an Englishman with several loyalties, Miliband echoed the traditions of radical patriotism that emphasised conflict, instead of nostalgic views of a pastoral England of green and pleasant lands. As such, it was not a conception of Englishness that suited all political sensibilities. Echoing E. P. Thompson's take on English national identity, Miliband claimed that Englishness was based on a 'history of solidarity' and on 'traditions of fairness' (but also of dissent and promotion of progressive causes) exemplified by 'the Battle of Cable Street against Oswald Mosley and the black shirts to the spirit of the Blitz', as well as by the Ford workers' fight for equal pay.[63] For him, the English national identity included traits such as the 'spirit of quiet determination in the face of adversity'; the tradition of a trading island open to the world as well as the cooperative traditions of the early trade unionists; and the dissenting spirit of those who fought for universal suffrage, for equality and equal rights.[64]

This conception of progressive patriotism informed Labour's reassessment of its approach to immigration. In his first speech as Labour leader, he admitted that New Labour did not 'do enough to address concerns about some of the consequences of globalisation, including migration'.[65] In a direct reference to the party's loss of working-class supporters he admitted too that immigration was having a negative impact on wages, and for that reason voters were right to be disillusioned with Labour. As he put it, 'the poorest and the low paid felt we had nothing to say to them about the challenges in their lives'.[66] Thus, he signalled that the party had to change its policies on immigration but also on labour market liberalisation. Labour had to challenge 'the old thinking that flexible labour markets are always the answer', and as a result it should not allow employers to 'exploit migrant labour in order to undercut wages', he said.[67] With that goal in mind, Labour defended the rise of the minimum wage and reforms to zero-hours contracts, and sought to address the cost-of-living crisis with a series of micro-policies that tackled pay-day lenders, exploitative landlords, and extortionist energy companies. On the other hand, he warned against the temptation to 'out-UKIP UKIP'. He claimed that UKIP's views on immigration needed to be challenged on the grounds that they represented 'a vision of the past' that was 'rooted in the same failed ideas that have let our country down'.[68]

This critical reassessment of New Labour's legacy reflected Miliband's re-engagement with older Labour traditions of radical patriotism that were espoused by some of the figures associated with Blue Labour. His thinking reflected as well Blue Labour debates on the impact of commodification on the lives of communities and on Labour's loss of working-class voters. That engagement was visible in his choice of words, themes, and even some of the policies he advocated, such as the defending of a 'controlled and managed' approach to immigration and his appraisal of Englishness.

But Miliband departed from Blue Labour in two important areas. He did not engage in debates about the alleged crisis of masculinity and he did not endorse the underlying patriarchal and conservative values defended by Blue Labour. During the electoral campaign, he was also keen to emphasise the positive contribution of migrants and the fact that Britain was a tolerant country.[69] In fact, Miliband's approach to patriotism was closer to Tim Soutphommasane's liberal patriotism. As such, it offered a nuanced take on the complex challenge of managing diversity in a liberal society. Its starting point was the recognition of cultural and ethnic diversity, but he also addressed the need to promote a type of patriotism that could negotiate those differences. This was done through the promotion of a robust national culture based on the liberal values of equality and liberty but that accepted accommodation of other cultures and values through democratic deliberation. Miliband's narrative was also translated into a new focus on

Englishness, on a new approach to diversity that tried to go beyond the debates between advocates of multiculturalism and liberalism; however, its main component was a reassessment of Labour's approach to immigration, which I will now analyse.

Changing the tone on immigration

Miliband indicated in several speeches that he wanted to change the party's approach to immigration. His critique of New Labour suggested a subtle change of direction that reflected voters' concerns with immigration but sought to be loyal to the party's traditions of internationalism. But because the party was bitterly divided on the issue, Ed Miliband developed his approach slowly and with typical caution.

He accepted that voters had reasons to be legitimately concerned with immigration,[70] and that New Labour had been 'too starry-eyed about the benefits of globalisation'.[71] According to him, New Labour had made the mistake of not introducing restrictions to the freedom of movement of migrants coming from the new EU accession countries. As a result of this new migrant influx – which was much larger than expected – the country struggled with a hugely changed population and under-resourced public services, namely in housing, in access to health care, and in education. In a speech delivered following the 2014 local and European Parliament elections, Ed Miliband recognised that New Labour had let people down:

> Our embrace of the future meant that some people thought we didn't respect the loss they felt from the past. Our embrace of openness made some people feel we didn't understand the pressures immigration put on them ... Labour was founded on standing up for working people. But for too many that link was lost. That is what UKIP has sought to exploit.[72]

This analysis guided Labour's change of policy on migration. Labour's new approach sought to balance Britain's needs to recruit, as the shadow home secretary Yvette Cooper put it, the 'best international talent',[73] whilst at the same time it addressed the concerns of voters who felt 'powerless, ignored, let down'.[74] As she argued, 'the pace of change in local neighbourhoods can cause anxiety for settled communities, create pressure on local services, drive down wages in some jobs and lead to exploitation'.[75] As Miliband and Cooper sought to demonstrate that they were addressing voters' anxieties, they were very careful in their use of language. For example, they promised that under Labour immigration would be 'controlled and managed'.[76]

Labour's balanced approach to immigration had three main strands.[77] The first strand was about abolishing the immigration targets imposed by the Coalition Government and reinforcing instead the visa points system affecting migrants coming from outside the EU. In particular, Labour proposed changing the visa system for student visitors and imposing stronger border controls to tackle illegal immigration.

To show the party's commitment to 'stronger border controls', Cooper announced that a Labour Government would recruit more border control staff and re-introduce exit controls to count people in and out of Britain.[78]

The second, and perhaps more problematic strand, was about tackling EU immigration. Because the British Government cannot decide unilaterally to ban EU citizens from moving into Britain, or restrict their access to public services and welfare benefits, Labour was forced to base its approach on a set of promises it was not certain to deliver, as they required the approval of the remaining twenty-seven EU member states.[79] Nonetheless, Labour – and in particular Yvette Cooper, Ed Balls, and Rachel Reeves – used strong words to indicate that Labour's policy had changed. For example, in her 2014 Labour Annual Conference speech, Cooper claimed that Labour's approach was about 'not free movement, but fair movement'. In a speech to Progress, Ed Balls echoed the same idea and hinted that Labour would seek reforms to the Single Market rules that might require a treaty change.[80] Balls and Cooper's choice of words seemed to be deliberate, given that it was the EU's single-market principle of free movement that was the point of contention. In similar vein, the shadow work and pensions secretary, Rachel Reeves, used an article published in the *Daily Mail* to outline Labour's proposals to change EU rules on the freedom of movement of workers. In this article, Reeves argued that EU migrants settling in Britain should first contribute to the tax and social security system for two years before they could access in-work benefits and unemployment benefits. She justified Labour's stance on the grounds that 'people should work and contribute before drawing on the system'.[81] She also proposed banning the practice of paying child benefit to families whose children did not live in Britain.

Aware that a Labour Government could not change the Single Market rules singlehandedly, Reeves claimed to have had conversations with German, French, and Irish officials who seemed to be supportive of her plans. But if it is true that Germany and France face similar problems and could therefore be inclined to support Labour's plans, there are twenty-five remaining EU member states that need to agree to those changes. Moreover, amongst those twenty-five European countries there are several that do not support those ideas. Thus, the only promises on EU immigration that Labour could deliver were about imposing 'maximum transitional controls' for any new countries joining the EU, and about introducing legislation to prevent employers from recruiting only from outside Britain.

The third strand of Labour's new approach to migration sought to mitigate the impact of migration on low-skilled workers. In this area, Labour proposed stronger penalties for employers who abused the rules on the minimum wage and introducing minimum custodial sentences for any employer that exploits migrant workers.[82] Labour was also committed to protecting and investing in public services such as the NHS, and to building 200,000 houses per year until 2020. The purpose of this strand was twofold: first, to tackle what Labour perceived to be the reason why so many voters thought immigration was a problem; and second, to address the concerns of those alleged left-behind voters who were now voting, or considering voting, UKIP.

As a balancing act, Miliband's proposals were nuanced; however, they were barely noticeable to the public and they also failed to unite the party. Even those who supported him, like John Denham, would have liked the Labour leader to be more explicit about his desire to reduce the number of migrants coming from Europe.[83] Denham had seen the impact of EU immigration in his constituency and noted that it 'had a very big impact in a very short space of time and made a lot of people's lives worse'.[84] He also contended that Labour had 'no credibility' on migration and that the only way to regain it was to make access to public services and benefits conditional on contributions to the tax system.[85]

Those opposing Miliband's new approach on migration fell into three main categories. The first category was composed of MPs such as Frank Field, Ronnie Campbell, John Mann, Graham Stringer, Kate Hoey, Ian Davidson, and Roger Godsiff, who would like to see even stricter limits to immigration from some EU countries. The second category of opponents, which included figures such as Diane Abbott and David Lammy, argued instead that the party would pay a heavy price if it followed such a strategy. Diane Abbott warned that Labour's new narrative on immigration 'would be disastrous' for the party, and she was particularly critical of Ed Miliband who, according to her, sounded 'like a milk and water version of Nigel Farage'.[86] The shadow business secretary, Chuka Umunna, also seemed uncomfortable with some of Labour's stances. In a radio interview he condemned the practice of blaming migrants for everything that was wrong in Britain: 'All the problems that you have, whether it's a getting an appointment at your GP, the fact you aren't earning enough at work, the fact your child can't get a house round the corner from you, is down to Eastern European immigration. It isn't. It's a con. It is misleading and wrong.'[87]

The third category of critics included MPs and think-tanks close to the Blairite circles who argued that Labour's focus on the core vote was misguided. Just before the 2014 local and European elections the think-tank Policy Network published a pamphlet where it warned Labour about the dangers of overreacting against the Third Way experience, and in particular of becoming 'over-obsessed with this communitarian/cosmopolitan dividing line'.[88] The authors of the pamphlet argued that Blue Labour was wrong in its identification of the new insecure electorate. Basing their stance on demographic data, Policy Network argued that an electoral strategy centred on attracting white, working-class, and middle-aged voters, who only represented a small percentage of the electorate, would be disastrous. Instead, they argued that Labour should focus its strategy in targeting the new class of the insecure – middle-class professionals – who represented 75 per cent of the electorate.[89] The influential Labour strategist John McTernan agreed with this stance, and warned the party against pandering to the UKIP voter, in particular to the so-called 'left behind' Labour voter. Those voters, he argued, 'are no longer numerically, or spiritually, the Labour party's base'[90] Instead, Labour should focus on targeting the professional middle classes, together with the young, and black and minority ethnic voters, whom he saw as Labour new core vote.[91] In a similar vein, Anthony Painter argued that Labour's strategy of targeting what he called 'blue-collar voters' was not working, as the party was still losing working-class supporters. Painter argued that Labour could only win if it targeted a 'broad and plural coalition' of voters.[92]

The divisions within the party about immigration were illustrative of Labour's electoral dilemmas. If Labour was to harden its stance on immigration in the hope of winning UKIP supporters, the party risked alienating women, young professionals, and ethnic minorities who could switch allegiance to the Greens, the Liberal Democrats or the SNP; but on the other hand, if it neglected its old core voters it risked losing some safe seats. According to research conducted by the Fabian Society, Labour had reasons to be worried about the UKIP insurgency. The flow of Labour votes to UKIP had the potential 'to boost Conservative prospects in a large number of important marginal seats'.[93]

Managing diversity

Miliband's stance on immigration was directly related to the party's approach to Britain's ethnic and cultural diversity. In this area, Ed Miliband did not start on a blank page. Labour had been reassessing British multiculturalism since the racial riots of 2001 in the north-east of England, and since the debates on the radicalisation of young British Muslims that had come to the foreground of British politics in the wake of the terrorist attacks in New York in 2001 and in London in 2005. As a result, Miliband's approach reflected not only party discussions but national debates on how to manage a diverse society.

Labour did not present a clear and definite vision of what such policies would entail; however, it did not endorse the policies of robust integration favoured by other European countries and by the Conservative prime minister, David Cameron. Instead, Labour defended an approach that was close to Soutphommasane's liberal patriotism, and which offered a corrective to Britain's multiculturalism. As explained in the previous pages, liberal patriotism is based on a robust civic patriotism that recognises cultural, ethnic, and religious diversity but expects citizens to accept certain national values. In addition, liberal patriotism accepts that those national values are subject to permanent democratic negotiation among all citizens.

For Labour politicians this kind of liberal patriotism was epitomised in Danny Boyle's London Olympics opening ceremony, which presented a social democratic view of Britain, with the celebration of the trade union movement, the Suffragettes, the NHS, and Campaign for Nuclear Disarmament, amongst other British icons. Thus, the London Olympics opening ceremony, but also the achievements of British athletes and the spirit of togetherness that the Games promoted, were used as examples of the patriotism Miliband wanted to project.

In a speech on immigration he made several references to how Britain's ethnic diversity was behind the country's achievements during the 2012 Olympic Games. As he put it, 'social, cultural and ethnic diversity has made us stronger'.[94] Similarly, for the MP Rushanara Ali, the Olympics opening ceremony 'painted the picture of an open, outward-looking and dynamic country' that had 'travelled on a long journey since its colonial past'.[95] Invoking the atmosphere of London 2012 Yvette Cooper presented a view of a modern Britain that prized diversity: 'The modern history of Britain is the triumph of friendships across cultures and ethnicities over racism and prejudice.'[96]

The perception that Britain's ethnic diversity was something to be valued led Miliband to reassess the party's approach to the integration of minorities. His approach, which he defined as 'living together across communities', rejected the policies of both assimilation and multiculturalism but reflected the insights of Tim Soutphommasane and of the IPPR's report on migration. His One Nation vision was of 'a Britain where people of all backgrounds, all races, all ethnicities, all cultures, can practice their own religion, continue their own customs, but also come together to forge a new and better identity'.[97]

Echoing Miliband's thinking and the IPPR's recommendations, Yvette Cooper also emphasised the need to integrate minorities. Making immigration work, she said, 'means making sure that people can come together in local communities, building common bonds, sharing British values, not living segregated lives'.[98] Similarly, Miliband recognised that integration was a process rooted in the lives of communities. The first step to a successful integration strategy was the requirement that all migrants should speak English, especially those who worked in the public services. Interestingly, the requirement to speak English was not justified on purely economic grounds. The economic rationale was there, but in his speech Miliband emphasised the need for dialogue across communities. 'We all know that the beginning of any real connection with a neighbour or colleague, work-mate or friend is a conversation', he said.[99]

Stronger integration would also imply the development of housing and employment policies rooted in a sense of 'shared citizenship'.[100] That notion of 'shared citizenship' meant, according to Cooper, that migrants were expected to 'work hard, obey the law, and contribute to our economy and society'.[101] However, Labour was less explicit about what it meant by 'shared citizenship'. Miliband and Cooper advocated building more affordable housing that would promote mixed communities, and banning employment practices that segregated workers along national and ethnic lines, but their thinking on how to develop that sense of shared citizenship was not fully developed. Apart from a vague notion of what British citizenship values would entail, Labour had no specific proposals on how to promote the common bonds of citizenship or a national dialogue across communities. And yet, the IPPR report made a number of recommendations on how local communities, schools, and other public institutions were best placed to teach the values of citizenship, not to mention the proposal to promote British citizenship to new migrants. Similarly, Soutphommasane's approach emphasised the importance of democratic dialogue among the different communities that were part of Britain.

Addressing the 'English Question'

In several speeches delivered throughout his leadership of the Labour Party, Miliband made references to the multiple identities of British citizens and argued that people can be 'patriotically British without abandoning their cultural roots';[102] however, he seemed to be uncomfortable with the rise of the English national identity. As Simon Lee noted, the Labour Party 'remains overwhelmingly hostile to the idea of an English narrative of democracy, despite England's long traditions both of radicalism and republicanism'.[103]

Miliband's shyness about England was also the result of political circumstances. Indeed, the referendum on Scottish independence, and the subsequent rise in popularity of the SNP, forced the party to stress its pro-unionist credentials. This meant that instead of talking about the special features of Britain's four nations, Labour focused on a message that emphasised the need to strengthen the union.

But Labour had to react, or at least acknowledge that the emergence of a distinct English national identity was an important, if complex, political phenomenon. Indeed, this was a phenomenon with a variety of causes. The impact of devolution in Westminster was often quoted as a cause but there were others. According to Michael Kenny, Euroscepticism, the demise of Britishness as a national identity that offered sufficient social glue to unite the different British nations, and the impact of globalisation on those of lower skills, as well as the rise of identity politics visible in people's political behaviour and popular culture, were factors that contributed to the emergence of a distinct English national identity.[104]

This was a new phenomenon that for electoral reasons Labour could not afford to ignore. Scottish and Welsh devolution had exposed one of Labour's electoral weaknesses, namely that the party was not particularly strong in English constituencies. This electoral weakness led the outgoing Labour MP John Denham to call on the party leader to address the English Question. He wrote extensively on how devolution to Scotland (in particular), but also to Wales and Northern Ireland, left the English feeling they had no voice. To address this problem he called on Miliband to develop a 'progressive English story that is inclusive and confident of our role in the union, Europe, and the wider world'.[105]

Similarly, Jon Cruddas was concerned with the English Question, but he emphasised the sense of dispossession and alienation felt by English voters. Thus, instead of attributing the rise of Englishness to devolution he linked it to the dramatic social and economic changes brought by globalisation and immigration. Cruddas identified the 'loss of a sense of belonging, a feeling among people that something has been lost from their lives that they will never get back. They feel abandoned, and UKIP is exploiting this mood in Labour's English heartlands, the ex-industrial areas in which decent work and the old culture of the working class have been devastated.'[106] To fight the perception that conceding to English nationalism was equivalent to accepting a reactionary take on patriotism, Cruddas highlighted the radical patriotism of English radicals like Thomas Paine, the Levellers, Lansbury, and 'even Michael Foot'. However, he conceded that the prospect could be 'very disconcerting to sections of the Labour Party'.[107]

Miliband's approach to Englishness drew from this radical tradition. At the 2014 Labour Annual Conference, he paid homage to the English traditions of solidarity, fairness, and internationalism, but his response to the English question was timid.[108] It was also very slow. Though he acknowledged the rise in English national identity in a few speeches, his policy response was only unveiled in 2014 when he proposed the devolution of new powers to English cities and towns (analysed in the previous chapter). In the aftermath of the referendum on Scottish independence, he promised devolution for local government 'from Cornwall to Cumbria'.[109] Under Labour's plans, local councils would acquire new powers and resources to design and deliver public services, in particular in the areas of housing, development of skills, transport, and business support.[110] In addition, those local councils that form combined authorities would be able to retain the totality of the income raised by their business rates.

Miliband compared Labour's proposals, entitled *New Deal for England*, to Scottish and Welsh devolution; however, they were far less ambitious.[111] In the eyes of one observer, Labour's proposals offered 'centralist solutions to localism, built on the idea that Whitehall gives permission for cities and regions to act'.[112] Indeed, under Labour's plans local councils would have to earn their right to that administrative freedom by meeting targets set by Whitehall. Critics also did not trust Labour's willingness to devolve power, given that historically the party had been a great supporter of a centralising model of government.[113] Furthermore, these proposals for English devolution were not radically different from the policies enacted by the Coalition Government, and were modest in comparison with the Conservative Party's proposals for English home rule and for English-votes-for-English-laws. More importantly, the proposals were presented as a way of promoting the economic development of neglected English regions, and as a technocratic response to the failings of the unresponsive central State. They were not presented as a response to the rise in salience of the English national identity as a cultural phenomenon.

Following the referendum on Scottish independence, Miliband slightly changed tack. He admitted that English devolution had to go beyond the devolution of fiscal powers to local authorities. In the party's 2015 manifesto, Labour sought to address the famously intractable West Lothian Question by promising 'to consider how English MPs can have a greater role in the scrutiny of legislation that only affects England'.[114] Perhaps aware of the timidity of this proposal, Miliband proposed organising a democratic convention on constitutional reform, where devolution for England as well as the codification of the constitution and other constitutional issues would be decided. He also proposed that this constitutional convention welcome the participation of citizens, as 'these issues can no longer be fixed solely by politicians or Prime Ministers trying to shore up their position in their own party'.[115] Miliband's approach seemed democratic enough, but it also suggested that the party was still trying to make sense of what had happened in Scotland and of its wider implications for the rest of the union.

Concluding remarks

The rise of immigration as a top voter concern, the emergence of a distinct English national identity, the rise of UKIP as an electoral force, the party's own electoral concerns with its vulnerable position in England (not only in the south but also in the north-east, where the party had many safe seats), and challenges posed by governing an ethnically diverse society made the politics of belonging an important plank of Labour's One Nation agenda. However, this was a sensitive area of politics, and as a result the party's response was cautious; in some areas nebulous; and, considering the 2015 electoral results, also a case of 'too little, too late'.

Labour's One Nation narrative weaved together the different aspects of the party's approach to the politics of identity and belonging. As a corrective to the neoliberal excesses of New Labour, One Nation politics recognised that globalisation did not work for everyone. With its embrace of flexible labour markets, it had promoted economic, social, and cultural anxieties. More importantly, many core Labour voters stopped voting for the party because they felt it no longer addressed their concerns or understood their lives. One Nation politics had also to respond to the unintended consequences of New Labour's constitutional reforms, namely to the rise of English national identity. The party had to address too the impact of the independence referendum in Scotland and the apparently unstoppable rise of the SNP.

Labour's approach sought to respond to these challenges and reflected a variety of ideas and traditions. Blue Labour's concerns with the impact of globalisation on the lives of working-class voters informed the party's approach to immigration in terms of narrative and, to a certain extent, also in terms of policies. Similarly, Blue Labour's approach to England and apprehensions about the party's neglect of identity issues found their way into Miliband's rhetoric about Englishness and constitutional reform.

By the same token, Soutphommasane's ideas on liberal patriotism also impacted on Miliband's approach to patriotism, diversity, and immigration. Indeed, if he accepted the Blue Labour framing of these issues, his own approach was also partly shaped by his personal background (to which he referred several times during the campaign, including in the party's electoral broadcasts), and Soutphommasane's ideas. Thus, the patriotism that the Labour Party under Ed Miliband defended was one that emphasised the added value of multiple and overlapping identities, but valued a robust conception of shared citizenship built around respect for Britain's liberal values and for democratic dialogue.

Debates within and around Labour recognised the need to address these different challenges by articulating a conception of patriotism that reflected the party's values but also the ethnic and cultural diversity of contemporary Britain. But having agreed that the party needed to address the politics of belonging did not mean that there was a consensus about how to go about it. Whereas some in the party continued to promote the politics of open borders, others defended robust approaches to immigration. And whilst some insisted on asserting Labour's commitment to a multicultural Britain, others emphasised a conception of patriotism marked by nostalgia and patriarchal values.

In his trademark consensual and cautious style, Miliband's approach sought to strike a balance between the polarised positions within the party and to address the competing electoral challenges. But the result was not as coherent or persuasive as the Labour leader desired. Miliband's consolation was that the Conservatives were no longer seen by voters as the most trusted party to tackle the problems associated with immigration.

In terms of policies, Miliband's patriotism was translated into a nuanced approach to immigration that simultaneously recognised the legitimacy of citizens' concerns with recent migratory flows but valued the contribution of migrants. To mitigate the pressures on public services imposed by immigration, Labour proposed an enforcement of labour laws to avoid the exploitation of migrants and the undercutting of wages of British workers, and the introduction of a contributory principle to migrants' access to benefits and public services. In terms of reaching a balance between addressing the new popular anxieties with immigration and keeping the party's traditions of internationalism and support for ethnic minorities, Labour's proposals hit the right buttons. However, this carefully calibrated message was insufficient to win the vote of 'left behind' voters. As Tim Bale argued, these voters cared far more about immigration than they did about the minimum wage, access to social housing, or the NHS, and did not trust Labour to deliver on these issues.[116]

Labour insisted as well on promoting a conception of citizenship based on shared values and on reciprocity. Migrants were expected to 'play by the rules' and to speak English. However, Miliband's proposals were short on detail about how to promote that conception of shared citizenship. More importantly, the party's new policies were barely visible to voters. Miliband and Cooper addressed this theme in many speeches, but the London-based media showed little interest in them.

Last but not least, Labour under Ed Miliband sought to respond to the English Question. But for a variety of reasons its response was timid. Whilst Labour recognised the dissident and democratic traditions of English nationalism, its response to the English question was on the whole technocratic. The party's proposals to devolve power to English cities and towns were a far cry from the devolution of powers given to Scotland and Wales. But more importantly, they did not engage with the important question of English national identity. Instead the proposals were clothed in the language of democracy, power devolution, and decentralisation, and they did not recognise that this question was as much about political representation as about an insecure national identity.

In conclusion, Miliband's conception of progressive patriotism sought to address the different challenges posed by the politics of belonging that manifested itself in the salience of immigration and in the rise of English national identity. However, the concessions Miliband had to make to accommodate the different strands of opinion in the party, as well as the conflicting electoral challenges, led to a very slow policy development process that in turn suggested the party was struggling to respond to events. Moreover, if the new approach developed by the party was ideologically cogent and comprehensible it was too subtle to persuade those disillusioned voters who seemed to prefer UKIP's and the SNP's strident style of politics.

Notes

1 Ed Miliband, 'Ed Miliband's Speech on Scottish Independence', 11 September 2014, http://www.totalpolitics.com/print/speeches/292477/ed-milibands-speech-on-scottish-independence-in-glasgow.thtml (accessed 13 December 2014).

2 Robert Ford and Matthew Goodwin, *Revolt on the Right: Explaining Support for the Radical Right in Britain* (London: Routledge, 2014), p. 131.

3 Lauren M. McLaren, 'Immigration and Perceptions of the Political System in Britain', *Political Quarterly* 84:1 (January–March 2013): 90–100 (pp. 94–96). Lauren M. McLaren, 'Immigration and Political Trust in the UK', *Political Insight* 4:3 (December 2013): 14–17 (p. 17).

4 Robert Ford and Anthony Heath, 'Immigration', in Alison Park, Caroline Bryson, and John Curtice (eds), *British Social Attitudes 31* (London: NatCen Social Research, 2014), p. 78.

5 Ford and Goodwin, *Revolt on the Right*, p. 152.

6 Ford and Goodwin, *Revolt on the Right*, p. 152.

7 Ford and Goodwin, *Revolt on the Right*, p. 173.

8 Robert Ford and Matthew Goodwin, 'Now Ukip Is Gunning for Labour, What's Ed Miliband Going to Do about It?', *Guardian*, 30 May 2013, http://www.theguardian.com/comment-isfree/2013/may/30/ukip-gunning-labour-ed-miliband (accessed 3 August 2015). See also Marcus Roberts, *Revolt on the Left: Labour's UKIP Problem and How It Can Be Overcome* (London: Fabian Society, 2014).

9 Jonathan Rutherford, 'The Future Is Conservative', in Maurice Glasman, Jonathan Rutherford, Marc Stears, and Stuart White (eds), *The Labour Tradition and the Politics of Paradox: The Oxford London Seminars 2010–11* (n.p.: Oxford London Seminars, 2011), pp. 88–105 (p. 89).

10 Rutherford, 'The Future Is Conservative', p. 97.

11 Jon Cruddas, 'Speech to Compass', 13 June 2010, http://liberalconspiracy.org/2010/06/13/his-best-speech-ever-jon-cruddas-on-how-labour-needs-to-reinvent-itself/ (accessed 3 August 2015).

12 Cruddas, 'Speech to Compass'.

13 Rutherford, 'The Future Is Conservative', p. 89.

14 Rutherford, 'The Future is Conservative', p. 104.

15 Jon Cruddas, 'Democracy of the Dead', in Glasman, Rutherford, Stears, and White, *The Labour Tradition*, pp. 140–142 (p. 140).

16 Cruddas, 'Democracy of the Dead', p. 141.

17 Jon Cruddas, 'Radical Hope: Speech to the Radical Society of the Arts', 1 July 2014, http://www.joncruddas.org.uk/jon-cruddas-mp-radical-hope-speech-rsa (accessed 28 August 2014).

18 Jon Cruddas, private interview, 4 March 2015.

19 Jon Cruddas, 'Speech to the Resolution Foundation: Earning and Belonging', 7 February 2013, http://www.joncruddas.org.uk/jon-cruddas-mp-dagenham-and-rainham-earning-and-belonging (accessed 28 August 2014).

20 Rowenna Davis, 'Shades of Blue', in John Denham (ed.), *The Shape of Things to Come: Labour's New Thinking* (London: Fabian Society, 2012), pp. 84–93 (p. 86).

21 Davis, 'Shades of Blue', p. 87.

22 Philip Collins, 'Why I Am Not a Conservative', in Glasman, Rutherford, Stears, and White, *The Labour Tradition*, pp. 114–118 (p. 118).

23 Hazel Blears, 'Hope Will Always Triumph over Fear', in Glasman, Rutherford, Stears, and White, *The Labour Tradition*, pp. 143–152 (pp. 145–146).

24 Collins, 'Why I Am Not a Conservative', p. 115.

25 Maurice Glasman, 'Labour as a Radical Tradition', in Glasman, Rutherford, Stears, and White, *The Labour Tradition*, pp. 14–34 (pp. 22–23).

26 Rutherford, 'The Future Is Conservative', p. 88.

27 Rutherford, 'The Future Is Conservative', p. 100.

28 Rutherford, 'The Future Is Conservative', p. 101.

29 Helen Goodman, 'Tradition and Change: Four People – A Response to the Politics of the Paradox', June 2011, http://leftfootforward.org/images/2011/06/Helen-Goodman-MP-Tradition-and-Change.pdf (accessed 3 August 2015).

30 Blears, 'Hope Will Always Triumph over Fear', pp. 146–147.

31 Rutherford, 'The Future Is Conservative', p. 91.

32 Rutherford, 'The Future Is Conservative', p. 103.

33 Jon Cruddas and Jonathan Rutherford, 'Labour Must Fashion a New Patriotism', *Guardian*, 1 July 2011.

34 Jon Cruddas, private interview, 2 September 2013.

35 Cruddas and Rutherford, 'Labour Must Fashion a New Patriotism'.

36 Mary Riddell and Tom Whitehead, 'Immigration Should Be Frozen, Says Miliband Adviser', *Daily Telegraph*, 18 July 2011. See also Rowenna Davis, *Tangled Up in Blue: Blue Labour and the Struggle for Labour's Soul* (London: Ruskin Publishing, 2011), pp. 195–196.

37 Michael Kenny, 'Faith, Flag and the British Left – One Nation?', OurKingdom, 28 June 2013, www.opendemocracy.net/ourkingdom/michael-kenny/faith-flag-and-british-left-one-nation (accessed 3 August 2015).

38 Michael Kenny, 'Faith, Flag and the "First" New Left: E. P. Thompson and the Politics of "One Nation"', *Renewal* 21:1 (2013): 15–23 (p. 22).

39 Kenny, 'Faith, Flag and the "First" New Left', p. 22.

40 Kenny, 'Faith, Flag and the "First" New Left', p. 21.

41 Stuart White, 'The Dignity of Dissent: E. P. Thompson and One Nation Labour', 2 August 2013, https://www.opendemocracy.net/ourkingdom/stuart-white/dignity-of-dissent-ep-thompson-and-one-nation-labour (accessed 6 August 2015).

42 Tim Soutphommasane, *The Virtuous Citizen: Patriotism in a Multicultural Society* (Cambridge: Cambridge University Press, 2012), p. 71.

43 Soutphommasane, *The Virtuous Citizen*, p. 43.

44 Soutphommasane, *The Virtuous Citizen*, p. 230.

45 Soutphommasane, *The Virtuous Citizen*, p. 75.

46 Soutphommasane, *The Virtuous Citizen*, p. 229.

47 Soutphommasane, *The Virtuous Citizen*, p. 8.

48 Soutphommasane, *The Virtuous Citizen*, p. 196.

49 Soutphommasane, *The Virtuous Citizen*, p. 197. However, these restrictions are only justified when an incoming group is large and cohesive enough to make its own claims on nationhood or when the rate of immigration is so high that it threatens social cohesion. Soutphommasane, *The Virtuous Citizen*, p. 200.

50 Soutphommasane, *The Virtuous Citizen*, p. 211.

51 Soutphommasane, *The Virtuous Citizen*, p. 75.

52 IPPR, *A Fair Deal on Migration for the UK* (London: IPPR, 2014), p. 7.

53 IPPR, *A Fair Deal*, p. 67.

54 IPPR, *A Fair Deal*, pp. 4–6.

55 IPPR, *A Fair Deal*, p. 61.

56 Mark Wickham-Jones, 'The Modernising Antecedents and Historical Origins of One Nation Labour', *Political Quarterly* 84:3 (July–September 2013): 321–329.

57 Ed Miliband, 'Full Transcript: Ed Miliband, Speech to the Fabians', 15 January 2011, http://www.newstatesman.com/blogs/the-staggers/2011/01/labour-government-politics (accessed 12 March 2012).

58 Ed Miliband, 'The New Generation: Speech to the 2010 Labour Party Annual Conference', 28 September 2010, www2.labour.org.uk/ed-miliband---a-new-generation,2010-09-28 (accessed 10 January 2012).

59 Ed Miliband, 'Speech on Englishness', *New Statesman*, 6 June 2012, http://www.newstatesman.com/print/node/186474?title=&text= (accessed 21 July 2012).

60 Miliband, 'Speech on Englishness'.

61 Miliband, 'Speech on Englishness'.

62 Miliband, 'Speech on Englishness'.

63 Ed Miliband, '2014 Labour Conference Speech', 23 September 2014, http://www.labour.org.uk/blog/entry/2014-labour-conference-speech (accessed 25 September 2014).

64 Miliband, 'Speech on Englishness'.

65 Miliband, 'The New Generation'.

66 Ed Miliband, 'A Mandate for Change', 30 August 2010, http://www.labourincoventry.org.uk/index.php?option=com_content&view=article&id (accessed 24 January 2014).

67 Miliband, 'The New Generation'.

68 Ed Miliband, 'Ed Miliband Speech at Senate House', 13 November 2014, http://press.labour.org.uk/post/102524244299/ed-miliband-speech-at-senate-house (accessed 14 November 2014).

69 In a speech devoted to immigration he said: 'I know immigration can benefit our country. But I also know that for that to happen there have to be proper controls on immigration.' Ed Miliband, 'Ed Miliband's Speech on Immigration', 18 April 2015, http://press.labour.org.uk/post/116721382454/ed-milibands-speech-on-immigration (accessed 28 April 2015).

70 Ed Miliband, 'Britain Needs Real Change, Not False Promises – Ed Miliband', 27 May 2014, http:///www.press.labour.org.uk/post/86997808779/britain-needs-real-change-not-false-promises (accessed 28 May 2014).

71 Ed Miliband quoted in Patrick Wintour and Alexandra Topping, 'Change Rules on Migrant Workers, Says Ed Miliband', *Guardian*, 21 June 2012, http://www.theguardian.com/uk/2012/jun/21/change-rules-migrant-workers-miliband (accessed 25 August 2015).

72 Miliband, 'Britain Needs Real Change'.

73 Yvette Cooper, 'Speech to the IPPR', 7 March 2013, http://archive.labour.org.uk/speech-by-yvette-cooper-to-the-ippr (accessed 24 June 2014).

74 Yvette Cooper, 'Speech to the 2014 Labour Party Conference', 24 September 2014, http://press.labour.org.uk/post/98301589749/speech-by-yvette-cooper-mp-to-labours-annual (accessed 25 September 2014).

75 Yvette Cooper, 'Speech on Immigration', 10 April 2014, http://labourlist.org/2014/04/yvette-coopers-immigration-speech-full-text/ (accessed 3 August 2015).

76 Cooper, 'Speech to the 2014 Labour Party Conference'.

77 Ed Miliband, 'Ed Miliband Remarks in Rochester and Strood', 23 October 2014, http://press.labour.org.uk/post/100742025549/ed-miliband-remarks-in-rochester-and-strood (accessed 4 August 2015). In this speech Miliband presented a five-point plan to tackle immigration.

78 Yvette Cooper, 'Labour Approach to Immigration', 18 November 2014, http://press.labour.org.uk/post/102953239474/yvette-cooper-speech-labours-approach-to (accessed 13 December 2014).

79 Douglas Alexander, 'How Labour Will Work for Real Change in Europe', *New Statesman*, 14 March 2014.

80 Ed Balls, 'Winning a Mandate for Change: In Conversation with Ed Balls MP', 14 October 2014, http://www.progressonline.org.uk/event/winning-a-mandate-for-change-in-conversation-with-ed-balls-mp/ (accessed 21 October 2014).

81 Rachel Reeves, 'Changing Rules to Ban Jobseekers from Claiming Benefits for Two Years', *Daily Mail*, 18 November 2014.

82 *Britain Can Be Better: The Labour Party Manifesto 2015* (London: Labour Party, 2015), pp. 49–50.

83 John Denham, 'Home Truths on Migration', 2 June 2014, http://labourlist.org/2014/06/home-truths-on-migration/ (accessed 3 August 2015).

84 John Denham, private interview, 16 July 2013.

85 Denham, private interview, 16 July 2013.

86 Diane Abbott, 'Labour Shouldn't Stoop to UKIP's Level for the Anti-Immigrant Vote', *Guardian*, 28 May 2014.

87 Chuka Umunna quoted in Matt Chorley, 'Ukip are "Absolutely Vile" for Blaming Immigrants for Every Problem in Britain, Warns Labour's Chuka Umunna', *Mail Online*, 22 October 2014, http://www.dailymail.co.uk/news/article-2802843/ukip-absolutely-vile-blaming-immigrants-problem-britain-warns-labour-s-chuka-umunna.html (accessed 13 December 2014).

88   Policy Network, 'How Social Democracy Can Triumph in the 5-75-20 Society', Policy Network, 24 April 2014, http://www.policy-network.net (accessed 6 August 2015).

89   Policy Network, 'How Social Democracy Can Triumph'.

90   John McTernan, 'Immigration Will Not Be the Issue to Split the Labour Party', *Financial Times*, 8 June 2014.

91   McTernan, 'Immigration Will Not Be the Issue to Split the Labour Party'.

92   Anthony Painter, 'Labour's Real "Blue Collar" Problem', LabourList, 12 June 2014, http:// labourlist.org/2014/06/labours-real-blue-collar-problem/ (accessed 12 June 2014).

93   Roberts, *Revolt on the Left*.

94   Ed Miliband, 'Full Text: Ed Miliband Immigration Speech', 14 December 2012, http://www. newstatesman.com/staggers/2012/12/full-text-ed-miliband-immigration-speech (accessed 4 August 2015).

95   Rushanara Ali, 'Everyday Life and National Renewal', in Owen Smith and Rachel Reeves(eds), *One Nation: Power, Hope, Community* (London: One Nation Register, 2013), pp. 77–88 (p. 77).

96   Cooper, 'Speech to the IPPR'.

97   Miliband, 'Immigration Speech'.

98   Cooper, 'Speech to the IPPR'.

99   Miliband, 'Immigration Speech'.

100 Cooper, 'Speech to the IPPR'.

101 Cooper, 'Speech to the IPPR'.

102 Miliband, 'Immigration Speech'.

103 Simon Lee, 'Towards an English Narrative of Democracy?', *Policy Studies* 33:2 (March 2012): 173–191 (p. 188).

104 Michael Kenny, *The Politics of English Nationhood* (Oxford: Oxford University Press, 2014), pp. 31–49.

105 John Denham, 'Speak for the English, Ed Miliband', *Guardian*, 12 November 2013.

106 Jon Cruddas, 'Ukip Isn't a Tory Movement. It's a Party of the Disenfranchised English', *Guardian*, 8 May 2014.

107 Cruddas, private interview, 4 March 2015.

108 Miliband, '2014 Labour Conference Speech'.

109 Miliband, 'Devolution Is for Everyone'.

110 Labour's detailed plans are outlined in Local Government Innovation Taskforce, 'Final Report: People Powered Public Services', July 2014, http://lgalabour.local.gov.uk/ documents/330956/6335671/INNOVATION+TASKFORCE+FINAL+REPORT.pdf (accessed 26 August 2015); and the final report of the Adonis Review, *Mending the Fractured Economy: Smarter State, Better Jobs* (London: Policy Network, 2014). See also *Britain Can Be Better: The Labour Party Manifesto 2015* (London: Labour Party, 2015), p. 64.

111 Ed Miliband, 'The Future is Local – If Labour Is Elected', *Guardian*, 7 July 2014.

112 Richard Vize, 'The Fatal Flaw in Labour's Plan to Give Large Cities More Power', *Guardian*, 4 July 2014.

113 Patrick Diamond, *Governing Britain: Power, Politics and the Prime Minister* (London: I.B. Tauris, 2014), pp. 67–69.

114   *Britain Can Be Better*, p. 64.

115   Ed Miliband quoted in 'A Constitutional Convention for the UK', 19 September 2014, http:// press.labour.org.uk/post/97885913129/a-constitutional-convention-for-the-uk-a-dynamic (accessed 13 December 2014).

116   Tim Bale, 'Putting It Right? The Labour Party's Big Shift on Immigration since 2010', *Political Quarterly* 85:3 (July–September 2014): 296–303 (p. 302).

Conclusion

Trying but failing to renew social democracy

Ideas do matter. Our political culture doesn't sufficiently appreciate them. But they change the world. But ideas are not enough. You need to stick to them even when times are hard. Even when those who disagree are big and powerful.

Ed Miliband[1]

It is a convention of modern politics that leaders of opposition parties start their mandates by promising change. This promise is easy enough to understand. Change is a requirement to move from the opposition benches to a position of power. In order to win, opposition parties need to demonstrate that they have 'changed' their ways that led to defeat, but also that they offer 'change' to voters. In this regard, Ed Miliband's bid for the leadership of the Labour Party in 2010 followed a well-established pattern. But perhaps less conventional was his insistence on challenging 'established thinking' to develop a 'transformative' agenda that would move the party into a more clearly defined social democratic mould.

This book has sought to establish whether he was successful in that task during his short term as leader of the Labour Party. From the onset, this was a difficult question to ask, given that transformative change does not happen overnight and parties in opposition have limited resources to do so. However, as this was Miliband's stated intention, it seems fair to take him to task. Moreover, the global financial crisis offered that critical juncture moment that could have opened the way for transformative change.

As the results of the 2015 general election make clear, Miliband failed to deliver that transformative change. The party obtained its worst results since 1987, winning only 30.4 per cent of the vote (which represents a mere 1.4 per cent increase from the 2010 results). Labour lost all but one of its seats in Scotland and had disappointing results in suburban England. If the party registered gains in London and other urban centres in the south of England, its results in the Midlands, the south-east, and the north of England were disappointing to say the least. In the

Labour heartlands in the north-east of England, UKIP dented Labour's majority, and in some cases, such as in Ed Balls's old constituency of Morley and Outwood, it led to humiliating losses.

Labour's surprising but colossal defeat has a myriad of causes. Some are directly related to Ed Miliband's leadership and to the strategic mistakes he made, but others, such as the emergence of identity politics, the resilience of neoliberalism following the global financial crisis, the legacy of New Labour, the decline of European social democracy, and the explosion of multiparty politics would have negatively impacted the Labour Party regardless of the personality or political inclinations of its leader. Though it will take time fully to understand the causes of Labour's shocking defeat, the fact that Miliband's agenda lacked definition, in some areas intellectual consistency, and was less than the sum of its parts played a role in that defeat. The remaining pages of this final chapter seek to explain why Miliband failed to deliver the transformative change he promised in the early days of his leadership. The chapter will conclude by tentatively suggesting that if Milibandism failed as a political project, it succeeded in identified the key political issues that the Labour Party needs to address if it wants to win the 2020 general election.

The importance of timing

It was not hubris that led Ed Miliband to believe that he was on course to capture a new social 'democratic moment'. Transformative change often occurs in periods of crisis. In those periods that are characterised by instability and often great social, economic, political, and cultural disruption, the principles and assumptions that have guided political action thus far are questioned, because the old recipes no longer seem to work. It is rational, then, to expect political actors to search for new ideas that will help them to make sense of what is happening, but also to find a reasonably clear road map that will guide their way out of the crisis and into a new form of stability. At such times, new ideas, and in this context new economic ideas, enable political actors to reduce uncertainty. They do so because, as Mark Blyth argued, 'such ideas provide agents with both a scientific and a normative critique of the existing economy and polity, and a blueprint that specifies how these elements should be constructed'.[2]

The global financial crisis of 2007–08 was one of those moments. As argued in the introduction, this was not an ordinary crisis.[3] Indeed, it was one that shook the foundations of modern capitalism and that resonated across the world, leaving a destructive trail in its wake. In Europe and the United States, millions of people lost their homes and their jobs; thousands saw their living standards collapse; and governments spent billions of pounds saving failing banks, creating huge public deficits in the process. Across the political spectrum, political and economic actors sought to understand what had provoked the crisis, but also attempted to find ways to respond to it. Like Miliband, other social democratic leaders, and the left in general,

believed that the global financial crisis had opened the way to a new social democratic moment.

Ed Miliband's bid for the leadership of the Labour Party suggests that he thought
the global financial crisis had created the space for paradigmatic change. It was in
those terms that he justified entering the leadership contest. In his first speech as
Labour leader, he talked about the need to choose between returning 'to business
as usual' or challenging 'old thinking to build the new economy we need'.[4] He also
believed that there was a 'centre-left moment' – that is, a moment when Labour
could 'bring the vested interests to heel' and 'change the way the economy works'.[5]

Miliband's transformative goals were genuine. His friend and speech-writer
Marc Stears claimed that Miliband's ambition was 'to create a new paradigm',[6] and
Labour's chair of the Policy Review, Jon Cruddas, took very seriously the task of
're-imagining social democracy'. In other words, Miliband was not aiming just to
tinker with the system. Instead, he wanted to use the space left open by the crisis to
bring big reforms.

In several speeches and articles the Labour leader offered an ideologically cogent
analysis of the causes of the global financial crisis and talked about the need to
implement radical reforms that would amount to a policy paradigm shift. However,
he only had a broad idea about the direction of travel. As he admitted in his first
speech as Labour leader, 'we do not start the journey by claiming we know all the
answers now. We do so by setting a direction of change'.[7] But setting that direction of
change was far more difficult than he anticipated.

The supply of ideas

If the global financial and economic crisis of 2007–08 had opened the way for the
emergence of new ideas, and new ways of thinking about the role of the market
and the State in democratic societies, or about what constitutes the good society,
it did not automatically follow from there that that open space would be occupied.
As Blyth explained, moments of opportunity for fundamental change 'do not lay
courses of action'.[8] Indeed, a number of things need to happen, but the first condition, as Margaret Weir presciently argued, is the availability of ideas that 'provide
the rationale for policy departures'.[9] This seems to be a very obvious condition but it
turns out that it was the first obstacle Miliband encountered.

The political right was quick to adapt and to fill that space with the old ideas
that were at the origin of the crisis. Indeed, the political centre-right was interested
in changing the status quo as little as possible. To that effect, centre-right parties,
assisted by a sympathetic media, quickly refashioned what undoubtedly had been
a crisis of capitalism into a crisis created by a profligate and irresponsible State.
If anything, the political right used the crisis to try to implement the 'small State'
agenda that hitherto they had been too shy to advocate. Across Europe, centre-right
parties convinced voters that the deficit crisis had been created by irresponsible

government spending and could only be addressed by a harsh dose of austerity and State retrenchment. With the support of understanding voters, centre-right governments slashed welfare budgets, eliminated thousands of public sector jobs, and eroded labour rights. Perhaps more surprisingly, voters continued to support this policy mix despite its evident failure to eliminate public deficits and public debt or to promote economic growth.

This turn of events has surprised many social democrats, but it may well be, as Andrew Gamble suggested, that neoliberal ideas 'have become embedded both at the level of common sense, helped by the modern media, and as operational codes through the influence of modern economics'.[10] Vivian A. Schmidt and Mark Thatcher reached a similar conclusion. They argued that neoliberal ideas predominate because 'their simplicity and apparent good sense provide cognitive and normative resonances in policy debates and political discourse'.[11] Neoliberalism has also benefited from the flexibility of its core principles, and the force of institutions in embedding it in political practices and discourse.[12] Furthermore, the neoliberal consensus also prevails because there are no longer many political economy alternatives to it.[13] Hence, as Schmidt and Thatcher argued, the 'dominance of neoliberalism has ensured that it has come to define the terms of discussion and contestation'.[14]

This latter factor is particularly apt to explain the absence of a social democratic response to the global financial crisis in Europe. As Chapter 1 showed, the social democratic left was disorientated and had no coherent or cohesive response to the crisis. Social democratic parties failed to contest the false idea that the global financial crisis and the European debt crisis were caused by State profligacy, and as a result were forced to endorse austerity. In addition, their long-standing support for the process of European integration did not help. Challenging the austerity dogma (and the ideas that underpin it) was tantamount to question the foundations of the Single Market and of the single currency. But as they painfully learnt, not challenging that austerity dogma condemned them to the opposition, as they were unable to respond to the electoral challenges that were emerging from the radical left and the populist right. In short, if many social democrats felt, like Ed Miliband, that their moment had come, they had no road map that would assist them in making it a reality. For a variety of reasons (explained in Chapter 1), the responses that social democrats developed to the crisis were tentative, piecemeal, and ultimately inconsistent and inadequate.

The fact that European social democrats had not developed a viable policy alternative to the prevailing neoliberal ideas affected the Labour Party in a variety of ways. First, there were no successful examples of social democratic parties that had been able to challenge the idea that the deficit crisis had been created by profligate public spending. In fact, like Labour, several social democratic parties were blamed by voters for having created the crisis. Second, Labour was affected by the shortage of ideas around. Political actors, and in particular political parties, are rarely the 'makers of ideology'. As 'carriers' of ideologies, political parties draw inspiration and learn lessons from what similar actors have done in comparable circumstances. It is simply too costly to try an untested idea. Thus, political actors select and use ideas that address the specific circumstances they face, that match their programmatic goals, and that have demonstrated their viability. However, the lessons Miliband learnt from the experiences of other social democratic parties were on the whole negative, as they highlighted the ideational and institutional obstacles to challenging established thinking. Consequently, the state of intellectual and ideological disorientation of European social democracy also meant that the Labour leader could not rely on the ideational or institutional support of European social democratic parties to develop a programme of transformative change.

Miliband's blueprint

In these heavily constrained circumstances the Labour Party under Ed Miliband sought to develop a political programme that would address the policy puzzles created by the global financial crisis and that was consistent with the party's ideological traditions. For that purpose, the Labour leader actively searched for ideas and policy solutions. Interestingly, that search did not concentrate on Europe. Indeed, the party barely ventured into the desolate European political landscape. Instead, Miliband's team searched across the Atlantic – in particular in the United States, but also in the progressive circles of Brazil (via Harvard University) and Australia – and also in the party's keepsake box for the ideas that would form Labour's new agenda.

The starting point of that search was a diagnosis of the causes of the global financial crisis. Miliband drew two key lessons from it. First, he concluded that modern capitalism had created the seeds of the financial crisis and generated unsustainable and unacceptable levels of social inequality. Second, he believed that modern capitalism had to be reformed and regulated to deliver a stable, sustainable, balanced, and equitably shared economic growth. These two key lessons led the party to focus on four main areas of reform: reforming capitalism, addressing inequalities of wealth and power, devolving power and reforming the unresponsive State, and responding to popular anxieties about national identity and belonging that resulted from economic and cultural globalisation.

This particular understanding of the problems facing contemporary Britain shaped Miliband's search for ideas that would address those challenges in a manner that would be ideologically cogent, politically viable, and electorally appealing. That understanding was visible at the level of what Vivien Schmidt calls the 'coordinative discourse' that prevailed in the policy and public spheres and involved a variety of actors, but also at the level of 'communicative discourse', which defined the way the party presented and justified its ideas, and sought to galvanise the public at large.[15]

As this book has shown, the Labour Party under Ed Miliband threw itself into the task of challenging 'established thinking' with great intellectual and ideological gusto. Miliband sought answers from the public intellectuals of the day, and surrounded himself with advisers, such as Lord Wood, Marc Stears, and Jon Cruddas, whose main job was to think deeply about these matters. In their roles as advisers they introduced the Labour leader to new ideas and new intellectual 'gurus', and reacquainted him with those Labour traditions that had something relevant to say about contemporary political and policy challenges. They also relied on the assistance of think-tanks associated with the Labour Party – in particular the IPPR, the Resolution Foundation, Policy Network, and the Fabian Society – and with activist networks like Compass, Progress, LabourList, and not forgetting Blue Labour (there were others, but these were the more influential).

The result of the ideational activities of this epistemic community were dozens of pamphlets, media articles, open-door seminars, and closed-door workshops that dealt with both big-picture issues and minute policy recommendations. The underlying idea guiding these discussions was that their policy proposals would have to consider the financial constraints of a future Labour Government. Indeed, these discussions were often prefaced with a 'reforms for when there is less money around' or 'big reforms, not big spending' type of caveat. What this means is that the process of developing ideas for the Labour Party reflected the political and economic contexts as well as a particular perception about how voters and, crucially, relevant actors would react to them.

This process of reflecting and prioritising the issues, which would constitute the core of the party's agenda, had a clear influence on Miliband's narrative. The manner in which he discussed the challenges he wanted to tackle, as well as the vision he wanted to pursue, accommodated the different traditions and ideas within the party. But this came to be seen as a problem. Indeed, Neal Lawson from Compass argued that 'the problem with Miliband is that he tries to accommodate everyone'.[16] The result of this accommodation was sometimes a well-meaning agenda without a core or a main narrative pull. As Peter Mandelson argued in a nuanced analysis of Labour's catastrophic defeat, Miliband's case for an interventionist social democracy 'did not cohere or become a compelling vision of society'. Instead, he 'fell back on a string of financial offers' that came to sound 'more like populist, transactional, rather than principled, politics'.[17] As a result, that break with established thinking was not as radical as Ed Miliband intended.

If Miliband saw the global financial crisis as an opportunity to reform British capitalism, he failed to explain loud and clear how he would reform it. More importantly, the Labour Party under Ed Miliband failed to challenge the perception that the deficit crisis had been created by irresponsible public spending on the part of the previous Labour Government. This failure had three important and negative consequences. First, the party was never able to recover the mantle of economic credibility that it had lost in 2010. Second, Labour's failure to challenge the prevailing narrative on the causes of the public deficit led to the party's reluctant embrace of austerity. This in turn had the effect of obfuscating and confusing the party's agenda to develop the foundations of a more balanced and productive economy. If the party had signed up to more public spending cuts – in which it did not believe – how could it invest in the transformation of British capitalism? In other words, Labour's embrace of austerity did not enhance the party's economic credibility. In truth, given that Labour was still seen as the party that had led the country to bankruptcy (as some members of the public put it during the televised debates) voters were not the least interested in hearing what Labour had to say about its reform plans.

Similarly, if Miliband's focus on inequality marked a departure from New Labour, he did not develop a cogent narrative and a set of policies that would substantially address the widening gap between rich and poor. Instead, Labour preferred to focus on a list of micro-policies – such as the ban on the bedroom tax, the freeze on energy bills, the reform of zero-hours contracts, and a modest increase in the minimum wage – that failed either to galvanise social democratic voters or to reassure undecided 'Middle England' voters.

Labour's departure from New Labour's and from the party's traditional centralised statecraft was equally half-hearted. Again, Miliband had put his finger on a key issue but failed to take the logic of his analysis to its full conclusion. His agenda for public sector reform was totally invisible (this being said, this is hardly an issue that decides elections) and his plan to devolve powers to local communities in England was over-shadowed by the Coalition's approach to regional development, and in particular by George Osborne's 'Northern Powerhouse' agenda. Finally, Labour's take on the politics of identity and belonging was too bureaucratic and subtle. Miliband understood voters' concerns with immigration as a consequence of globalised capitalism (which was the correct diagnosis) and sought to address them with socio-economic policies. But in the process Labour failed to demonstrate it understood the sense of cultural displacement and insecurity felt by the voters who had been adversely affected by immigration. Thus, 'Milibandism' constitutes an incremental leftward shift from New Labour in its approach to equality, to capitalism, to the State, and to the politics of belonging, but it is far from being the 're-imagined social democracy' able to challenge 'stale' ideas.

A lone rider

Miliband's half-hearted and timid agenda was mostly the result of the multiple compromises he made with different Labour factions. This process of accommodating the different currents of opinion suggests that his grip on the party was weak. In truth, throughout his leadership, he was never in a position of power where he could impose his vision on the party.

This difficulty pointed to the existence of institutional and political constraints that rendered more difficult the process of developing the paradigm-shifting agenda that Miliband desired. To use Peter A. Hall's terminology, the Labour leader did not benefit from 'positional advantages' within the broader institutional framework, nor did he possess the 'ancillary resources' to address relevant conflicts.[18] Indeed, as leader of the main opposition party, he had limited resources to set the political agenda. That role tends to be reserved for the party or parties of government, which control information flows and have the advantage of 'doing things' instead of just 'saying things' or 'stating intentions'.

In addition, Miliband's position within the Labour Party was not one that granted him great autonomy. When he was elected leader the party was exhausted and demoralised. This defeatist mindset became a fertile ground for party feuds and internal wars. As party members readily admit, Labour is not good at accepting the role of opposition, as it quickly 'retreats into factions, all of which are very conservative and are not sites of innovation and contest and renewal'.[19] To prevent Labour going into civil war he devoted considerable energy to party management issues, neglecting the process of developing a strong political agenda.

As the book has shown, throughout his leadership Miliband struggled to attract the support of the relevant actors in the party. Labour backbenchers seemed keen to remind him (and the media) on a regular basis that they did not back him to become party leader. The Blairite wing was particularly effective at undermining his authority by leaking stories about Miliband's blunders or by giving unsolicited advice to the party leader via the pages of the right-wing media and the microphones of the national broadcasters.

Several members of the frontbench team seemed equally sceptical. Some of them, in particular those associated with the New Labour governments, believed that the party could win by offering incremental changes to its outlook. According to Jon Cruddas, the 'dominant method of thinking within the party' argued that cash offers such as raising the minimum wage, pegging energy prices, and getting rid of the bedroom tax would suffice to secure an electoral victory.[20]

This suggests that Labour was – and remains – divided about its future direction. The main schism in the party (there were others) divided those who did not question New Labour's economic model and those who argued for a more social democratic agenda. This schism informed Labour debates about how to deal with the New Labour legacy of a huge public deficit. Another important dividing line separated the 'centralisers' from the 'devolvers' of power. This schism was not just about Ed Balls's resistance to devolving power to English cities and towns. It was also about the culture of the party. Whereas Miliband, Cruddas, and McNicol were eager to inject a more democratic and pluralist culture into Labour politics, others like the former chair of Labour's electoral strategy, Douglas Alexander, favoured a more centralised, hierarchical, and tribalist electoral strategy, and managed to side-line the architects of 'movement politics'. Similarly, there was no consensus within the party about how to respond to the electoral threat posed by UKIP. If the wing associated with Blue Labour had identified the concerns of 'left behind' voters with immigration as a key electoral challenge, other factions of the party underestimated the threat UKIP posed.

It did not help that Miliband was ambivalent about many of these issues. If this ambivalence can be partly explained by his attempt to build a large consensus around him, it is also true that he was undecided about many of these crucial questions. His indecision and typically cautious style led many of his supporters to despair. In short, he looked, and often was, a lone rider.

Image problems

His isolation in the party was quickly picked up and exploited by the media. Throughout Miliband's leadership, countless stories about party divisions, about his shortcomings as a party leader, not forgetting the several plot attempts to oust him, dominated the media coverage of the Labour Party. This coverage contributed to the perception that he was a weak leader, who lacked authority and who was not even able to persuade his party to support his agenda.

The news media focus was not limited to Miliband's psychological profile, though this was a dominant media frame. The news media also assessed his ideas and proposals, and generally concluded that they were either too left-wing and dangerous (in particular for the right-wing press) or not sufficiently credible (the diagnosis of most of the press). The most sympathetic media coverage he obtained came from *The Mirror*, the *New Statesman* and the *Guardian*, but even these publications judged Miliband's ideas to be 'good' in principle but 'vague' or 'undeveloped' in practice.

Though it is hard to establish whether media coverage of Ed Miliband had a direct impact on public opinion, it is possible to point to the similarities between voters' perceptions of the Labour leader and the frames used by the media. A poll commissioned by BuzzFeed and conducted by YouGov reflected the media framing when it asked voters whether the three main party leaders were 'weird'. Unsurprisingly, Ed Miliband topped the poll with 41 per cent of respondents agreeing with the question.[21]

Leaving aside the 'weird' media frame, voters could not imagine Ed Miliband as prime minister. A YouGov poll suggested that one in four voters regarded him as weak rather than strong, and one in three voters said he was simply not up to the job of prime minister.[22] Similarly, an opinion poll conducted by Ipsos MORI in November 2014 revealed that only 13 per cent of Labour supporters thought Ed Miliband was ready to become prime minister,[23] and just a few days before the general election another Ipsos MORI poll showed that only 34 per cent of voters thought Miliband 'was doing a good job as leader of the Labour Party.[24] In addition, a majority of voters questioned the party's competence in economic affairs.[25]

During the electoral campaign the 'weak and dangerous leader' frame dominated the media coverage of the Labour campaign. Taking their cues from the Conservatives' electoral strategy, the right-wing media liked to suggest that a Labour Government would put the unity of the country at risk because it would depend on the SNP to govern. This particular line of attack was quite effective at persuading floating voters. According to a poll conducted by Greenberg Quinlan Rosner Research right after the general election, 24 per cent of voters believed a Labour Government would have been 'bossed around' by the SNP.[26]

But Miliband's image problems were not only the result of negative media coverage or of a divided and unenthusiastic party. They were also of his own making. He refused to play the media game of offering photo-ops or personally revealing stories that would help to 'humanise' or 'normalise' his reputation as 'weird' and too intellectual. Moreover, the Labour leader was not the most media-savvy or most effective and engaging communicator. His performance in television interviews was often wooden and he had Gordon Brown's tendency to answer questions by using slogans or rehearsed sentences. His poor communication skills were seen as a liability for the party. Labour activists and parliamentary candidates reported that Miliband's image problems were often quoted by voters as reasons not to vote Labour.

During the electoral campaign he surprised his party colleagues but also media commentators and his opponents with effective, strong, and articulate media interviews. He even managed to bring some passion to his delivery during the televised debates. But by then, it was too late. Most voters had made up their minds. And most had decided that Ed Miliband was not prime-ministerial. Again, the opinion poll conducted by Greenberg Quinlan Rosner Research revealed that a majority of voters preferred to have David Cameron as prime minister.[27]

His leadership style also partly explains his image problems. Miliband was able to set the political agenda on a number of issues – namely on energy prices, the 'cost of living crisis', and the 'squeezed middle' – however, he was not able to capitalise on these successes. Often, there were long periods of silence until he made a new speech or announced a new proposal. When this happened, Labour was not only invisible to voters but was also unable to set the political agenda. These periods of silence also had a demoralising effect on the party. It was usually during these times that rumours about leadership challenges started to emerge.

There was also a paradox at the heart of his leadership. Miliband tried to be a deliberative type of leader who led by consensus, who was open to debate, and who valued pluralism, and yet he gave little room for other Labour voices to flourish. His team controlled the development of the party's programme and also its media strategy. As a result, several frontbenchers were not given an adequate platform to promote the party's programme. Some, like Tristram Hunt, resented it. In a candid interview with the *Daily Mail*, Hunt argued that such strategy was damaging: 'I never believed the answer to Labour's problems was to show people more of Ed Miliband. It was a ridiculous idea dreamed up by his advisers who have served him badly.'[28] Thus, in the end, Ed Miliband was neither a dialogical nor an authoritative leader able to command loyalty and enthusiasm from either the party, the media, or voters.

Persuasion and comprehension

The fact that Miliband did not obtain support from 'relevant actors' had a spill-over effect for the two other factors that, according to Peter A. Hall, can determine the success of ideas. Because he had few cheerleaders inside or outside the party, the Labour leader was forced to compromise his vision on a number of crucial areas. As a result, his proposals, which had not been fully developed, were robbed of the persuasiveness and comprehensibility they required to be successful.

More importantly, the programme he eventually was able to develop lacked the boldness and radicalism that he had promised. A typical comment made by his supporters was that 'Ed talks a good talk but where's the beef?'. In other words, the gap between the narrative and the policy proposals was quite wide. More than that, the narrative about the resetting of social democracy was totally obfuscated by an electoral strategy that focused on micro-policies such as the bedroom tax, the mansion tax, and zero-hours contracts. The result was what Jon Cruddas defined as 'a dice-and-slice strategy that balkanised the electorate'.[29] In short, there was no compelling and overarching narrative with the potential to galvanise or at least to reassure a large number of voters.

But Miliband also faced legacy problems. The fact that the deficit crisis emerged under the watch of a Labour Government was hugely problematic. The prevailing narrative was that the big hole in the public finances had been created by the irresponsible overspending of the previous Government. The leadership of the Labour Party did little to dispel this perception. Miliband and his team used several speeches to explain that the deficit had been created by the global financial crisis that had started in the United States, but very few people were paying attention. In fact, the media accepted nothing else but an admission of guilt. Thus, Miliband was advised to 'concede and move on'. The assumption was that if Labour admitted to some responsibility in creating the deficit, the party would be allowed to develop its economic strategy. But such an option was a huge gamble as it opened the way for a new set of questions about Labour's economic record.

In the end, Miliband and Balls did not 'concede and move on', but neither did they defend Labour's economic record. This proved to be problematic for the party's economic policy. As Labour was still perceived as the party that had overspent, it was cornered into accepting austerity as the only viable policy option to eliminate the deficit. Labour's reluctant acceptance of austerity undermined its plans to develop the foundations for a more productive, stable, and balanced economy. Moreover, the fact that the party channelled its communicative strategy into emphasising its commitment to fiscal probity and downplaying its plans to raise public borrowing to invest in apprenticeships, economic infrastructure, and investments in key industries raised important questions about the feasibility of such an ambitious agenda. The party attempted to quell these doubts by arguing that many of its big reforms did not require big State investment, but the problem was that no one was listening.

But the acceptance of austerity had other effects. Labour's rhetoric on the deficit was barely distinguishable from the Conservatives'. This had the effect of alienating centre-left voters who preferred the anti-austerity message of the SNP in Scotland and of the Greens in England. It also failed to convince undecided voters, who ended up voting Conservative because they did not believe the economy was safe in Labour's hands.

Similarly, Miliband's egalitarian agenda was compromised by Labour's endorsement of austerity and by its concern with developing a pro-business agenda. This was particularly visible with regard to the party's commitment to the living wage. Indeed, in many speeches delivered in the first years of his leadership, Miliband argued that the living wage and the plight of the low-paid were top priorities for Labour. But as time passed, his proposals for the living wage lost pre-eminence and were eventually watered down. The party's position was limited to encouraging private companies and Labour-led councils to pay a living wage to all of their employees. In the months leading to the general election, the living wage disappeared from Miliband's speeches. Instead, the Labour leader announced a rather modest commitment to increase the minimum wage by £1.50 over a period of five years. This cautious approach was all the more surprising because the Conservative London mayor, Boris Johnson, had campaigned for the living wage, and the governor of the Bank of England, Mark Carney, had warned several times about the negative impact of low pay on Britain's economic growth.

Likewise, the party's confused message on immigration did little to improve its electoral appeal. As the countdown to the general election accelerated, Labour tried to develop an approach that simultaneously sought to respond to the concerns of UKIP supporters with immigration, and to placate those progressive voters who might be tempted to shift their allegiances to the Greens, the SNP, or the Liberal Democrats. Labour attempted to navigate this electoral minefield with a subtle message (sometimes too subtle) that on the one hand stressed the positive role of immigration, but on the other addressed voters' concerns about EU migrants' access to welfare benefits.

This being said, Labour's message was not always subtle or clear. Indeed, in the space of a week in autumn 2014, the party managed simultaneously to declare its support for immigration (in a speech delivered by Miliband) and to announce a series of stringent policy proposals (announced by Rachel Reeves) that framed EU migrants as a drain on the British welfare state. It is fair to conclude that this mixed message was neither comprehensible nor persuasive as voters were left none the wiser about Labour's position on immigration.

 There were also problems with Labour's agenda for State reform. This was an important component of 'Milibandism', however it lacked visibility and salience. If, a priori, voters were supportive of the idea of a more responsive and relational State, it was clearly not a top public concern. Moreover, the policy proposals were too minute to be able to galvanise important sectors of the electorate, apart from *Guardian* readers and the minuscule pool of political activists.

In short, Miliband encountered several ideational, political, and institutional obstacles to putting in place the transformative agenda that challenged the established thinking of his time. In particular, on the issues that would decide the election – the economy and immigration – the differences between Labour and the Conservatives were barely noticeable (though there were substantial differences in their concrete approaches to these issues). By contrast, in the areas where Labour had something distinct to say, Miliband was under pressure to downplay the radicalism of his ideas.

So what does explain Miliband's incremental and cautious agenda? Well, to start with, his timing was not auspicious. He became leader of the Labour Party at the time when the 'social democratic moment' was quickly vanishing. The political right was able successfully to transform what had started as a crisis of capitalism into a crisis of the State. Second, the problem of timing affected the supply of ideas in social democratic circles. The social democratic left, which had been in decline since the 1970s, was not able to develop a credible and coherent alternative to the policy puzzles of the day. This suggests that Labour's difficulties were not unique, nor were they created by a single individual. Instead, they are part of a bigger trend in social democratic politics.

The social democratic embrace of neoliberalism that took place in the late 1990s was successful for a while but eventually it created the conditions for the shrinking of its electoral basis. The still existent working-class voters who had been adversely affected by the economic globalisation that Third Way politics promoted sought refuge in the xenophobic but reassuring policies of the populist right, or stopped voting altogether. On the other hand, the progressive middle-class voters upon whom social democratic parties depended to get elected discovered that there were left-wing alternatives to the neoliberalisation of European social democracy.

In Britain, those trends were evident before 2010. At the 2007 Scottish Parliament elections the SNP replaced Labour as the main party of Scotland. In 2014 the campaign for the Scottish independence referendum hammered the last nail into Labour's coffin in Scotland. The SNP had skilfully succeeded in portraying Labour as 'Red Toryism' and in presenting the SNP as the representatives of social democratic values. Similarly, in 2005 some Labour figures had rightly identified immigration as a key issue to the party's electoral base, but the issue was ignored by the leadership. In 2015, Labour suffered the consequences of that neglect.

Labour's defeat was also the result of Miliband's shortcomings as leader. The fact that he won the leadership of the party in the wrong way, the fact that he ruffled the feathers of the Blairite wing by disowning the legacy of New Labour in strong terms, and the fact that he was not a charismatic and authoritative leader had a key role in explaining Labour's colossal defeat. Simply put, voters thought that Ed Miliband did not have the attributes of an authoritative prime minister.

What now for Labour?

At the time of writing, the party is in the middle of a simultaneously introspective and cacophonous debate about the causes of its defeat and about the future road ahead. Understandably, the recriminations and the finger-pointing play a big role in these debates. Some party grandees, media commentators, leadership contenders, and wannabes were quick to blame Miliband's decision to abandon the ubiquitous but ill-defined centre-ground of politics as the factor that decided Labour's catastrophic defeat. According to this viewpoint, forcefully made by furious Blairites, Miliband's ideas were too left-wing, too anti-business, and failed to win the support of 'aspirational voters'. In order to win again, they say, Labour needs to develop an 'aspirational message' that appeals to the suburban, lower middle classes who would like to shop at John Lewis, though the policies they advocate do not necessarily target those aspirational voters. Indeed they would mostly benefit Britain's wealthiest citizens.

But another wing claimed that Labour lost because Miliband had neglected the 'left behind' voters who voted UKIP because they were against immigration and mistrusted Westminster politics. A few Labour backbenchers argued that Labour's embrace of austerity politics had alienated core Labour voters who did not bother to vote or voted for the SNP or the Greens, whilst others felt Labour lost because the party did not offer a unifying message that could galvanise all types of voters. But most agreed that Ed Miliband did not have what it takes to convince voters that he was prime-ministerial.

These different analyses of the causes of Labour's defeat reflect the mixed messages voters sent to the party on 7 May. In Scotland, Labour was decimated, losing all but one MP. In England, the electoral landscape was more complex. Voters from suburban constituencies in the south of England were still blaming Labour for the deficit crisis and decided to place their trust in the Conservatives' long-term economic plan, which thus far had failed to eliminate the public deficit. In the south-west and south-east, disillusioned Liberal Democrat voters, whom Miliband sought to woo, voted for other parties. In the Midlands, the UKIP surge helped the Conservatives and harmed Labour. And even in the party's heartlands in the north-east of England, Labour failed to enthuse their traditional voters (the twenty seats with the lowest turnouts were won by Labour candidates) and shed votes to UKIP. The only areas of the country where Labour made significant gains were in London, where it won forty-five out seventy-three seats, and other prosperous cities in the south of England.

This changed electoral landscape means that the next Labour leader will face a very challenging task. Simply put, Labour faces electoral challenges from the left, from the centre, and from the populist right. As Labour found out in 2015, developing a programme and a message that convince different sets of voters will be challenging to say the least. To win the 2020 election the party will have to do far more than to appeal to 'aspirational' voters with a unifying message. Some of these voters will not be the least inspired by centrist platitudes. It will be even more difficult to win the support of those 'left behind' voters who saw their lives transformed by the impact of economic globalisation. Promises of more protection at work or of affordable housing will not address their sense of cultural displacement and unease. On the other hand, Labour cannot promise to impose more controls on immigration. Thus, a large chunk of this electorate may be lost forever.

Labour's difficulties go beyond finding a unifying message that will obtain the support of a balkanised electorate. Like other social democratic parties in Europe, the Labour Party is in decline. As Britain's multiparty and multinational politics seems now to be a permanent fixture, it is very likely that Labour's survival will depend on the party's adoption of a more pluralist culture. This implies that Labour has to consider the possibility of starting dialogues and/or forming alliances with other progressively minded parties and movements.

In the short term, the main task Labour faces will be about regaining economic credibility, though that is easier said than done. As the Conservatives and the Liberal Democrats demonstrated, the concept of 'economic credibility' is unrelated to evidence-based policies and is totally dependent on how the conventional wisdom of the time defines it. Large sections of the electorate are convinced that Labour's overspending led to the rise of the public deficit and yet consider credible the Government that failed its deficit targets. Without powerful supporters in the media, it will be very difficult to challenge this narrative. The only hope for Labour is that the national obsession with the public deficit will abate in the coming years.

There are signs that the public debate is slowly shifting. The Bank of England has tried to move the national conversation on the economy by publishing reports that highlight Britain's low-productivity problem, and these concerns are starting to percolate through political discussions. For example, the former Conservative cabinet minister Kenneth Clarke told the *New Statesman* that 'getting a rebalanced economy isn't just debt'.[30] Similarly, in the pages of the *Financial Times* the columnist Philip Stephens lamented the national obsession with austerity when low productivity was a far more serious economic problem.[31] But Labour should not rely on others to carry this debate. It has to lead it, and with far more confidence and conviction than it has shown since 2010.

In the rush to find a road map to electoral success the Labour Party is tempted to condemn Milibandism to the dustbin of the party's history, but this would be a serious mistake. If Miliband and the frontbench team committed grave errors in terms of electoral strategy and emphasis, the party should not ditch Milibandism altogether. As Blair and Mandelson admitted in their election post-mortems, Miliband was right on a number of things. In particular, he was correct in identifying three particular issues – the rise of inequalities, the need to develop a more balanced economy based on an active industrial policy and on high-skilled workforce, and the need to decentralise the State and reform public services – that will continue to dominate the political agenda in the coming years.

As Blair recognised, Miliband was 'absolutely right to raise the issue of inequality and to say that Labour should focus anew on it'.[32] But as we saw, Miliband's approach to equality was minimalist, though it was presented in an angry and divisive language that was bound to be badly received by the right-wing press. The fact remains that the widening gap between rich and poor is an issue that negatively affects Britain's economic prospects and that worries many voters. It is also true that many of Labour's minimalist labour market reforms and redistributive policies were popular. So popular, in fact, that the Conservatives are moving quickly to occupy this territory. The prime minister's focus on 'blue-collar workers' with policy commitments on the living wage and zero-hours contracts, and Steve Hilton's attack on what he defined as 'obscene' executive pay, suggest that the Tories will try to neutralise Labour in this particular area. More crucially, this is a defining aspect of Labour's ideology. If the party is no longer the standard-bearer for egalitarian politics and for workers' rights it may as well consider closing its doors.

The right of the party is also busy accusing Miliband of not having developed a strategy for economic growth. This is not exactly true. Miliband, together with Lord Adonis, Ed Balls, and even Chuka Umunna, developed plans to rebalance the economy and address the long-term problems of low productivity with an active industrial policy and new focus on apprenticeships and market-regulating policies.[33] But this policy was obfuscated by Labour's convoluted stances on the deficit. It is also true that a deficit-obsessed mainstream media was not the least interested in hearing Labour's plans to rebalance the economy.

Miliband was also attacked for his lack of interest in public sector reform. But the party's manifesto tells a different story. In fact, the manifesto brought to the centre stage Labour's 'power agenda', though – and for good electoral reasons – this theme was hardly addressed during the electoral campaign. Finally, Miliband tried but failed to turn the party into a movement that was open to other progressive forces and grassroots movements. The electoral landscape suggests that if Labour wants to survive as a major political party in Britain it should revisit Miliband's movement politics and open its doors to dialogues with other progressives and like-minded parties such as the Liberal Democrats, the Greens, and even the SNP. Thus, if Milibandism failed to renew social democracy, it has identified the key political battlegrounds upon which its renewal will rely.

Notes

1 Ed Miliband, 'The Choice: Leadership. Speech by Ed Miliband MP', 25 July 2014, http://press.labour.org.uk/post/92819342334/the-choice-leadership-speech-by-ed-miliband-mp (accessed 28 July 2014).

2 Mark Blyth, *Great Transformations: Economic Ideas and Institutional Change in the Twentieth Century* (Cambridge: Cambridge University Press, 2002), p. 37.

3 Andrew Gamble offers a lucid explanation of the magnitude of the global financial and economic crisis and also explains why the crisis is far from over. Andrew Gamble, *Crisis without End? The Unravelling of Western Prosperity* (Houndmills: Palgrave Macmillan, 2014), pp. 18–27.

4 Ed Miliband, 'The New Generation: Speech to the 2010 Labour Party Annual Conference', 28 September 2010, www2.labour.org.uk/ed-miliband---a-new-generation,2010-09-28 (accessed 10 January 2012).

5 Jason Cowley, 'Ed Miliband Interview: He's Not for Turning', *New Statesman*, 5 September 2012.

6 Marc Stears quoted in Cowley, 'Ed Miliband Interview'.

7 Miliband, 'The New Generation'.

8 Blyth, *Great Transformations*, p. 275.

9 Margaret Weir, 'Ideas and Politics: The Acceptance of Keynesianism in Britain and the United States', in Peter A. Hall (ed.), *The Political Power of Economic Ideas: Keynesianism across Nations* (Princeton: Princeton University Press, 1989), pp. 53–86 (p. 54).

10 Gamble, *Crisis without End?*, p. 14.

11 Mark Thatcher and Vivian A. Schmidt, 'Conclusion: Explaining the Resilience of Neoliberalism and Possible Pathways Out', in Vivian A. Schmidt and Mark Thatcher (eds), *Resilient Liberalism in Europe's Political Economy* (Cambridge: Cambridge University Press, 2013), pp. 403–431 (p. 413).

12 Vivien A. Schmidt and Mark Thatcher, 'Theorizing Ideational Continuity: The Resilience of Neo-Liberal Ideas in Europe', in Schmidt and Thatcher, *Resilient Liberalism*, pp. 1–50 (pp. 15–16).

13 Gamble, *Crisis without End?*, p. 14.

14 Schmidt and Thatcher, 'Theorizing Ideational Continuity', p. 19.

15 Vivien Schmidt, 'Discursive Institutionalism: The Explanatory Power of Ideas and Discourse', *Annual Review of Political Science* 11 (2008): 303–326 (p. 310).

16 Neal Lawson, private interview, 10 May 2013.

17 Peter Mandelson, 'Labour Will Never Be Credible without Convincing People of Its Economic Credentials', LabourList, 10 May 2015, http://labourlist.org/2015/05/labour-will-never-be-credible-without-convincing-people-of-its-economic-credentials/ (accessed 11 May 2015).

18 Hall argues that 'the movement from one paradigm to another will ultimately entail a set of judgements that is more political in tone, and the outcome will depend not only on the arguments of competing factions, but on their positional advantage within a broader institutional framework, on the ancillary resources they can command in the relevant conflicts, and on exogenous factors affecting the power of one set of actors to impose its paradigm over others'. Peter A. Hall, 'Policy Paradigms, Social Learning, and the State: The Case of Economic Policymaking in Britain', *Comparative Politics* 25:3 (April 1993): 275–296 (p. 280).

19 Jon Cruddas, private interview, 2 September 2013.

20 Jon Cruddas, private interview, 4 March 2015.

21 Jim Waterson, 'The British Public Still Thinks Ed Miliband Is Weird', BuzzFeed, 23 March 2014, http://www.buzzfeed.com/jimwaterson/the-british-public-still-think-ed-miliband-is-weird (accessed 27 August 2015).

22 Peter Kellner, 'The Trouble with Labour Leader Ed Miliband', *Prospect*, 19 June 2014, http://www.prospectmagazine.co.uk/features/the-trouble-with-ed-miliband (accessed 20 June 2014).

23   Alberto Nardelli, 'Ed Miliband Is Most Unpopular Leader among His Own Party's Supporters Ever', *Guardian*, 12 November 2014, http://www.theguardian.com/news/datablog/2014/nov/12/ed-miliband-is-the-most-unpopular-leader-among-labour-supporters-ever (accessed 27 August 2015).

24   Ipsos MORI, 'Political Monitor: Satisfaction Ratings 1997–Present', 29 April 2015, https://www.ipsos-mori.com/researchpublications/researcharchive/88/Political-Monitor-Satisfaction-Ratings-1997Present.aspx?view=wide (accessed 18 May 2015).

25   Kellner, 'The Trouble with Labour Leader Ed Miliband.

26   Greenberg Quinlan Rosner Research, 'UK Post-Election Poll for the TUC', May 2015, http://www.gqrr.com/uk-post-election-1 (accessed 15 May 2015).

27   Greenberg Quinlan Rosner Research, 'UK Post-Election Poll'.

28   Simon Walters, 'Now a Shadow Minister Plunges in the Dagger: Tristram Hunt Joins Labour Revolt', *Daily Mail*, 8 November 2014, http://www.dailymail.co.uk/news/article-2826937/Ed-shadow-minister-plunges-dagger-Tristram-Hunt-joins-Labour-revolt-poll-says-Miliband-liability.html (accessed 27 August 2015).

29   Jon Cruddas quoted by Toby Helm, 'Jon Cruddas: This Could Be the Greatest Crisis the Labour Party Has Ever Faced', *Guardian*, 16 May 2015, http://www.theguardian.com/politics/2015/may/16/labour-great-crisis-ever (accessed 3 August 2015).

30   Anoosh Chakelian, 'An Interview with Ken Clarke: "The Iron of the Treasury Has Entered My Soul"', *New Statesman*, 16 April 2015.

31   Philip Stephens, 'Lies, Damned Lies and the British Election', *Financial Times*, 15 April 2015.

32   Tony Blair, 'Labour Must Be the Party of Ambition as Well as Compassion', *Observer*, 10 May 2015.

33   Patrick Diamond, 'Labour Is Proposing a Sensible Reform of British Capitalism', *Independent*, 9 February 2015, http://www.independent.co.uk/voices/comment/labour-is-proposing-a-sensible-restructure-of-british-capitalism-10034855.html (accessed 27 August 2015).

Bibliography

Abbott, Diane. 'Labour Shouldn't Stoop to UKIP's Level for the Anti-Immigrant Vote', *Guardian*, 28 May 2014.

Adonis, Andrew. 'Youth Unemployment: It's Not the Age that Matters but Lack of Skills', *Guardian*, 1 July 2013.

Adonis Review. *Mending the Fractured Economy: Smarter State, Better Jobs*, London: Policy Network, 2014.

Alexander, Douglas. 'How Labour Will Work for Real Change in Europe', *New Statesman*, 14 March 2014.

Alexander, Douglas, and Ed Miliband. 'We Will Defend the State', *Guardian*, 5 February 2010, http://www.theguardian.com/commentisfree/2010/feb/05/defend-state-osborne-nudge-equality (accessed 17 August 2015).

Ali, Rushanara. 'Everyday Life and National Renewal', in Owen Smith and Rachel Reeves (eds), *One Nation: Power, Hope, Community*, London: One Nation Register, 2013, pp. 77–88.

Anderson, Elizabeth S. 'What Is the Point of Equality?', *Ethics* 109 (January 1999): 287–337.

Anderson, Perry. 'The Europe to Come', in Peter Gowan and Perry Anderson (eds), *The Question of Europe*, London: Verso, 1997.

Atkins, Judi. 'Narrating One Nation: The Ideology and Rhetoric of the Miliband Labour Party', *Politics* 35:1 (February 2015): 19–31.

Bale, Tim. 'Concede and Move On? One Nation and the Welfare State', *Political Quarterly* 84:3 (October 2013): 342–352.

Bale, Tim. *Five Year Mission: The Labour Party under Ed Miliband*, Oxford: Oxford University Press, 2015.

Bale, Tim. 'Four Reasons Ed Miliband Is Still a Good Opposition Leader', *Guardian*, 16 October 2014.

Bale, Tim. 'Putting It Right? The Labour Party's Big Shift on Immigration since 2010', *Political Quarterly* 85:3 (July–September 2014): 296–303.

Balls, Ed. 'Beyond the Third Way: A New Inclusive Prosperity for the 21st Century', 30 June 2014, http://www.edballs.co.uk/blog/?p=5244 (accessed 28 August 2014).

Balls, Ed. 'Conservative Complacency Won't Help Working People', *Guardian*, 24 July 2014.

Balls, Ed. 'Don't Cripple the City', *Evening Standard*, 31 October 2011, http://www.standard. co.uk/news/dont-cripple-the-city-london-can-lead-the-recovery-6363131.html (accessed 16 August 2015).

Balls, Ed. 'Now Let's Offer a Real Choice – and Nail the Tory Lie on Cuts', *Guardian*, 26 September 2010, www.guardian.co.uk/commentisfree/2010/sep/26/offer-choice-nail-tory-cuts-lie (accessed 10 January 2012).

Balls, Ed. 'My Speech to the Fabian Society', 24 January 2014, http://www.edballs.co.uk/blog/?p=4747 (accessed 4 February 2014).

Balls, Ed. 'Speech to the Labour Party Conference', 22 September 2014, http://press.labour. org.uk/post/98137818419/speech-by-ed-balls-mp-to-labour-party-annual (accessed 23 September 2014).

Balls, Ed. 'Striking the Right Balance for the British Economy', 3 June 2013, http://www.labour.org. uk/striking-the-right-balance-for-the-british-economy (accessed 5 June 2013).

Balls, Ed. 'There Is an Alternative – Speech to Bloomberg', 27 August 2010, http://www.edballs. co.uk/blog/?p=907 (accessed 10 January 2012).

Balls, Ed. 'Winning a Mandate for Change: In Conversation with Ed Balls MP', 14 October 2014, http:// www.progressonline.org.uk/event/winning-a-mandate-for-change-in-conversation-with-ed-balls-mp/ (accessed 21 October 2014).

Balls, Ed, and Ed Miliband. 'Ed Miliband and Ed Balls Press Conference', 14 March 2011, http://www.labour.org.uk/ed-miliband-and-ed-balls-press-conference,2011-03-14 (accessed 20 January 2012).

Behr, Rafael. 'Milibandism's Next Chapter: Reforming the State', *New Statesman*, 7 February 2014.

Behr, Rafael. 'Miliband's Reshuffle Was Post-Blairite, Not Anti-Blairite', *New Statesman*, 8 October 2013, http://www.newstatesman.com/politics/2013/10/milibands-reshuffle-was-p ost-blairite-not-anti-blairite (accessed 1 August 2015).

Behr, Rafael. 'Miliband's Sheet Is Still Blank on Public Service Reform', *New Statesman*, 18 December 2013, http://wwwnewstatesman.com/print/politics/2013/12/milibands-sheet-st ill-blank-public-service-reform (accessed 20 December 2013).

Béland, Daniel. 'The Idea of Power and the Role of Ideas', *Political Studies* 8 (2010): 145–154.

Béland, Daniel, and Robert Henry Cox. 'Introduction: Ideas and Politics', in Daniel Béland and Robert Henry Cox (eds), *Ideas and Politics in Social Science Research*, Oxford: Oxford University Press, 2011, pp. 1–26.

Bennett, Owen. '"Windfall Tax on Energy Companies to Stop Heating or Eating Choice" Argues Sir John Major', *Express*, 22 October 2013, http://www.express.co.uk/news/uk/438504/ Windfall-tax-on-energy-companies-to-stop-heating-or-eating-choice-argues-Sir-John-Major (accessed 18 August 2015).

Berman, Sheri. *The Primacy of Politics: Social Democracy and the Making of Europe's Twentieth Century*, Cambridge: Cambridge University Press, 2010.

Bevir, Mark. 'New Labour: A Study in Ideology', *British Journal of Politics and International Relations* 2:3 (2000): 277–301.

Blair, Tony. 'Labour Must Be the Party of Ambition as Well as Compassion', *Observer*, 10 May 2015.

Blair, Tony. 'Labour Must Search for Answers and Not Merely Aspire to Be a Repository for People's Anger', *New Statesman*, 11 April 2013.

Blears, Hazel. 'Hope Will Always Triumph over Fear', in Maurice Glasman, Jonathan Rutherford, Marc Stears, and Stuart White (eds), *The Labour Tradition and the Politics of Paradox: The Oxford London Seminars 2010–11*, n.p.: Oxford London Seminars, 2011, pp. 143–152.

Blyth, Mark. ' "Any More Bright Ideas?" The Ideational Turn of Comparative Political Economy', *Comparative Politics* 29:2 (January 1997): 229–250.

Blyth, Mark. 'The Austerity Delusion: Why a Bad Idea Won Over the West', *Foreign Affairs* 92:3 (May/June 2013): 41–56.

Blyth, Mark. *Austerity: The History of a Dangerous Idea*, Oxford: Oxford University Press, 2013.

Blyth, Mark. *Great Transformations: Economic Ideas and Institutional Change in the Twentieth Century*, Cambridge: Cambridge University Press, 2002.

Blyth, Mark. *Britain Can Be Better: The Labour Party Manifesto 2015* (London: Labour Party, 2015).

Brown, Gordon. 'The Mansion House Speech', 20 June 2007, http://ukingermany.fco.gov.uk/en/news/?view=Speech$id=4616377 (accessed 10 October 2012).

Buckler, Steve, and David P. Dolowitz. 'Ideology, Party Identity and Renewal', *Journal of Political Ideologies* 14:1 (February 2009): 11–30.

Budge, Ian. 'A New Spatial Theory of Party Competition: Uncertainty, Ideology and Policy Equilibria Viewed Comparatively and Temporally', *British Journal of Political Science* 24:4 (October 1994): 443–467.

Burnham, Andy. 'Labour's 10-Year Plan for Health and Care', 27 January 2015, http://www.andy-burnham.blogspot.co.uk/2015/02/andy-burnham-speech-on-labour's-10-year-plan-for-health-and-care (accessed 20 February 2015).

Byrne, Liam. 'Eliminating "Power Failures": A New Agenda for Tackling Inequality', in Robert Philpot (ed.), *The Purple Book: A Progressive Future for Labour*, London: Biteback Publishing, 2011, pp. 129–143.

Chakelian, Anoosh. 'An Interview with Ken Clarke: "The Iron of the Treasury Has Entered My Soul" ', *New Statesman*, 16 April 2015.

Chang, Ha-Joon, and Antonio Andreoni. 'Rebuilding the UK Industrial Base', in Chuka Umunna (ed.), *Owning the Future: How Britain Can Make It in a Fast-Changing World*, London: Policy Network, 2014, pp. 103–112.

Chorley, Matt. 'Ukip are "Absolutely Vile" for Blaming Immigrants for Every Problem in Britain, Warns Labour's Chuka Umunna', *Mail Online*, 22 October 2014, http://www.dailymail.co.uk/news/article-2802843/ukip-absolutely-vile-blaming-immigrants-problem-britain-warns-labour-s-chuka-umunna.html (accessed 13 December 2014).

Clarke, Eoin, and Owain Gardner (eds). *The Red Book: Labour Left*. Cambridge: Searching Finance, 2012.

Coll, Steve. 'The Whole Intellectual Edifice', *New Yorker*, 23 October 2008, http://www.newyorker.com/news/steve-coll/the-whole-intellectual-edifice (accessed 20 August 2014).

Collins, Philip. 'Why I Am Not a Conservative', in Maurice Glasman, Jonathan Rutherford, Marc Stears, and Stuart White (eds), *The Labour Tradition and the Politics of Paradox: The Oxford London Seminars 2010–11*, n.p.: Oxford London Seminars, 2011, pp. 114–118.

'A Constitutional Convention for the UK', 19 September 2014, http://press.labour.org.uk/post/97885913129/a-constitutional-convention-for-the-uk-a-dynamic (accessed 13 December 2014).

Cooke, Graeme. 'New and Blue', in Maurice Glasman, Jonathan Rutherford, Marc Stears, and Stuart White, *The Labour Tradition and the Politics of Paradox*, n.p.: Oxford London Seminars, 2011, pp. 133–139.

Cooke, Graeme, and Rick Muir. 'The Possibilities and Politics of the Relational State', in Graeme Cooke and Rick Muir (eds), *The Relational State: How Recognising the Importance of Human Relationships Could Revolutionise the Role of the State*, London: IPPR, 2012, pp. 3–19.

Cook, Graham, Adam Lent, Anthony Painter, and Hopi Sen. *In the Black Labour*, London: Policy Network, 2011, http://www.policy-network.net/publications/4101/-in-the-black-labour (accessed 3 August 2015).

Cooper, Yvette. 'Labour Approach to Immigration', 18 November 2014, http://press.labour.org.uk/post/102953239474/yvette-cooper-speech-labours-approach-to (accessed 13 December 2014).

Cooper, Yvette. 'Speech to the IPPR', 7 March 2013, http://archive.labour.org.uk/speech-by-yvette-cooper-to-the-ippr (accessed 24 June 2014).

Cooper, Yvette. 'Speech on Immigration', 10 April 2014, http://labourlist.org/2014/04/yvette-coopers-immigration-speech-full-text/ (accessed 3 August 2015).

Cooper, Yvette. 'Speech to the 2014 Labour Party Conference', 24 September 2014, http://press.labour.org.uk/post/98301589749/speech-by-yvette-cooper-mp-to-labours-annual (accessed 25 September 2014).

Cowley, Jason. 'Ed Miliband Interview: He's Not for Turning', *New Statesman*, 5 September 2012.

Cramme, Olaf, and Patrick Diamond (eds). *After the Third Way: The Future of Social Democracy in Europe*. London: I.B. Tauris, 2012.

Crawford, Rowena, Carl Emmerson, Soumaya Keynes, and Gemma Tetlow. *Post-Election Austerity: Parties' Plans Compared*, London: Institute for Fiscal Studies, 2015.

Crouch, Colin. *The Strange Non-Death of Neoliberalism*, Cambridge: Polity Press, 2011.

Cruddas, Jon. 'Democracy of the Dead', in Maurice Glasman, Jonathan Rutherford, Marc Stears, and Stuart White (eds), *The Labour Tradition and the Politics of Paradox: The Oxford London Seminars 2010–11*, n.p.: Oxford London Seminars, 2011, pp. 140–142.

Cruddas, Jon. 'Power and Belonging: Speech to Acevo Conference', 7 May 2014, http://www.joncruddas.org.uk/jon-cruddas-mp-power-and-belonging (accessed 28 August 2014).

Cruddas, Jon. 'Power and One Nation: Speech to the NLGN Annual Conference', 12 February 2014, http://www.joncruddas.org.uk/node/595 (accessed 28 August 2014).

Cruddas, Jon. 'Radical Hope: Speech to the Radical Society of the Arts', 1 July 2014, http://www.joncruddas.org.uk/jon-cruddas-mp-radical-hope-speech-rsa (accessed 28 August 2014).

Cruddas, Jon. 'Speech on Love and Work', 29 January 2015, http://www.joncruddas.org.uk/sites/joncruddas.org.uk/files/FINAL%20Love%20and%20Work%2028.1.15.pdf (accessed 2 February 2015).

Cruddas, Jon. 'Speech to Compass', 13 June 2010, http://liberalconspiracy.org/2010/06/13/his-best-speech-ever-jon-cruddas-on-how-labour-needs-to-reinvent-itself/ (accessed 3 August 2015).

Cruddas, Jon. 'Speech to the Resolution Foundation: Earning and Belonging', 7 February 2013, http://www.joncruddas.org.uk/jon-cruddas-mp-dagenham-and-rainham-earning-and-belonging (accessed 28 August 2014).

Cruddas, Jon. 'Ukip Isn't a Tory Movement. It's a Party of the Disenfranchised English', *Guardian*, 8 May 2014.

Cruddas, Jon, and Andrea Nahles. *Building the Good Society: The Project of the Democratic Left*, London: Compass, 2009.

Cruddas, Jon, and Lisa Nandy. 'Only Labour Can Build the Big Society', *New Statesman*, 9 May 2014.

Cruddas, Jon, and Jonathan Rutherford. 'Labour Must Fashion a New Patriotism', *Guardian*, 1 July 2011.

Cruddas, Jon, and Jonathan Rutherford. *One Nation: Labour's Political Renewal*, London: One Nation Register, 2014, http://www.joncruddas.org.uk/sites/joncruddas.org.uk/files/OneNation%20 by%20Jon.pdf (accessed 3 August 2015).

Dahlgreen, Will. 'Voters: Energy Prices Are Number One Threat', YouGov, 25 September 2013, http://yougov.co.uk/news/2013/09/25/energy-prices-economic-threat/ (accessed 3 August 2015).

Davis, Rowenna. 'Arnie Graf: The Man Ed Miliband Asked to Rebuild Labour', *Guardian*, 21 November 2012, http://www.theguardian.com/politics/2012/nov/21/arnie-graf-labour-pa rty-miliband?cat=politics&type=article (accessed 3 August 2015).

Davis, Rowenna. 'Shades of Blue', in John Denham (ed.), *The Shape of Things to Come: Labour's New Thinking*, London: Fabian Society, 2012, pp. 85–93.

Davis, Rowenna. *Tangled Up in Blue: Blue Labour and the Struggle for Labour's Soul*, London: Ruskin Publishing, 2011.

Denham, John. 'Home Truths on Migration', 2 June 2014, http://labourlist.org/2014/06/ home-truths-on-migration/ (accessed 3 August 2015).

Denham, John. 'Speak for the English, Ed Miliband', *Guardian*, 12 November 2013.

Diamond, Patrick. *Governing Britain: Power, Politics and the Prime Minister*, London: I.B. Tauris, 2014.

Diamond, Patrick. 'Labour Must Wise Up to What Voters Really Want', *Guardian*, 24 January 2014.

Diamond, Patrick. 'Mutualism and Social Democracy', in *What Mutualism Means for Labour: Political Economy and Public Services*, London: Policy Network, 2011, pp. 7–13.

Diamond, Patrick. 'Wanted: A Tax-and-Spend Policy that Makes Sense', *Guardian*, 27 March 2014.

Dimitrakapoulos, Dionyssis G. 'Introduction: Social Democracy, European Integration and Preference Formation', in Dionyssis G. Dimitrakapoulos (ed.), *Social Democracy and European Integration: The Politics of Preference Formation*, Abingdon: Routledge, 2011, pp. 1–22.

Dobbin, Frank, Beth Simmons, and Geoffrey Garrett. 'The Global Diffusion of Public Policies: Social Construction, Coercion, Competition, or Learning?', *Annual Review of Sociology* 33 (2007): 449–472.

Eagle, Angela. 'Why We Need a People's Politics Inquiry', LabourList, 24 April 2013, http:// labourlist.org/2013/04/why-we-need-a-peoples-politics-enquiry/ (accessed 27 March 2015).

Eaton, George. 'Jacob Hacker: Ed Miliband's Wonkish Pin-Up', *New Statesman*, 11 July 2013.

Eaton, George. 'Who Will Pay for Labour's Next Election Campaign?', *New Statesman*, 12 September 2013, http://www.newstatesman.com/politics/2013/09/who-will-pay-labours- next-election-campaign (accessed 21 February 2014).

Emanuel, Rahm. 'You never want a serious crisis to go to waste', 18 November 2008, https://www. youtube.com/watch?v=1yeA_kHHLow (accessed 22 August 2014).

Escalona, Fabien, and Mathieu Vieira. ' "It Does Not Happen Here Either": Why Social Democrats Fail in the Context of the Great Economic Crisis', in David J. Bailey, Jean-Michel de Waele,

Fabien Escalona, and Mathieu Vieira (eds), *European Social Democracy during the Global Economic Crisis: Renovation or Resignation?*, Manchester: Manchester University Press, 2014, pp. 19–41.

Evans-Pritchard, Ambrose. 'France Cautions Germany Not to Push Europe Too Far on Austerity', *Daily Telegraph*, 6 October 2014, http://www.telegraph.co.uk/finance/economics/11144769/ France-cautions-Germany-not-to-push-Europe-too-far-on-austerity.html (accessed 9 August 2015).

Ferguson, Mark. 'Cut to the Chase, Ed – and Raise the Minimum Wage to the Living Wage', LabourList, 4 November 2013, http://labourlist.org/2013/11/cut-to-the-chase-ed-and-raise-the-minimum-wage-to-the-living-wage/ (accessed 20 November 2013).

Ferguson, Mark. 'Ed Miliband Interview, Part Two: On Selections, Community Organising and the Future of the Labour Party', LabourList, 1 April 2013, http://labourlist.org/2013/04/ ed-miliband-interview-part-two-on-selections-community-organising-and-the-future-of-the-labour-party/ (accessed 3 August 2015).

Freeden, Michael. 'Conclusion: Ideology – Balances and Projections', in Michael Freeden (ed.), *Reassessing Political Ideologies: The Durability of Dissent*, London: Routledge, 2001, pp. 193–208.

Freeden, Michael. *Ideologies and Political Theory: A Conceptual Approach*, Oxford Clarendon Press, 1998.

Freeden, Michael. 'Ideology and Political Theory', *Journal of Political Ideologies* 11:1 (February 2006): 3–22.

Freeden, Michael. 'Practising Ideology and Ideological Practices', *Political Studies*, special issue, 48:2 (2000): 302–322.

Fielding, Steven. 'Labour's Campaign: Things Can Only Get …Worse?', *Parliamentary Affairs* 63:4 (2010): 653–666.

Finlayson, Alan. 'From Blue to Green and Everything in Between: Ideational Change and Left Political Economy after New Labour', *British Journal of Politics and International Relations* 15 (2013): 70–88.

Finlayson, Alan. 'Rhetoric and the Political Theory of Ideologies', *Political Studies* 60:4 (2012): 751–767.

Finlayson, Alan. 'Should the Left Go Blue? Making Sense of Maurice Glasman', 27 May 2011, https:// www.opendemocracy.net/ourkingdom/alan-finlayson/should-left-go-blue-making-sense-of-maurice-glasman (accessed 3 August 2015).

Fominaya, Cristina Flesher. ' "Spain Is Different": Podemos and 15-M', 29 May 2014, https://www. opendemocracy.net/can-europe-make-it/cristina-flesher-fominaya/%E2%80%9Cspain-is-different%E2%80%9D-podemos-and-15m (accessed 3 August 2015).

Ford, Robert, and Matthew Goodwin. 'Now Ukip Is Gunning for Labour, What's Ed Miliband Going to Do about It?', *Guardian*, 30 May 2013, http://www.theguardian.com/commentis-free/2013/may/30/ukip-gunning-labour-ed-miliband (accessed 3 August 2015).

Ford, Robert, and Matthew Goodwin. *Revolt on the Right: Explaining Support for the Radical Right in Britain*, London: Routledge, 2014.

Ford, Robert, and Anthony Heath. 'Immigration', in Alison Park, Caroline Bryson, and John Curtice (eds), *British Social Attitudes 31*, London: NatCen Social Research, 2014.

Gaber, Ivor. 'The "Othering" of "Red Ed", or How the *Daily Mail* "Framed" the British Labour Leader', *Political Quarterly* 85:4 (October–December 2014): 471–479.

Gamble, Andrew. *Crisis without End? The Unravelling of Western Prosperity*, Houndmills: Palgrave Macmillan, 2014.

Gamble, Andrew. 'The Legacy of Thatcherism', in Mark Perryman (ed.), *The Blair Agenda*, London: Lawrence and Wishart, 1996, pp. 18–38.

Gamble, Andrew. 'Neo-Liberalism and Fiscal Conservatism', in Vivian A. Schmidt and Mark Thatcher (eds), *Resilient Liberalism in Europe's Political Economy*, Cambridge: Cambridge University Press, 2013, pp. 53–76.

Gamble, Andrew. *The Spectre at the Feast: Capitalist Crisis and the Politics of Recession*, Houndmills: Palgrave Macmillan, 2009.

Gentleman, Amelia. 'Labour Vows to Reduce Reliance on Food Banks if It Comes to Power', *Guardian*, 17 March 2015.

Glasman, Maurice. 'Ed Miliband Must Trust His Instincts and Stand Up for Real Change', *New Statesman*, 5 January 2012.

Glasman, Maurice. 'Labour as a Radical Tradition', in Maurice Glasman, Jonathan Rutherford, Marc Stears, and Stuart White (eds), *The Labour Tradition and the Politics of Paradox: The Oxford London Seminars 2010–11*, n.p.: Oxford London Seminars, 2011, pp. 14–34.

Glasman, Maurice. 'My Blue Labour Vision Can Defeat the Coalition', *Observer*, 24 April 2011.

Glasman, Maurice, and Duncan Weldon. 'German Lessons for Miliband's Growth Agenda', *Financial Times*, 3 August 2011.

Goes, Eunice. *A era Blair em exame*, Lisbon: Quimera, 2003.

Goes, Eunice. 'The Left and the Global Financial Crisis: The Labour Party in Search of a New Economic Narrative', in João Cardoso Rosas and Ana Rita Ferreira (eds), *Left and Right: The Great Dichotomy Revisited*, Cambridge: Cambridge Scholars, 2013, pp. 183–200.

Goodman, Helen. 'Tradition and Change: Four People – A Response to the Politics of the Paradox', June 2011, http://leftfootforward.org/images/2011/06/Helen-Goodman-MP-Tradition-and-Change.pdf (accessed 3 August 2015).

Graham, Georgia. 'Ed Miliband Is Confused and Unconvincing, Lord Mandelson Says', *Daily Telegraph*, 19 June 2014, http://www.telegraph.co.uk/news/politics/ed-miliband/10911015/Ed-Miliband-is-confused-and-unconvincing-Lord-Mandelson-says.html (accessed 3 September 2014).

Greenberg Quinlan Rosner Research. 'UK Post-Election Poll for the TUC', May 2015, http://www.gqrr.com/uk-post-election-1 (accessed 15 May 2015).

Grice, Andrew. 'New Labour, New Danger: Tony Blair Leads Party Grandees in Attack on Ed Miliband', *Independent*, 12 April 2013, http://www.independent.co.uk/news/uk/politics/new-labour-new-danger-tony-blair-leads-party-grandees-in-attack-on-ed-miliband-8568148.html (accessed 11 August 2015).

Haas, Peter M. 'Introduction: Epistemic Communities and International Policy Coordination', *International Organization* 46:1 (Winter 1992): 1–35.

Habermas, Jürgen. 'Germany and the Euro-Crisis', *The Nation*, 28 June 2010.

Hacker, Jacob. 'The Free Market Fantasy', Policy Network, 23 April 2014, http://www.policy-network.net/pno_detail.aspx?ID=4628&title=The-Free-Market-Fantasy (accessed 28 August 2014).

Hacker, Jacob S. 'The Institutional Foundations of Middle-Class Democracy', Policy Network, 6 May 2011, http://www.policy-network.net/pno_detail.aspx?ID=3998&title=The+institutional+foundations+of+middle-class+democracy (accessed 7 September 2012).

Hacker, Jacob S., and Paul Pierson. *Winner-Take-All Politics: How Washington Made the Rich Richer – and Turned Its Back on the Middle Class*, New York: Simon and Schuster, 2010.

Hacker, Jacob, Ben Jackson, and Martin O'Neill. 'The Politics of Predistribution: Jacob Hacker Interviewed by Ben Jackson and Martin O'Neill', *Renewal* 21:2–3 (28 August 2013): 54–64.

Hain, Peter. *Back to the Future of Socialism*, Bristol: Policy Press, 2015.

Johnson, Alan. "The Unions' No-Cuts Agenda Is Delusional", *Guardian*, 17 January 2012.

Hall, Peter A. 'Conclusion: The Politics of Keynesian Ideas', in Peter A. Hall (ed.), *The Political Power of Economic Ideas: Keynesianism across Nations*, Princeton: Princeton University Press, 1989, pp. 361–391.

Hall, Peter A. 'Policy Paradigms, Social Learning, and the State: The Case of Economic Policymaking in Britain', *Comparative Politics* 25:3 (April 1993): 275–296.

Hasan, Mehdi. 'Miliband's Vision Is Bold – But Now It's Time to Convince the Country', *New Statesman*, 3 October 2011.

Hasan, Mehdi, and James Macintyre. *Ed: The Milibands and the Making of a Labour Leader*, London: Biteback Publishing, 2011.

Hay, Colin. 'Treating the Symptom Not the Condition: Crisis Definition, Deficit Reduction and the Search for a New British Growth Model', *British Journal of Politics and International Relations* 15:1 (February 2013): 23–37.

Heffernan, Richard. 'Labour's New Labour Legacy: Politics after Blair and Brown', *Political Studies Review* 9 (2011): 163–177.

Heffernan, Richard. *New Labour and Thatcherism: Political Change in Britain*, Houndmills: Palgrave Macmillan, 2001.

Heffernan, Richard. 'UK Party Leaders Are "Preeminent", but Can Also Be "Predominant": Cameron and the Conservatives, 2005–2010', *British Politics* 9:1 (April 2014): 51–67.

Helm, Toby. 'Jon Cruddas: This Could Be the Greatest Crisis the Labour Party Has Ever Faced', *Guardian*, 16 May 2015, http://www.theguardian.com/politics/2015/may/16/labour-great-crisis-ever (accessed 3 August 2015).

Helm, Toby. 'Labour Will Be Tougher than Tories on Benefits, Promises New Welfare Chief', *Observer*, 13 October 2013.

Helm, Toby, Jamie Doward, and Daniel Boffey. 'Murdoch's Empire Must Be Dismantled – Ed Miliband', *Observer*, 16 November 2011, http://www.theguardian.com/politics/2011/jul/16/rupert-murdoch-ed-miliband-phone-hacking (accessed 3 August 2015).

Hills, John. 'Labour's Record on Cash Transfers, Poverty, Inequality and the Lifecycle 1997–2010', CASE Working Paper 5 (July 2013).

Hirst, Paul. *From Statism to Pluralism*, London: Routledge, 1997.

Hodges, Dan. 'Miliband Has Told the Blairites: There's No Place for You in This Party. He'd Better Watch His Back', *Daily Telegraph*, 7 October 2013, http://blogs.telegraph.co.uk/news/danhodges/100240240/ed-miliband-has-told-the-blairites-theres-no-place-for-you-in-this-party-hed-better-watch-his-back/ (accessed 3 August 2015).

Hough, Dan. 'From Pariah to Prospective Partner? The German Left Party's Winding Path towards Government', in Jonathan Olsen, Dan Hough, and Michael Koß (eds), *Left Parties in National Governments*, Houndmills: Palgrave Macmillan, 2010, pp. 138–154.

Hunt, Tristram. 'Big Society, Big Danger', in *What Mutualism Means for Labour*, London: Policy Network, 2011, pp. 15–25.

Hunt, Tristram. 'One Nation Labour', in Owen Smith and Rachel Reeves (eds), *One Nation: Power, Hope, Community*, London: One Nation Register, 2013, pp. 145–159.

Hunt, Tristram. 'Reviving Our Sense of Mission: Designing a New Political Economy', in Robert Philpot (ed.), *The Purple Book: A Progressive Future for Labour*, London: Biteback Publishing, 2011, pp. 61–79.

Institute for Public Policy Research (IPPR). *A Fair Deal on Migration for the UK*, London: IPPR, 2014.

Ipsos MORI. 'Political Monitor: Satisfaction Ratings 1997–Present', 29 April 2015, https://www. ipsos-mori.com/researchpublications/researcharchive/88/Political-Monitor-Satisfaction-Ratings-1997Present.aspx?view=wide (accessed 18 May 2015).

Jackson, Ben. *Equality and the British Left: A Study in Progressive Political Thought, 1900–64*, Manchester: Manchester University Press, 2007.

Jackson, Ben. 'The Masses against the Classes', *Public Policy Research* 19:3 (2012): 160–165.

Jobson, Richard, and Mark Wickham-Jones. 'Gripped by the Past: Nostalgia and the 2010 Labour Party Leadership Contest', *British Politics* 5:4 (2010): 525–548.

Kellner, Peter. 'A Quiet Revolution', *Prospect* 192 (March 2012): 30–34.

Kellner, Peter. 'The Trouble with Labour Leader Ed Miliband', *Prospect*, 19 June 2014, http://www. prospectmagazine.co.uk/features/the-trouble-with-ed-miliband (accessed 20 June 2014).

Kendall, Liz, and Steve Reed. 'People-Powered Public Services', in John Woodcock and Liz Kendall (eds), *Laying the Foundations for a Labour Century*, London: Policy Network, 2014, pp. 29–34.

Kennedy, Paul. 'Back to the Drawing Board: The PSOE after the 2011 Elections', in in David J. Bailey, Jean-Michel de Waele, Fabien Escalona, and Mathieu Vieira (eds), *European Social Democracy during the Global Economic Crisis: Renovation or Resignation?*, Manchester: Manchester University Press, 2014, pp. 176–192.

Kenny, Michael. 'Faith, Flag and the British Left – One Nation?', OurKingdom, 28 June 2013, https://www.opendemocracy.net/ourkingdom/michael-kenny/faith-flag-and-british-le ft-one-nation (accessed 3 August 2015).

Kenny, Michael. 'Faith, Flag and the "First" New Left: E. P. Thompson and the Politics of "One Nation"', *Renewal* 21:1 (2013): 15–23.

Kenny, Michael. *The Politics of English Nationhood*, Oxford: Oxford University Press, 2014.

Kingemann, Hans-Dieter, Richard I. Hofferbert, and Ian Budge. *Parties, Policies and Democracy*, Oxford: Westview Press, 1994.

Kitschelt, Herbert. *The Transformation of European Social Democracy*, Cambridge: Cambridge University Press, 1994.

'Labour MPs Revolt over Miliband's Economic Policy', *Northern Echo*, 17 June 2014, http:// www.thenorthernecho.co.uk/news/local/northdurham/11281657.Labour_MPs_revolt_over_ Miliband_s_economic_policy/ (accessed 23 August 2015).

'Labour's New Leader: Ed Miliband's Moment', *Guardian*, 27 September 2010, http://www. theguardian.com/commentisfree/2010/sep/27/labours-new-leader-ed-miliband-editorial (accessed 11 August 2015).

Lapavitsas, Costas, Annina Kaltenbrunner, Duncan Lindo, J. Mitchell, Juan Pablo Painceira, Eugenia Pires, et al. 'Eurozone Crisis: Begga Thyself and Thy Neignbour', *Journal of Balkan and Near Eastern Studies* 12:4 (December 2010): 321–373.

Lavelle, Ashley. 'Postface: Death by a Thousand Cuts?', in David J. Bailey, Jean-Michel de Waele, Fabien Escalona, and Mathieu Vieira (eds), *European Social Democracy during the Global Economic Crisis: Renovation or Resignation?* Manchester: Manchester University Press, 2010, pp. 270–283.

Lawson, Neal. 'Labour and the Tories – Spot the Difference', *Guardian*, 24 June 2013, http://www.guardian.co.uk/commentisfree/2013/jun/24/labour-tories-austerity-investing-grow-economy (accessed 24 June 2013).

Lawson, Neal, Patrick Diamond, Anna Coote, Andrew Harrop, David Clark, Mark Ferguson, *et al.* 'Labour Must Adopt New Principles', *Guardian*, 24 March 2014.

Lawton, Kayte, Graeme Cooke, and Nick Pearce. *The Condition of Britain: Strategies for Social Renewal*, London: IPPR, 2014.

Lee, Simon. 'Towards an English Narrative of Democracy?', *Policy Studies* 33:2 (March 2012): 173–191.

Lent, Adam, Hopi Sen, and Anthony Painter, 'Moving Labour "into the Black"', Policy Network, 19 June 2013, http://www.policy-network.net/pno_detail.aspx?ID=4422&title=Moving-Labour-%E2%80%98into-the-black- (accessed 16 August 2015).

Levy, Geoffrey. 'The Man who Hated Britain: Red Ed's Pledge to Bring Back Socialism Is a Homage to His Marxist Father …', *Mail Online*, 27 September 2013, http://www.dailymail.co.uk/news/article-2435751/Red-Eds-pledge-bring-socialism-homage-Marxist-father-Ralph-Miliband-says-GEOFFREY-LEVY.html (accessed 11 August 2015).

Liddle, Roger. 'Is Social Democracy in Need of a New Economic Model?', 9 December 2010, http://www.social-europe.eu/2010/12/is-social-democracy-in-need-of-a-new-economic-model/ (accessed 16 June 2013).

Liddle, Roger, and Patrick Diamond. 'Towards a Progressive Capitalism', Policy Network, 2 July 2014, http://www.policy-network.net/pno_detail.aspx?ID=4696&title=Towards-a-progressive-capitalism (accessed 5 September 2014).

Local Government Innovation Taskforce. 'Final Report: People Powered Public Services', July 2014, http://lgalabour.local.gov.uk/documents/330956/6335671/INNOVATION+TASKFOR CE+FINAL+REPORT.pdf (accessed 26 August 2015).

'Lord Mandelson Attacks Ed Miliband for "Taking Labour Backwards"', *Huffington Post UK*, 26 September 2013, http://www.huffingtonpost.co.uk/2013/09/26/mandelson-miliband-taking-labour-backwards_n_3993694.html (accessed 7 February 2014).

McLaren, Lauren M. 'Immigration and Perceptions of the Political System in Britain', *Political Quarterly* 84:1 (January–March 2013): 90–100.

McLaren, Lauren M. 'Immigration and Political Trust in the UK', *Political Insight* 4:3 (December 2013): 14–17.

McTernan, John. 'Ed Miliband's Big, Bold Plan', *The Scotsman*, 13 February 2014.

McTernan, John. 'Immigration Will Not Be the Issue to Split the Labour Party', *Financial Times*, 8 June 2014.

Mandelson, Peter. 'Labour Will Never Be Credible without Convincing People of Its Economic Credentials', LabourList, 10 May 2015, http://labourlist.org/2015/05/labour-will-never-be-credible-without-convincing-people-of-its-economic-credentials/ (accessed 11 May 2015).

March, Luke. 'The European Radical Left and the International Economic Crisis: Opportunity Wasted?', 5 February 2013, https://www.opendemocracy.net/luke-march/european-radical-le ft-and-international-economic-crisis-opportunity-wasted (accessed 4 August 2015).

March, Luke. 'Os partidos radicais da esquerda radical após a crise: Marxismo, mainstream ou marginalidade', in Luke March and Andre Freire, *A esquerda radical em Portugal e na Europa*, Vila do Conde: Quidnovi, 2012, pp. 25–104.

Marlière, Philippe. 'The Decline of Europe's Social Democratic Parties', 16 March 2010, https://www.opendemocracy.net/philippe-marliere/decline-of-europes-social-democratic-parties (accessed 4 August 2015).

Marlière, Philippe. 'The French Socialist Party and European Integration: Faltering Europeanism', in Dionyssis G. Dimitrakopoulos (ed.), *Social Democracy and European Integration: The Politics of Preference Formation*, Abingdon: Routledge, 2011, pp. 51–82.

Marquand, David. *Britain since 1918: The Strange Career of British Democracy*, London: Weidenfeld and Nicolson, 2008.

Mazower, Mark. 'The Great Reckoning: Why the European Ideal Is under Threat', *New Statesman*, 15–25 April 2013.

Mazzucato, Mariana. *The Entrepreneurial State: Debunking Public vs. Private Sector Myths*, London: Anthem Press, 2013.

Mazzucato, Mariana. 'Small and Inclusive Growth', in Chuka Umunna (ed.), *Owning the Future: How Britain Can Make It in a Fast-Changing World*, London: Policy Network, 2014, pp. 63–72.

Meagher, Kevin. 'Sorry Arnie, Labour's a Political Party, Not a Community Group', LabourList, 23 April 2013, http://labourlist.org/2013/04/sorry-arnie-labours-a-political-party-not-a-community-group/ (accessed 4 August 2015).

Mehta, Jal. 'The Varied Roles of Ideas in Politics: From "Whether" to "How"', in Daniel Béland and Robert Henry Cox (eds), *Ideas and Politics in Social Science Research*, Oxford: Oxford University Press, 2011, pp. 23–46.

Miliband, Ed. '2014 Labour Conference Speech', 23 September 2014, http://www.labour.org.uk/blog/entry/2014-labour-conference-speech (accessed 25 September 2014).

Miliband, Ed. 'Britain Can Be Better: The Full Text of Miliband's Manifesto Launch Speech', LabourList, 13 April 2015, http://labourlist.org/2015/04/britain-can-be-better-the-full-text-of-milibands-manifesto-launch-speech/ (accessed 14 April 2015).

Miliband, Ed. 'Britain Needs Real Change, Not False Promises – Ed Miliband', 27 May 2014, http://press.labour.org.uk/post/86997808779/britain-needs-real-change-not-false-promises-ed (accessed 28 May 2014).

Miliband, Ed. 'Building a Responsible Capitalism', *Public Policy Research* 19:1 (2012): 17–25.

Miliband, Ed. 'The Choice: Leadership. Speech by Ed Miliband MP', 25 July 2014, http://press.labour.org.uk/post/92819342334/the-choice-leadership-speech-by-ed-miliband-mp (accessed 28 July 2014).

Miliband, Ed. 'The Cost of Living Crisis in Britain: Speech to the Resolution Foundation', 28 February 2011, http://www.labour.org.uk/the-cost-of-living-crisis-facing-britain-ed-miliband (accessed 20 March 2011).

Miliband, Ed. 'Devolution Is for Everyone: A No Vote Will Change All of Britain', *Guardian*, 14 September 2014, http://www.theguardian.com/commentisfree/2014/sep/14/scotland-has-shown-change-whole-country (accessed 4 August 2015).

Miliband, Ed. 'The Discipline to Make a Difference', 22 June 2013, http://www.labour.org.uk/the-discipline-to-make-a-difference–ed-miliband (accessed 24 June 2013).

Miliband, Ed. 'Ed Miliband MP's Speech to the Labour Party Annual Conference 2013,' 24 September 2013, http://press.labour.org.uk/post/62160282657/ed-miliband-mps-speech-to-labour-party-annual (accessed 25 September 2013).

Miliband, Ed. 'Ed Miliband Remarks in Rochester and Strood', 23 October 2014, http://press.labour.org.uk/post/100742025549/ed-miliband-remarks-in-rochester-and-strood (accessed 4 August 2015).

Miliband, Ed. 'Ed Miliband Speech at Senate House', 13 November 2014, http://press.labour.org.uk/post/102524244299/ed-miliband-speech-at-senate-house (accessed 14 November 2014).

Miliband, Ed. 'Ed Miliband Speech in Salford', 5 January 2015, http://press.labour.org.uk/post/107208138389/ed-miliband-speech-in-salford (accessed 1 May 2015).

Miliband, Ed. 'Ed Miliband Speech in Warrington', 4 April 2015, http://press.labour.org.uk/post/115482192359/ed-miliband-speech-in-warrington (accessed 9 April 2015).

Miliband, Ed. 'Ed Miliband Speech Launching Labour's General Election Campaign', 27 March 2015, http://press.labour.org.uk/post/114747701274/ed-miliband-speech-launching-labours-general-election-campaign (accessed 27 March 2015).

Miliband, Ed. 'Ed Miliband Speech on the NHS', 27 January 2015, http://press.labour.org.uk/post/109289243889/ed-miliband-speech-on-the-nhs (accessed 2 February 2015).

Miliband, Ed. 'Ed Miliband's "Cost of Living Crisis" Speech – Full Text', LabourList, 5 November 2013, http://labourlist.org/2013/11/ed-milibands-cost-of-living-crisis-speech-full-text (accessed 5 November 2013).

Miliband, Ed. 'Ed Miliband's Economy Speech in Full', 17 January 2014, http://www.politics.co.uk/comment-analysis/2014/01/17/ed-miliband-s-economy-speech-in-full (accessed 4 August 2015).

Miliband, Ed. 'Ed Miliband's Speech in Stockton-on-Tees', 27 April 2015, http://press.labour.org.uk/post/117508448409/ed-milibands-speech-in-stockton-on-tees (accessed 1 May 2015).

Miliband, Ed. 'Ed Miliband's Speech on Immigration', 18 April 2015, http://press.labour.org.uk/post/116721382454/ed-milibands-speech-on-immigration (accessed 28 April 2015).

Miliband, Ed. 'Ed Miliband's Speech on Scottish Independence in Glasgow', 11 September 2014, http://www.totalpolitics.com/print/speeches/292477/ed-milibands-speech-on-scottish-independence-in-glasgow.thtml (accessed 13 December 2014).

Miliband, Ed. 'Ed Miliband's Speech to Labour Party Conference', 27 September 2011, http://archive.labour.org.uk/ed-milibands-speech-to-labour-party-conference (accessed 3 April 2015).

Miliband, Ed. 'Ed Miliband's Speech to the CBI', 10 November 2015, http://press.labour.org.uk/post/102276146664/ed-milibands-speech-to-the-cbi (accessed 14 November 2014).

Miliband, Ed. 'Ed Miliband's Speech to the Fabian Conference', 17 January 2015, http://press.labour.org.uk/post/108338079199/ed-milibands-speech-to-fabian-conference (accessed 2 February 2015).

Miliband, Ed. 'Ed Miliband's Speech to the Policy Network Inclusive Prosperity Conference', 3 July 2014, http://press.labour.org.uk/post/90646112699/ed-miliband-speech-to-the-policy-network-inclusive-propserity-conference (accessed 4 July 2014).

Miliband, Ed. 'The Fabric of Our Country – Speech by Ed Miliband', 8 April 2015, http://press.labour.org.uk/post/115841294434/the-fabric-of-our-country-speech-by-ed-miliband (accessed 12 August 2015).

Miliband, Ed. 'Full Text: Ed Miliband Immigration Speech', 14 December 2012, http://www.newstatesman.com/staggers/2012/12/full-text-ed-miliband-immigration-speech (accessed 4 August 2015).

Miliband, Ed. 'Full Transcript: Ed Miliband, Speech to the Fabians', 15 January 2011, http://www.newstatesman.com/blogs/the-staggers/2011/01/labour-government-politics (accessed 12 March 2012).

Miliband, Ed. 'The Future is Local – If Labour Is Elected', *Guardian*, 7 July 2014.

Miliband, Ed. 'The Hugo Young Lecture', LabourList, 10 February 2014, http://labourlist.org/2014/02/ed-milibands/hugo-young-lecture-full-text/ (accessed 15 April 2014).

Miliband, Ed. 'Interview with Ed Miliband: "We Need to Tax the Better-Off"', *Independent*, 30 August 2010.

Miliband, Ed. 'The Living Wage Benefits All, Not Just the Low-Paid', *Evening Standard*, 4 November 2013.

Miliband, Ed. 'A Mandate for Change', 30 August 2010, http://www.labourincoventry/org.uk/index.php?option=com_content&view=article&id (accessed 24 January 2014).

Miliband, Ed. 'Margaret Thatcher Tribute', 10 April 2013, http://www.labour.org.uk/ed-milibands-statement-on-margaret-thatcher,2013-04-10 (accessed 7 May 2013).

Miliband, Ed. 'My Vision to Rebuild Trust', *Sunday Telegraph*, 25 September 2010.

Miliband, Ed. 'The New Generation: Speech to the 2010 Labour Party Annual Conference', 28 September 2010, www2.labour.org.uk/ed-miliband---a-new-generation,2010-09-28 (accessed 10 January 2012).

Miliband, Ed. 'One Nation Labour: Britain Can Prevent a Lost Decade', 23 March 2013, http://www.labour.org.uk/one-nation-labour-britain-can-prevent-a-lost-decade (accessed 7 May 2013).

Miliband, Ed. 'One Nation Plan for Social Security Reform', 6 June 2013, http://www.labour.org.uk/one-nation-social-security-reform-miliband-speech (accessed 21 June 2013).

Miliband, Ed. 'One Nation Politics', 9 July 2013, http://www.labour.org.uk/one-nation-politics-speech (accessed 10 July 2013).

Miliband, Ed. 'Preface', in Owen Smith and Rachel Reeves (eds), *One Nation: Power, Hope, Community*, London: One Nation Register, 2013, pp. 7–9.

Miliband, Ed. 'Rebuilding Britain with a One Nation Economy', 14 February 2013, https://www.labour.org.uk/rebuilding-britain-with-a-one-nation-economy-ed-miliband (accessed 7 May 2013).

Miliband, Ed. 'Rebuilding Scotland, Rebuilding Britain', 19 April 2013, http://www.labour.org.uk/ed-miliband-scottish-conference (accessed 7 May 2013).

Miliband, Ed. 'Responsibility in 21st Century Britain', 13 June 2011, http://www.labour.org.uk/ed-miliband-speech-responsibility-2011-06-13 (accessed 25 November 2013).

Miliband, Ed. 'Speech by Ed Miliband MP on the Deficit', 11 December 2014, http:// http://press.labour.org.uk/post/104918318074/speech-by-ed-miliband-mp-on-the-deficit (accessed 11 December 2014).

Miliband, Ed. 'Speech in Huddersfield', 1 April 2015, http://press.labour.org.uk/post/115200074924/ed-miliband-remarks-zero-hours-contracts (accessed 17 August 2015).

Miliband, Ed. 'Speech on Englishness', *New Statesman*, 6 June 2012, http://www.newstatesman.com/print/node/186474?title=&text= (accessed 21 July 2012).

Miliband, Ed. 'Speech on Social Mobility to the Sutton Trust', 21 May 2012, http://www.labour. org.uk/ed-milibands-speech-on-social-mobility-sutton-trust,2012-05-21 (accessed 21 July 2012).

Miliband, Ed. 'Ed Miliband's Speech on Tackling the Cost-of-Living Crisis', 8 April 2014, http:// press.labour.org.uk/post/82080311502/ed-milibands-speech-on-tackling-the (accessed 8 April 2014).

Miliband, Ed. 'Speech to Labour's Youth Conference', 16 March 2013, http://www.labour.org.uk/ ed-milibands-speech-to-labours-youth-conference,2012-03-16 (accessed 2 December 2013).

Miliband, Ed. 'Speech to London Citizens', 10 January 2013, http://www.labour.org.uk/ labour-will-deliver-fairness (accessed 15 January 2013).

Miliband, Ed. 'Speech to Policy Network – Labour's New Agenda', 6 September 2012, http://www. labour.org.uk/labours-new-agenda (accessed 22 August 2013).

Miliband, Ed, 'Speech to Progress Annual Conference', 21 May 2011, http://www.labour.org.uk/ ed-milibands-speech-to-progress-annual-conference (accessed 14 May 2013).

Miliband, Ed. 'Speech to the CBI', 25 October 2010, http://www.labour.org.uk/leader-of- the-labour-party-ed-milibands-speech-to-the-cbi,2010-10-25 (accessed 10 January 2012).

Miliband, Ed. 'Speech to the IPPR', 24 November 2011, http://www.labour.org.uk/ economic-gamble-has-failed,2011-11-24 (accessed 30 November 2011).

Miliband, Ed. 'Speech to the Labour Party Annual Conference 2012', 2 October 2012, http://www. labour.org.uk/ed-miliband-speech-conf-2012,2012-10-02 (accessed 4 October 2012).

Miliband, Ed. 'Speech to the TUC', 10 September 2013, http://www.labour.org.uk/speech-by- ed-miliband-to-the-tuc (accessed 2 December 2013).

Miliband, Ed. 'Statement on the Leveson Inquiry', 29 November 2012, http://www.labour.org.uk/ statement-on-the-leveson-inquiry,2012-11-29 (accessed 11 January 2013).

Miliband, Ed. 'Taking Big Money out of Politics', 15 April 2012, http://www.labour.org.uk/ taking-big-money-out-of-politics,2012-04-05 (accessed 23 May 2012).

Miliband, Ed. 'We Need to Tax the Better-Off', *Independent*, 30 August 2010.

Miliband, Ed. 'When Leveson Reports, Parliament Must Act Swiftly', *Guardian*, 25 November 2012, http://www.guardian.co.uk/commentisfree/2012/nov/25/leveson-reports-parliament- act-swiftly (accessed 8 July 2013).

Miliband, Ed. 'Why I Want to Lead the Labour Party', *Guardian*, 15 May 2010.

Miliband, Ed. 'Yes, I Am Socialist', Channel4.com, 26 November 2010, http://www.channel4. com/news/ed-miliband-yes-i-am-a-socialist (accessed 7 February 2014).

Moschonas, Gerassimos. *In the Name of Social Democracy: The Great Transformation. 1945 to the Present.* London: Verso, 2002.

Moschonas, Gerassimos. 'Reforming Europe, Renewing Social Democracy? The PES, the Debt Crisis and the Euro-Parties', in David J. Bailey, Jean-Michel de Waele, Fabien Escalona, and Mathieu Vieira (eds), *European Social Democracy during the Global Economic Crisis: Renovation or Resignation?*, Manchester: Manchester University Press, 2014, pp. 252–269.

Moschonas, Gerassimos. 'When Institutions Matter: The EU and the Identity of Social Democracy', *Renewal* 17:2 (Summer 2009): 11–20.

Mount, Ferdinand. *The New Few; or, A Very British Oligarchy*, London: Simon and Schuster, 2012.

Mulgan, Geoff. 'Government with the People: The Outlines of a Relational State', in Graeme Cooke and Rick Muir (eds), *The Relational State: How Recognising the Importance of Human Relationships Could Revolutionise the Role of the State*, London: IPPR, 2012, pp. 20–34.

Münchau, Wolfgang. 'Eurozone Stagnation Is a Greater Threat than Debt', *Financial Times*, 19 October 2014.

Murphy, Joe. 'Labour MPs Tell Ed Miliband to Toughen Up on Welfare', *Evening Standard*, 8 April 2013.

Nardelli, Alberto. 'Ed Miliband Is Most Unpopular Leader among His Own Party's Supporters Ever', *Guardian*, 12 November 2014, http://www.theguardian.com/news/datablog/2014/nov/12/ed-miliband-is-the-most-unpopular-leader-among-labour-supporters-ever (accessed 27 August 2015).

Olsen, Jonathan, Dan Hough, and Michael Koß. 'Conclusion: Left Parties in National Governments', in Jonathan Olsen, Dan Hough, and Michael Koß (eds). *Left Parties in National Governments*, Houndmills: Palgrave Macmillan, 2010, pp. 173–205.

Painter, Anthony. 'Co-operatism as a Means to a Bigger Society', in *What Mutualism Means for Labour: Political Economy and Public Services*, London: Policy Network, 2011, pp. 27–35.

Painter, Anthony. 'Labour's Real "Blue Collar" Problem', LabourList, 12 June 2014, http://labourlist.org/2014/06/labours-real-blue-collar-problem/ (accessed 12 June 2014).

Painter, Anthony, and Hopi Sen. 'Labour Must Make Fiscal Honesty the Key to Responsible Capitalism', *Guardian*, 1 December 2011.

Paxman, Jeremy. Transcript of BBC *Newsnight* interview with Tony Blair, 2001, http://news.bbc.co.uk/1/hi/events/newsnight/1372220.stm (accessed 18 August 2015).

Pearce, Nick. 'Elizabeth Anderson: Juncture Interview', *Juncture* 19:3 (2012): 188–193.

Pearce, Nick. 'What Should Social Democrats Believe?', *Juncture*, 19 September 2013, www.ippr.org.uk/juncture/171/11280/what-should-social-democrats-believe (accessed 14 October 2013).

Pearce, Nick, and Eleanor Taylor. 'Government Spending and Welfare', in Alison Park, Caroline Bryson, Elizabeth Clery, John Curtice, and Miranda Phillips (eds), *British Social Attitudes 30*, London: NatCen Social Research, 2013, pp. 33–61.

Philpot, Robert (ed.). *The Purple Book: A Progressive Future for Labour*, London: Biteback Publishing, 2011.

Piketty, Thomas. *Capital in the Twentieth-First Century*, London: Belknap Press, 2014.

Polanyi, Karl. *The Great Transformation: The Political and Economic Origins of Our Time*, Boston, MA: Beacon Press, 2001.

Policy Network, 'How Social Democracy Can Triumph in the 5-75-20 Society', Policy Network, 24 April 2014, http://www.policy-network.net (accessed 6 August 2015).

Pope, Mike. 'The Rise of Podemos and Its People's Assembly', 7 November 2014, https://www.opendemocracy.net/can-europe-make-it/mike-pope/rise-of-podemos-and-its-people%27s-assembly (accessed 30 November 2014).

Rawnsley, Andrew. 'Ed Miliband Boldly Goes where Even Tony Blair Feared to Tread', *Observer*, 2 February 2014.

Reeves, Rachel. 'Changing Rules to Ban Jobseekers from Claiming Benefits for Two Years', *Daily Mail*, 18 November 2014.

Reeves, Rachel. 'The Labour Agenda for Tackling Low Pay', 4 September 2013, http://www.rachelreeves.mp.co.uk/the_labour_agenda_for_tackling_low_pay (accessed 4 May 2014).

Reeves, Rachel. 'Meeting the Fiscal Challenge', in John Denham (ed.), *The Shape of Things to Come: Labour's New Thinking*, London: Fabian Society, 2012.

Reeves, Rachel. 'Speech to Labour Party Annual Conference', 22 September 2014, http://press. labour.org.uk/post/98144482264/speech-by-rachel-reeves-mp-to-labours-annual (accessed 29 September 2014).

Rentoul, John. 'Recovery Means … Dumping Labour Policies', *Independent*, 23 June 2013, http://www.independent.co.uk/voices/comment/recovery-means-dumping-labour-policies-8669703. html (accessed 24 June 2013).

Riddell, Mary. 'Power to the People', 1 August 2013, *Fabian Review*, http://www.fabians.org.uk/power-to-the-people/ (accessed 6 August 2015).

Riddell, Mary. 'Will Ed Balls Back the Miliband Power Give Away?', *Telegraph* blog, 10 February 2014, http://blogs.telegraph.co.uk/news/maryriddell/100258930/will-ed-balls-back-the-miliband-power-giveway/ (accessed 6 August 2015).

Riddell, Mary, and Tom Whitehead. 'Immigration Should Be Frozen, Says Miliband Adviser', *Daily Telegraph*, 18 July 2011.

Roberts, Marcus. *Revolt on the Left: Labour's UKIP Problem and How It Can Be Overcome*, London: Fabian Society, 2014.

Rogers, Chris. '"Hang on a Minute, I've Got a Great Idea": From the Third Way to Mutual Advantage in the Political Economy of the British Labour Party', *British Journal of Politics and International Relations* 15 (2013): 53–69.

Rutherford, Jonathan. 'The Future Is Conservative', in Maurice Glasman, Jonathan Rutherford, Marc Stears, and Stuart White (eds), *The Labour Tradition and the Politics of Paradox: The Oxford London Seminars 2010–11*, n.p.: Oxford London Seminars, 2011, pp. 88–105.

Rutherford, Jonathan. 'The Labour Party and the New Left: The First New Left, Blue Labour and English Modernity', *Renewal* 21:1 (2013): 9–14.

Rutherford, Jonathan. 'Three Styles of Modern Leadership', in Maurice Glasman, Jonathan Rutherford, Marc Stears, and Stuart White (eds), *The Labour Tradition and the Politics of Paradox: The Oxford London Seminars 2010–11*, n.p.: Oxford London Seminars, 2011, pp. 72–74.

Sachs, Jeffrey, Charles Wyploss, Willem Buiter, Gerhard Fels, and George de Menil. 'The Economic Consequences of President Mitterrand', *Economic Policy* 1:2 (April 1986): 261–322.

Sandel, Michael J. *What Money Can't Buy: The Moral Limits of Markets*, London: Penguin, 2013.

Sassoon, Donald. *One Hundred Years of Socialism: The West European Left in the Twentieth Century*, London: Fontana Press, 1997.

Schmidt, Ingo. 'German Social Democracy: A Popular Project and an Unpopular Party', in David J. Bailey, Jean-Michel de Wael, Fabien Escalona, and Mathieu Vieira (eds), *European Social Democracy during the Global Economic Crisis: Renovation or Resignation?*, Manchester: Manchester University Press, 2014, pp. 132–152.

Schmidt, Vivien A. 'Discursive Institutionalism: The Explanatory Power of Ideas and Discourse', *Annual Review of Political Science Review* 11 (2008): 303–326.

Schmidt, Vivien A. 'Taking Ideas and Discourse Seriously: Explaining Change through Discursive Institutionalism as the Fourth "new institutionalism"', *European Political Science Review* 2:1 (2010): 1–25.

Schmidt, Vivien A., and Mark Thatcher. 'Theorizing Ideational Continuity: The Resilience of Neo-Liberal Ideas in Europe', in Vivien A. Schmidt and Mark Thatcher (eds), *Resilient Liberalism in Europe's Political Economy*, Cambridge: Cambridge University Press, 2013, pp. 1–50.

Serwotka, Mark. 'Miliband's Offer of Austerity in a Red Rosette Is Failing Voters', *New Statesman*, 24 June 2013, http://www.newstatesman.com/print/politics/2013/06/milibands-offer-austerit y-red-rosette-failing-voters (accessed 24 June 2013).

Skidelsky, Robert, and Edward Skidelsky. *How Much Is Enough? The Love of Money, and the Case for the Good Life*, London: Allen Lane, 2012.

Sloam, James, and Isabelle Hertner. 'The Europeanization of Social Democracy: Politics without Policy and Policy without Politics', in Henning Meyer and Jonathan Rutherford (eds), *The Future of European Social Democracy: Building the Good Society*, Houndmills: Palgrave Macmillan, 2012, pp. 27–38.

Soborski, Rafal. *Ideology In a Global Age: Continuity and Change*, Houndmills: Palgrave Macmillan, 2013.

Sotiropoulos, Dimitri A. 'Triumph and Collapse: PASOK in the Wake of the Crisis in Greece, 2009–13', in David J. Bailey, Jean-Michel de Waele, Fabien Escalona, and Mathieu Vieira (eds), *European Social Democracy during the Global Economic Crisis: Renovation or Resignation?* Manchester: Manchester University Press, 2014, pp. 193–214.

Soutphommasane, Tim. *The Virtuous Citizen: Patriotism in a Multicultural Society*, Cambridge: Cambridge University Press, 2012.

Stears, Marc. 'Active Equality: A Democratic Agenda for the British Left', in James Purnell and Graeme Cooke (eds), *We Mean Power: Ideas for the Future of the Left*, London: Demos, 2010, pp. 151–163.

Stears, Marc. 'The Case for a State that Supports Relationships, Not a Relational State', in Graeme Cooke and, Rick Muir (eds), *The Relational State: How Recognising the Importance of Human Relationships Could Revolutionise the Role of the State*, London: IPPR, 2012, pp. 35–44.

Stears, Marc. 'Democracy, Leadership and Organising', in Maurice Glasman, Jonathan Rutherford, Marc Stears, and Stuart White (eds), *The Labour Tradition and the Politics of Paradox*, n.p.: Oxford London Seminars, 2011, pp. 57–71.

Stears, Marc. 'In the Battle to Reshape Labour, a New Force Is Emerging', *Liberal Conspiracy*, 13 February 2011, http://www.liberalconspiracy.org/2011/02/13/in-the-battle-to-reshape-labour-a-new-force-is-emerging (accessed 17 June 2013).

Stears, Marc. 'The Personal Politics of Ed Miliband', in John Denham (ed.), *The Shape of Things to Come: Labour's New Thinking*, London: Fabian Society, 2012, pp. 123–132.

Stears, Marc. 'The Radical Potential of Conservatism', in Maurice Glasman, Jonathan Rutherford, Marc Stears, and Stuart White (eds), *The Labour Tradition and the Politics of Paradox: The Oxford London Seminars 2010–11*, n.p.: Oxford London Seminars, 2011, pp. 119–121.

Stephens, Philip. 'Lies, Damned Lies and the British Election', *Financial Times*, 15 April 2015.

Stiglitz, Joseph. *Freefall: Free Markets and the Sinking of the Global Economy*, London: Penguin, 2010.

Straw, Will, and Nick Anstead. 'Introduction', in Will Straw and Nick Anstead, *The Change We Need*, London: Fabian Society, 2009, pp. 1–5.

Syal, Rajeev. 'Labour Party's Falkirk Membership Inquiry Report – Analysis', *Guardian*, 3 February 2014.

Taylor-Gooby, Peter, and Eleanor Taylor. 'Benefits and Welfare', *British Social Attitudes* 32, http://www.bsa.natcen.ac.uk/media/38977/bsa32_welfare.pdf (accessed 5 May 2015).

Thatcher, Mark, and Vivien A. Schmidt. 'Conclusion: Explaining the Resilience of Neoliberalism and Possible Pathways Out', in Vivien A. Schmidt and Mark Thatcher (eds),

Resilient Liberalism in Europe's Political Economy, Cambridge: Cambridge University Press, 2013, pp. 403–431.

Theil, Stefan. 'Peer Steinbrück on the Global Economic Crisis', *Newsweek*, 5 December 2008.

Thelen, Kathleen. 'Historical Institutionalism in Comparative Politics', *Annual Review of Political Science* 2 (1999): 369–404.

Thompson, E. P. *The Making of the English Working Class*, London: Penguin, 2013.

Toynbee, Polly. 'Tories at Half-Time: Cruel and Inept, with Worse to Come', *Guardian*, 3 December 2012.

Umunna, Chuka. 'Future of Financial Services', 15 April 2013, http://www.labour.org.uk/future-of-financial-services–chuka-umunna.html (accessed 30 April 2013).

Umunna, Chuka. 'Introduction: How Britain Can Harness the Winds of Change', in Chuka Umunna (ed.), *Owning the Future: How Britain Can Make It in a Fast-Changing World*, London: Policy Network, 2014, pp. 1–9.

'Unemployment Statistics', March 2015, Eurostat, http://ec.europa.eu/eurostat/statistics-explained/index.php/Unemployment_statistics (accessed 21 May 2015).

Unger, Roberto. 'Deep Freedom: Why the Left Should Abandon Equality', *Juncture* 20:4 (Spring 2014): 93–100.

Weir, Margaret. 'Ideas and Politics: The Acceptance of Keynesianism in Britain and the United States', in Peter A. Hall (ed.), *The Political Power of Economic Ideas: Keynesianism across Nations*, Princeton: Princeton University Press, 1989, pp. 53–86.

Vincent, Andrew. *Modern Political Ideologies*, 2nd edn, Oxford: Blackwell, 1998.

Vize, Richard. 'The Fatal Flaw in Labour's Plan to Give Large Cities More Power', *Guardian*, 4 July 2014.

Walters, Simon. 'Now a Shadow Minister Plunges in the Dagger: Tristram Hunt Joins Labour Revolt', *Daily Mail*, 8 November 2014, http://www.dailymail.co.uk/news/article-2826937/Ed-shadow-minister-plunges-dagger-Tristram-Hunt-joins-Labour-revolt-poll-says-Miliband-liability.html (accessed 27 August 2015).

Waterson, Jim. 'The British Public Still Thinks Ed Miliband Is Weird', BuzzFeed, 23 March 2014, http://www.buzzfeed.com/jimwaterson/the-british-public-still-think-ed-miliband-is-weird (accessed 27 August 2015).

Watt, Nicholas, 'Peter Mandelson Hits Out at Ed Miliband's "Crowd-Pleasing" General Election Manifesto', *Guardian*, 19 September 2010, http://www.theguardian.com/politics/2010/sep/19/peter-mandelson-ed-miliband-manifesto (accessed 7 February 2014).

Wickham-Jones, Mark. 'The Modernising Antecedents and Historical Origins of One Nation Labour', *Political Quarterly* 84:3 (July–September 2013): 321–329.

White, Stuart. 'Blue Labour: A Republican Critique', 8 June 2011, https://www.opendemocracy.net/ourkingdom/stuart-white/blue-labour-republican-critique (accessed 6 August 2015).

White, Stuart. 'The Dignity of Dissent: E. P. Thompson and One Nation Labour', 2 August 2013, https://www.opendemocracy.net/ourkingdom/stuart-white/dignity-of-dissent-ep-thompson-and-one-nation-labour (accessed 6 August 2015).

Wilkinson, Richard, and Kate Pickett. *A Convenient Truth: A Better Society for Us and the Planet*, London: Fabian Society/Friedrich Ebert Stiftung, 2014.

Wilkinson, Richard, and Kate Pickett. *The Spirit Level: Why More Equal Societies Almost Always Do Better*, London: Allen Lane, 2009.

Williams, Michelle Hale. 'A New Era for French Far Right Politics? Comparing the FN under the Two Le Pens', *Análise social* 46: 201 (2011): 679–695.

Wintour, Patrick, and Alexandra Topping. 'Change Rules on Migrant Workers, Says Ed Miliband', *Guardian*, 21 June 2012, http://www.theguardian.com/uk/2012/jun/21/change-rules-migrant-workers-miliband (accessed 25 August 2015).

Wood, Stewart. 'Business, Government, and Patterns of Labor Market Policy in Britain and the Federal Republic of Germany', in Peter A. Hall and David Soskice (eds), *Varieties of Capitalism: The Institutional Foundations of Comparative Advantage*, Oxford: Oxford University Press, 2013, pp. 247–274.

Wood, Stewart. 'The God that Failed', *New Statesman*, 29 September 2011.

Wood, Stewart. 'Responsible Capitalism Is Labour's Agenda', *Guardian*, 9 January 2012, http://www.theguardian.com/commentisfree/2012/jan/09/responsible-capitalism-labour-david-cameron (accessed 17 August 2015).

Index